THE HURRICANE
NOTEBOOK

THE HURRICANE NOTEBOOK

Three Dialogues on the Human Condition

By Elizabeth M.

Edited by Alexander Jech

WISDOM/WORKS
Published by Wisdom Works
TomVMorris.com

Published 2019

Printed in the United States of America

ISBN: 978-0-9994813-9-4

Set in Adobe Garamond Pro
Designed by Abigail Chiaramonte
Cover Concept by Sara Morris
Edited by Megan Fritts

τῷ μαθητῷ

CONTENTS

PROVENANCE AND RECONSTRUCTION OF
THE HURRICANE NOTEBOOK

I.

The text of this "philosophical dialogue," "philosophical novel," or whatever label one may set on this tragic tale is drawn from the notebook of a recent student at the University of North Carolina at Wilmington. The notebook was first recovered by fisherman Thomas Marian following a recent tropical storm that struck the Carolinas. Mr. Marian found the brown-covered notebook down by the fishing piers, wrapped in plastic to keep the water out, tied together with repurposed elastic cord of the sort one might find tucked about somewhere in many basements or garages. Mr. Marian was the proprietor of Windswept, a small bar and restaurant on Topsail Island near Wilmington, and he added the notebook to the collection of oddities he had discovered while fishing, which he kept there. On particularly auspicious and high-spirited nights, he frequently brought out one or another of his curiosities to customers, weaving together some fantastically tall fisherman's tale, usually improvised on the spot, to explain them. The notebook, however, was a challenge. Admittedly, it was in keeping with the spirit of the place for a notebook written by an unknown hand to suddenly appear on a Wilmington beach, which is after all also home of the so-called "Wrightsville Beach Mailbox"—a mailbox placed on the north end of Wrightsville beach, in which there is always kept a notebook and pens, with the invitation "Leave a note." This little mailbox has seen countless love letters, confessions, and reports of joy, sadness, religious conversions—in short, every type of human event and experience has been recorded in the little mailbox. Initially, Mr. Marian attempted to explain the notebook he found along those lines, as if someone had taken the notebook from the mailbox and simply had so much to say that she filled the whole thing. But this never quite made sense. Why, then, the plastic covering? Why not return the notebook to the mailbox? And of course the contents indicated that this was a private notebook, a journal or almost a diary, of some kind, and part of a long series of such notebooks.

But even when he gave up trying to connect it to the Wrightsville Beach Mailbox, he found that his explanations never came out quite right. Was it a practical joke of some kind? A put-on? Its passion, the desperation of its search, seemed too earnest for that. Was it the work of some student, lost at the beach? Then where was she and why hadn't she come for it? Had she died or even just sailed away, become a stowaway and left everything behind? But then, why couldn't even her identity be confirmed? He tried various variations on these, looking for the story that would make sense of it all, but finally the notebook came to seem inappropriate to be made the matter of a tall tale, told for the amusement of his bar-goers. The contents also puzzled him. Some of it was written in a sort of shorthand and was altogether indecipherable, whereas what he could read and make out for himself he found rather ambiguous, and often too solemn for a tale of the kind he liked to regale for his customers. For example, what entertainment was there in a statement like "The veil upon reality is like the skin of a human being. What lies beneath that covering is fit only for a surgeon's eyes, and perhaps not even for them"?

And even if there was some humor in the oft-repeated "Everyone is guilty"—a wit will know how to extract a good amount of fun from such material—what mirth was there in a conclusion that runs "When the pattern goes down, it comes back up dark, bloody, twisted"? Even the "re-dime me" joke, which was light enough, was incapable of being retold, and wasn't even set out in the right way in the manuscript itself to be funny to anyone but perhaps the author herself. He therefore soon took to locking it in a case away from curious eyes. It seemed to him the kind of book to be kept this way.

The book's period of solitude ended, as such things often do, by accident. I had been to Windswept a handful of times before, but on this occasion the waitress carded me. When I showed her my ID, it so happened that Mr. Marian was looking my way. The waitress walked away, and a moment later Mr. Marian wished to speak with me. He had seen my University of North Carolina identification—at the time, I did work there—and he said he had found something that belonged to a UNC student, but didn't know what to make of it, and University privacy rules had so far prevented him from getting any answers from the University itself. I agreed to look at the notebook more out of good nature than genuine enthusiasm, not thinking to find more than a curiosity. When he happened to read a bit from it, I became intrigued by the author's rather dark reflections on the nature of human life and the arguments over the human condition she portrayed herself as participating in. The notebook seems to contain records of three lengthy philosophical discussions, as well as the author's private reflections on various matters. I was on the verge of trying to convince him to allow me to take the notebook for examination, but was prevented by Mr. Marian, who rather suddenly decided, for his own reasons, that he wanted "the Hurricane's notebook" out of his hands and told me I must take it and return it to the student if possible, but in any case, take the notebook somewhere it could better be kept than his bar of curiosities. And so, bemused, I found myself in possession of the notebook hardly having uttered even a word.

II.

The author identifies herself only as "Elizabeth M." The notebook had suffered minor water damage from the storm and from subsequent handling and storage on the fishing boat, but large portions remain legible. The pages of the notebook were filled with notes written in a small, neat hand, along with items taped or pasted into its pages at various points. A substantial amount of the notebook, however, had been written in an idiosyncratic shorthand developed from *notae Tironianae*, or Tironian Notes—a system of symbols adapted for rapid writing developed in the late Roman Republic by Cicero's secretary, Marcus Tullius Tiro, and popular throughout much of the following millennium—which she had adapted to encompass English phonemes and common English words and phrases. This shorthand tested the ingenuity of my editorial assistant, Megan Fritts, who identified the shorthand and whose work was essential for unraveling and reconstructing these mysterious sections of the text, particularly when Elizabeth wished to write of Sarah or Joshua. According to the internal dating of the notebook, its contents were written between August 28 and September 9, but it has not been easy to pinpoint the correct year, which she lists only as "The year she died." The forms and genres employed vary from day to day, and yet the notebook maintains the unity of a single, overarching mood, and the earnest attempt to resolve a single, gradually articulated problem—"a record, a letter, and a poem, each of which confounds me, and somehow constitute the answer to the knotted, undanceable problem of my life"—a problem which, however, it is not clear she wholly resolves.

What is clear, however, is that Elizabeth herself is changed in the process of confronting this problem, and that this change is reflected in the notebook. The cramped, dense, and detached

—even cruel—writing of "Gnothi Seauton" flowers in the more expansive prose of "The Analysts" and the freer, more fully natural style, of "Jouska," mirroring the author's own change from the isolated, self-embittered individual of the notebook's first pages into the open but broken author of its final words, "I want to live." Yet, though accurate enough, it would also be deceptive to trace Elizabeth's own development strictly in parallel with the notebook's development; the notebook begins, as notebooks do, *in media res*: to tell her story, one would have to begin, not with notebook's opening, chance remarks about declining an invitation from someone named Sammy to go to the Outer Banks, but with events much earlier—with the summer when Sarah tumbled into the treehouse where Elizabeth was teaching herself Latin, with the sisters' many adventures in the Outer Banks, or even with Elizabeth's discovery (or was it "invention"?) of the "Sacrum Arcanum." Surely that moment, when she stood in front of the two walls of mirrors covered with her own words spread out before her in dry-erase marker, her two assumptions—"the ideal is articulable" and "the individual is sufficient for her relation to the ideal"— hovering over everything, surely this was the necessary preface to the events and arguments recorded in the present notebook, the first step on a way of life that would lead to the tragedy and disaster that preoccupies Elizabeth from the notebook's first to its last words. But we do not acquire any of this information until Elizabeth feels the need to revisit it and reevaluate its significance from her current perspective. The reader is instead left to feel, just as Elizabeth herself does, that she is tasked with solving a chess problem where "[what] is wanted is ruled out by the beginning."

III.

Elizabeth M.'s writing itself invites a few remarks. Aside from the stylistic changes—the increasing expansiveness and earnestness of the writing—that develop throughout the course of the notebook, there are other points to mention. Since she writes almost wholly for herself, Elizabeth makes few allowances for the reader. She drops in frequent quotations from favorite authors sometimes in translation, sometimes in the original Greek, Latin, or French, sometimes with attribution, sometimes without. This raised questions for the editorial team regarding how much to help the reader with an author whose only reader she presumed to have read everything and to know everything she had read and knew. Should we provide references for all of her quotations? Should we translate her selections from Latin, Greek, French? What about her "twig Latin"? Regarding her references, we thought it best to provide them wherever they appear by an editorial footnote providing standard bibliographical information. When it came to her quotations, however, there was some debate. This centered on whether she had a reason for using a quote in the original language instead of in English, and vice versa, for using an English quotation when she might have instead written it in Latin, or Greek, or French. Had she done this randomly, or on a whim? Was it a matter of what she had memorized, or had easily on hand at the time she was writing? Was it, perhaps, a kind of snobbery—did she identify with the time when "every educated person" could be counted upon to know these languages? In fact, her language is often almost pretentious in its imitation of a Victorian style—although perhaps this was simply because, bookish as she was, it was these authors' words that filled her mind, rather than those of her contemporaries. Or did she have some purpose, literary or philosophical, for arranging them as she did? Did her perfectionism lead her to choose only that form of the quote that served her purpose most fully in the context in which she placed it?

Our conclusion was that although one couldn't rule out any particular reason in a particular case, nonetheless, the last reasons seemed most reflective of Elizabeth's mind—lost in the past, tempted by its examples to the point almost of pretension, responding to literary and philosophical requirements that she, perhaps alone, sensed and thought made the particular choice necessary. Yet what should an editor do? The Victorian or Edwardian audience capable of reading untranslated Latin and French, and occasional Greek, sentences, no longer exists. Yet if there were some effect Elizabeth desired from having it untranslated, would this be served by translating it? Surely not. What if it were footnoted? This was our final debate, and insofar as I am, perhaps, as tempted by snobbery as Elizabeth, I was inclined to leave it as is; but Tom and Megan were for adding the footnotes, Megan remarking, "It's a difficult and esoteric enough book as is!" So add the footnotes we did.

However, there was a second major problem for the editorial team. Between "The Black Swan" and "The Rose-Garden," little in the notebook is completely coherent as it stands; the contents of "Jouska" are fragmentary, often written in shorthand, marked by frequently obscure editorial comments connecting one portion with another. It fell upon the editors to decipher and reassemble these fragments into something resembling coherence. Corresponding to the freer and more natural style mentioned above is a lack of what Elizabeth would term "iron" in the organization of the whole and an unfinished, open quality to the section itself, terminating as it does not with a concluding argument but a conclusive event. How much of this is due to the unsettled external conditions faced by the author while writing this section and how much to her turbulent internal condition is one of many open questions. We have assembled these materials in the way we thought would best communicate and correspond with her own final, if incompletely accomplished, intentions, but there may be other possible ways of organizing the material that would correspond to other possible purposes.

IV.

Did Elizabeth intend her notebook to be published? There is nothing in the first half or even first two thirds of the book to suggest that this is the case. On the basis of the material in "Gnothi Seauton" and "The Analysts" alone, one would conclude "no." The

final sections of the notebook, however, point in another direction. It is on the basis of Elizabeth's remarks here regarding her
hope that someone will learn from what she has written in the
notebook—and also on the basis of the scrambled editorial directions written throughout "Jouska," seemingly presupposing that
someone other than herself will need to comb through, decipher,
and recover what she has written—that we found grounds for publishing the notebook, from beginning to end, as a record of how
a soul, perplexed in the extreme and struggling to find a solution
to its most vexing questions, almost to the point of giving up,
endured, persevered, and *in extremis* found a kind of rebirth and
the possibility of new hope.

But precisely here the reader is likely to wish to ask: to what
extent is the notebook's content historical, as opposed to being
purely philosophical, literary, or imaginative? The answer remains
inconclusive. Whereas initially the individuals appearing in the
notebook seemed to be particular individuals, with distinct per-
sonalities and circumstances, many also bear a certain similarity,
and some readers may be able to find themselves in each of them,
as if they embodied something universal, or were creations of a
single mind, as if perhaps Elizabeth herself had dreamed them all
up merely for the sake of expressing in an external form her purely private, spiritual crisis, the better to make it capable of resolution. Perhaps Elizabeth, like Kierkegaard, knew that "anyone who
experiences anything primitively also experiences in ideality the
possibilities of the same thing and the possibility of the opposite,"
and that literary activity was a transmutation of the personal into

such ideal universality;[1] and perhaps she desired to do this precisely because it is by transmutation into the universally human that a person finally attains personal disclosure in a form in which one can recognize oneself. In the absence of facts, however, such statements are only speculation.

Where historical solidity appears most certain is in the place names, businesses, and streets Elizabeth mentions, which correspond to places in Wilmington or North Carolina generally (though in one or two cases I admit she has given something a nickname, e.g., Pinnacles). Her story also has the "feel" of a Wilmington tale, with its magic, danger, whimsy, and marvels. But this can't answer the main quandary, Mr. Marian's unanswered question: "What of the author herself? Who is this Elizabeth M., if she exists at all?" On this front, we met abject failure: despite some initially promising leads, it has so far proven impossible to locate "Elizabeth M." herself. Until this search is complete the strict historicity of her account remains undetermined. Whether there was indeed a young woman with the name Elizabeth M., enrolled in UNCW during the late 2000s or early 2010s, and living in Wilmington afterwards, her current whereabouts, and her fate subsequent to the writing of the notebook, remain unknown.

Alexander Jech
University of Notre Dame
October 2019

---

1 "Anyone who experiences anything primitively also experiences in ideality the possibilities of the same thing and the possibility of the opposite. These possibilities are his legitimate literary property. His own personal actuality, however, is not. His speaking and his producing are, in fact, born of silence." Søren Kierkegaard, *Two Ages: A Literary Review*, trans. Howard V. Hong and Edna H. Hong (Princeton, NJ: Princeton University Press, 1978), p. 98.

PHILOSOPHICAL GOTHIC: FORM AND GENRES OF *THE HURICANE NOTEBOOK*

I.

Elizabeth M.'s writings were sent to me in the summer of 2014 by Alexander Jech, who had been looking through them over the past year. Alexander had a vision for cleaning up the manuscript well enough to be published as more than just a pile of obscurities. The task seemed monumental, but necessary—a job you can't say "no" to, because you're the only people in charge of deciding whether someone's story lives or dies. I can honestly say that in the years we have spent working on this book, the labor has been as edifying for us as it has been constructive for the manuscript itself. Any editors of this book, it seems, needed to have been people who would change along the way—people who would change as they worked. We certainly did that.

Some advance readers of *The Hurricane Notebook* have wondered how to categorize the work into a literary genre. Here, I would like to introduce some clarity on this topic, or explain the lack thereof, before the book enjoys a larger readership. Straightforwardly, there is a real sense in which this manuscript transcends many genres and is not, strictly speaking, within any of them. The content appears to be non-fiction, even though some characters seem not to be obviously identifiable with existing individuals, and many of the conversations seem quite fantastical—vending machine suppliers who double as theologians, and bartenders willing to discuss Kant. So, a non-fiction genre like memoir is not, in my estimation, the correct literary genre within which we should place *The Hurricane Notebook*. If pressed, I would name three types of literature that the journals of Elizabeth M. can be broadly understood as exemplifying: philosophical dialogue, southern gothic, and Greek tragedy.

II.

Although one would be missing much if they understood this manuscript solely as serving a philosophical purpose, its function as a philosophical dialogue is undeniable. The meat of Elizabeth's journal is the recounting of conversations with her peers, and nearly every one of these conversations is explicitly philosophical in nature. The most important themes draw on existentialist and religious philosophers such as Augustine, Pascal, Kierkegaard, and Dostoevsky, but these dialogues often tackle more wide-ranging material, including traditional philosophical figures such as Plato, Aristotle, Kant, and themes from contemporary analytic philosophy. There is a sense in which these recorded conversations strike the reader as contrived; it is difficult to imagine such a cast of philosophically adept characters as Elizabeth portrays. Additionally, one often gets the idea that Elizabeth's interlocutors are sometimes speaking for her, and that her own recorded responses to "their" arguments are the worries and doubts with which she is plagued. Plato never placed himself within any of the dialogues he authored, and even Plato's Socrates cannot be comfortably assumed to speak for him; Berkeley and Hume follow Plato in this practice, so that, similarly, it's never entirely certain that Philonous and Philo speak for them. Aristotle and Cicero diverge from this pattern; they appear as characters in their own dialogues whose arguments and ideas do appear to represent the views of their authors. Elizabeth, as an author, falls in between these camps, like Diderot. She writes herself in as a character, yet in such a way that we cannot always be confident that the position the author takes is the view she puts into her own character's mouth.

This may be due to a difference in function between Elizabeth's dialogues and those of the aforementioned authors. A philosophical dialogue is a type of narrative in which argument constitutes the action, and the central conflict is a philosophical problem whose solution bears on human life. Thus, in the Socratic dialogues, ethical content predominates, and they continually feature dramatic portrayals of *aporia*—philosophical angst—over these questions. But an author may write in a philosophical mode either for the sake of teaching something the author has learned, or for the sake of addressing the author's own confusion and angst. *The Hurricane Notebook* is a work of discovery of this latter type. Perhaps Elizabeth therefore appears in her own dialogues, then, not as a teacher of some truth she wants to give the reader, but as an illustration of her efforts to discover that truth.

III.

Perhaps the least intuitive of my three genre suggestions is southern gothic. This categorization is generally applied to works of fiction, but the notebook often reads so much like a novel (albeit a fragmentary one) that it is difficult to avoid making such literary comparisons. Superficially, there is much to support such a categorization. Elizabeth M. lived in, and wrote about, North Carolina which, while far from the Deep South occupied by Capote's and O'Connor's characters, still retains a whiff of southern spirit. In this way, *The Hurricane Notebook* is more aesthetically similar to the work of Thomas Wolfe or Toni Morrison—work that contains a bit of southern aesthetic, but muted, or sitting awkwardly alongside a more stifling presence of midwestern starkness. This, in some ways, gives the audience an advantage—a strong regional aesthetic, like a strong accent, makes something interesting but easy to misinterpret. In *The Hurricane Notebook*, unlike typical southern gothics, there is no theme of natural decay; rather, the characters are decaying, while the natural world around them flourishes, unbothered.

Elizabeth's central concerns—redemption and the human capacity for evil—are paradigmatic southern gothic themes. Similarly type-typical is her propensity for discussing universal themes of love, guilt, and human nature, using overtly religious terminology and metaphor. Many of her questions—in fact, her deepest questions—are religious in nature, and her search for penance and redemption, while not confidently Christian, is no secular journey. Here we might make a comparison to writers like Walker Percy, John Updike, perhaps even Flannery O'Connor (though O'Connor's writing differs from Elizabeth M.'s in most other ways). But while fascinated with God and evil, the writing in the notebook is not what one could call dogmatic Christianity; it is haunted by these ideas but reflects a spirit uncertain of how to approach them. Elizabeth was heavily influenced by existentialist philosophy and themes of absurdism, and in these ways carries on the torch of Sherwood Anderson and Cormac McCarthy.

The characters of *The Hurricane Notebook* with whom Elizabeth discusses these ideas are likely the most obvious markers of the southern gothic nature of the work. Unlike her depiction of her sister, Sarah, or her friend, Joshua, Elizabeth's portrayal of her interlocutors—coworkers, college acquaintances, mysterious strangers—are essentially one-dimensional. Among those she debates only her old mentor Simon, to a degree, marks a partial exception. Her primary interest in keeping a record of these interactions seems to clearly be the ideas discussed therein. The result is that these characters are, for the reader, reduced to a single idea. If there were real individuals behind these characters, they have disappeared into the single thought that Elizabeth associated with their persons. This is one of the primary identifying features of gothic literature—featuring "grotesques" to keep the reader uneasy. Unlike a typical gothic, however, our protagonist does not become more distorted, more grotesque, as the story goes on. Instead, the notebook conveys her attempt to arrest her own movement toward grotesquery.

IV.

However, what struck me initially about *The Hurricane Notebook*, once all the pages were in order and all the shorthand translated, was that it has a very classical structure. In particular, the journals can be read like a Greek tragedy, in which guilt and fate are discovered together. That is, the reader knows of the terrible event that has occurred in Elizabeth's life, and it's clear early on from the entries that she is suffering with a sort of depression; yet, beyond these relative superficialities, Elizabeth does not, initially, actually write very much about the event. And so, the impact of the death on Elizabeth is slowly revealed to readers of the journals as Elizabeth acquires greater understanding of life, relationships, and human nature. It is not hard to imagine that this tragic structure was, if not intentional, a natural subconscious effect of her immersion in the classical world. Elizabeth knew Greek and Latin, she knew the great tragedies and comedies, she knew Greek and Roman philosophy; she was already thinking like an Ancient, and no doubt her writing naturally followed suit. It may, in fact, *have* been intentional—a sort of device for framing her musings, to aid her own investigations into these deep philosophical questions.

For an interesting literary comparison, one might look at Donna Tartt's inaugural novel *The Secret History* (1992). Like *The Hurricane Notebook,* Tartt's book also has an overtly tragic structure, but in this case expertly transposed into the form of a modern novel—a structure made even more obvious by the fact that the story focuses on a small group of young classics students who meet in Greek class. Also like Elizabeth's journals, Tartt's novel focuses largely on the post-tragedy condition of this group of students, especially on their guilt and the subsequent personal unraveling occasioned by this guilt. Despite these similarities, it should be noted that we have no reason to believe Elizabeth M. ever read *The Secret History*. Throughout her journals Elizabeth M. refers to almost no contemporary literature, preferring to get her fill of fiction from the classics, and such a story of sin and undoing would surely have been mentioned by our author at least once somewhere in her writings.

One obvious, and important, difference between *The Hurricane Notebook* and *The Secret History* is the trajectories of the characters. In Tartt's novel, guilt is shoved under the furniture, and the result is the eventual rotting, a dissolving into something near irredeemable, of each of the main characters. Elizabeth M.'s journals show no sign of such evasive maneuvers; indeed, our mysterious writer forcefully and repeatedly commands herself to face her guilt (or what she believes to be her guilt) honestly—"No lies." The results of these diametrically opposed responses to terrible guilt are equally opposed outcomes. Unlike Oedipus, she refuses to take her eyes out, and forces herself to see the truth she had suppressed so long. Rather than rotting from the inside out—an ending typical of a classical tragedy—Elizabeth experiences deep intellectual and spiritual growth, even as she walks close to, or perhaps even dances with, madness.

V.

Some readers, after having read *The Hurricane Notebook*, may want to make a case for other genres. I do not take myself to have covered all, or even most, of the important literary elements of Elizabeth M.'s writings. It is clear, however, that the writings were intended to be a record, not a masterpiece or authoritative statement. It also seems—evidenced by the stylistic changes that progress over the course of the book—that this manuscript was possibly written over the course of years. Such evolutions of style add yet another layer of difficulty when it comes to genre categorization. What begins as almost straightforwardly a philosophical novel is soon punctuated with mysterious letters, ruminations about her friend and sister, flashbacks, poetry, and the slow burn of deepening anxiety. By the end of the manuscript, scenes come at us quickly in the form of four-page chapters seemingly disconnected from the primary narrative. But the connection is, of course, Elizabeth herself. The Hurricane Notebook, ultimately, is a record of an individual trying to pull all the experiences of her life into a story that makes sense to her. And maybe there is not yet a genre for a work like that. Maybe this is the first of a new genre.

Megan Fritts
University of Wisconsin—Madison
October 2019

S.A. XIX

AUGUST, THE YEAR SHE DIED

ELIZABETH M.

Gnothi Seauton

For by necessity the gods above
Enjoy eternity in highest peace,
Withdrawn and far removed from our affairs;
Free of all sorrow, free of peril, the gods
Thrive in their own works and need nothing from us,
Not won by virtuous acts nor touched by rage.

Lucretius, *De Rerum Natura*[2]

---

2 Ed.: Lucretius, *On the Nature of Things: De Rerum Natura,* trans. Anthony M. Esolen (Baltimore, MD: The Johns Hopkins University Press, 1995), Book I, lines 43–49.

HYPERION

Aug. 28

Sammy asked me to go to the Outer Banks with everyone last weekend. Should I have said yes? "Suffering alone in one's garret" sounds so romantic, but then, it's so monotonous, life so monochromatic, one's discoveries so trivial. Yet even when going out, I can't always escape. In this respect, the Outer Banks would have been like quicksand. I would have suffocated on the past. I'm not ready for that.

୧୬

It's sunny today. Staring out of my apartment window, everyone on the street below seems to hurry about so. Did I once scurry like that? It's hard to imagine, but perhaps I made shift with just as much fervor, with only God knows what goal in mind. Now it feels impossible to go out at all. The 1920s brick apartments and little shops at street level are attractive enough but nothing about them calls to me. There's a group of tourists a few streets down. Someone has planted roses in the group of planters across the street. I would like to smell them. Perhaps they'd be sweet.

I could wish for a storm. At least that would be interesting.

୧୬

I have always felt profoundly alone. There has never been another person to whom I could entrust what was essential in my life; whenever I have attempted such, I have continually been put in the position of the pilot in *The Little Prince*—whose drawings and pictures, when he was a child, the grown-ups always misconstrued. So a submarine is the sun, a bridge a rainbow, a bride a windmill, and yes, a boa constrictor digesting an elephant is a hat. We laugh at the book, we feel we are insiders, we know what it is about. How distressing it is to realize that I am myself one of these grown-ups.

❧

I want to go to sleep, but as soon as I do I'll dream, and I'll see Sarah's eyes staring through me, past me, appealing to silent heaven beyond. Why can't you just—get drunk, leave me alone? One night alone isn't too much to ask. But since you won't leave, at least get drunk. I have some rum around. No doubt it will help us both.

❧

I went down to the Riverwalk two weeks ago, and it was unseasonably cold. I saw Sal when I was there, the first time I'd seen him since before the end of school. It was morning, but I'd been out all night. The lights along the Riverwalk, beautiful in the darkness half an hour ago, were now dead, turning off as the gray, ambiguous morning light spread over the river. I ran into him as I crossed one of the bridges, a narrow pedestrian bridge of thick, black wrought iron. He was wearing a long black overcoat and an out of season straw boater. The coat was open, displaying formal attire underneath.

He seemed preoccupied with some difficult thought he was struggling with, but he brightened when he saw me. "Elizabeth," he said, nodding as we approached each other.

"Hey, Sal," I said.

"What are you up to, now that we've graduated?" he said.

I hesitated because a flip answer would feel a lie.

He went on as if no answer were needed. "I haven't seen you

around any of the matches or tournaments recently. Not even at Pinnacles, and they assure me you're still working there. Nice coincidence finding you here; I'm only in the neighborhood because I had to drop my car off in the shop and have business to finish up here. In your absence from the scene, of course, I've been winning constantly."

"How wonderful for you," I said.

"I'm not happy with it," he said, frowning. "Most of the time, I feel like there isn't much of a point in playing. Just these dull victories."

"Then however are you occupying yourself?" I said.

"Oh, I've found ways," he said, ignoring the mockery in my question. "I've moved on from chess to life. I finally feel I have completed my apprenticeship. But, I don't suppose..." He looked around searchingly, though of course there are no chess tables at the Riverwalk.

"You want to break our tie?" I said. Our record against each other was 9-9-3. "I haven't played in months, so I would agree to play only under blitz rules."

He laughed. "I do best with time to contemplate, plan, and calculate, but I'd like the chance nonetheless. A kind of final farewell to my college days."

"Sadly for you, I've put off playing until I can deal with a more pressing problem," I said.

"What's that?" he asked.

"The human condition," I said. "I want to understand evil. Where it comes from. How to deal with it."

"Hmmm," he said, nonplussed, or perhaps thoughtful. "What's your thing? Are you going religious?" he asked.

"What does that have to do with it?"

Sal looked like he was on the verge of saying something, and then thought better of it. "Perhaps we'll talk again later," he said, smiling. Incongruously, a look of pain flashed over his face. "One must imagine Ahab happy! Remember that. May your step always be light, Elizabeth Hyperion."

What a strange thing to say.

⁙

I did once have a dream about Hyperion, Titan brother of Cronus and Oceanus, back when I was sixteen. It was all nonsense, of course, with him trying to tell me something that simply never became clear, no matter how he tried to clarify it. He would repeatedly ask, "Do you understand?" but I didn't respond, for I had no idea what he wished from me. He was staring at me, those earnest, searing eyes boring into me, so sad, their fire almost out. His too-full lips twisted in a kind of despairing grimace. We stared at one another, but finally, wailing with some great, undying pain, Hyperion wept, and with a crackling cry, he soared up among the sparkling stars. Then, just before he vanished from sight, there was a flash and a crack, a bolt of lightning sliced across the sky from east to west, and Zeus Palamnaeus, the punisher, struck and destroyed Hyperion the golden-haired. All the lights began to die. The stars winked out one by one. The silent moon fell back upon itself, sinking into the all-devouring sea, whose surface bore dim, shifting reflections of the stars, until they too faded away. Then I was alone upon the unlimited expanse of silent waves.

As I said, nonsense. Why have I become so inactive? I don't lack courage, but I lack will. I lack will because I lack resolution. I am so used to intellectual clarity that losing it has had an exaggerated effect on my actions. I can see this clearly, though it doesn't give me additional resolution. Sarah is an immense problem, such an immense one I simply cannot find my footing, and an idle thought even grazing her outline erodes decision. I must find resolution, a single decisive point, and then—leap! Whithersoever I should land!

My dreams about Sarah, of course, make all too much sense. I just wish they'd cease.

⁙

Whenever I read one of my old journals, I am surprised by how much I seem to be forgetting. My power of memory is not uniform, since I have no difficulty remembering in general, but I have lost many particular thoughts. Some of these forgotten moments are full of clarity and insight, and I remember them clearly when I read about them, but between the moment of writing and the moment of reading, they had somehow sunk into miry oblivion. And when I read what I wrote about Joshua, I not only feel an urge to stop reading, but even feel averse to writing new entries. I feel the walls of necessity closing in upon me especially closely, and I need to run, to go out somewhere, away from this.

Why should I run? I do not trust such instincts. *No lies.* I will therefore make an endeavor the opposite way. We shall see how that turns out.

Then I shall write of Joshua. But what shall I say? There's hardly anything left to discuss, except that little shrine in my mind where I keep my most precious memories, and every once in a while, especially in November, I let Joshua out so I may recollect those strange, beautiful hours we shared in the studio those years ago before we separated for school. Sometimes I envision myself seeing him again, and in my mind's eye I see us again in the studio back in Greenville, dancing a *pas de deux* from *Giselle* or *Sleeping Beauty*, and my body feels a sudden yearning for the daily barre exercises and the surpassing, strenuous beauty of dance. But it has been too long, I would dance clumsily, and I think he would be secretly ashamed. He would ask "What have you been up to these past five years?" leaving unsaid the obvious—*instead of dancing*. Oh, my friend, I have spent these years doing nothing but reading old books, working over my ideas, and following the crooked paths in and outside myself to their sources; I've grown ever so sharp at chess tactics, but I don't know what I gained from all this. Yet even when we practiced every day, I wasn't half the dancer you were.

ের

When I indulge these little fantasies about seeing Joshua again, I always get confused. He's the best, I admit it, but he's also a silly creature, with all a dancer's prejudices, and it's silly of me to spend so much time dreaming about someone I haven't seen in ages. Or is it? Why am I so quick to turn away from these memories? Why so determined to immediately lose myself in something else? I want an open-air mind that faces life honestly, not one full of hidden compartments and spring-closed doors. The hardness of the hard thought is the spring I would break.

Aug. 29

A very strange matter:

I received a mysterious letter in the mail from parts unknown with no return address, written in beautiful cursive script on bright, white paper—the paper is soft and heavy, not the cheap copier paper you find everywhere. The sender is identified merely as "Niakani." Who is this Niakani, and why did he write me?

Well, Mr. Niakani, what are you up to? (The writing feels masculine, so I will call him *mister*.) Why are you writing me under this pseudonym? This Niakani alludes to some problem in his past, some wrecked relationship or catastrophic error, without, however, ever clearly stating the situation. Is the pseudonym supposed to protect or hide his past? Am *I* even the original and intended recipient of this letter? In fact, there is something impersonal to the whole thing, as if the writer were occupied solely with himself, and had no thought of ever finding an audience. In which case, was it the author who sent it to me, or someone else? But whatever for?

Vexing problems. The content troubles me still more. The conclusion trails off into unresolved obscurity, but the main idea challenges one of my long-standing principles. Not that the author could have known that; I have never published my little system, my Arcanum—the Archimedean point I utilized to give me the leverage to move the world. I will have to mull the problem of this letter. Perhaps in the category of "the friend" I could find the resources to build again a point upon which to stand and form decisive resolution. I used to like making big revisions to my idea, but this will be especially big, and I'm not sure that just now my concentration has the steel in it to carry through the task today. This revision is probably just what I need to correct, or at least, to diagnose, everything that went wrong with Sarah. I feel my thoughts swirling, but they need to steep before I try to draw them up.

Even after reading the whole letter, I feel I am still missing something important about the idea. There is some note here I am not quite hearing, and what is this business about "the Delacroix case"? There is no explanation at all!

ↁ

Outside, a storm is wearing itself out, beating everything with its rain. Meanwhile here I am inside choking on dust. I should go out. Perhaps tomorrow.

A CONVERSATION
ABOUT CARROTS

Aug. 30, a Thursday

I went to work today, and, what's more, I arrived on time. It was a slow morning at Pinnacles,[3] as usual. I'm not sure how long the store is going to survive. We aren't part of a chain and we still keep up all of Bill Brixton's eccentricities (the 5¢ licorice, progressively accumulating discounts for regular customers, etc.). We cut into our own profits with these loyalty practices, but I can't call them a failure, as our regulars generally shoplift their models and books from our competitors.

One awkward customer came to me with this: "Have you heard the rumor that they are going to make Thor a woman?"

"No," I said.

"Don't you think that would be cool?" he said. "Like, to get another cool female superhero out there, a really strong one?"

"I don't," I said.

"But don't you think—I mean, um, don't we need more women in comics?"

---

3 Ed.: Pinnacles is a comic shop in Wilmington, located about a mile from UNCW, selling movies, card games, board games, pewter and plastic models, and hosting competitions and tournaments for Magic, Warhammer, and other games.

"What happens in comics is irrelevant to me," I said.

"Oh," he said. "I just thought, you know—"

"But you're right, I should be delighted for my gender that the best someone can do to imagine a female superhero is to draw breasts on a male superhero. That does sound like we're conquering pop-art."

I wasn't always so cruel to customers, but I have no patience for their absurd concerns. I feel trapped here. I found this place because of the biweekly chess tournaments, and then I became intrigued by the idea of approaching some of these other games from the standpoint of mathematical modeling, to see whether I could win through superior calculation. Warhammer was a particular challenge, as not only were the number of different armies and the variable terrain complicating factors, but an elegant and perfect strategy is made hideous by a slovenly army, and my attempts at painting the models were mind-boggling failures. I can't understand how anyone could be willing to play with an ugly army, no matter if they won or lost. This project of mathematical modeling had me spending so much time at the store that they offered to hire me, even without an application. I suppose they think having me around makes for a better atmosphere.

Now that I've abandoned the project, I could try to find a new job, but I can't spare the motivational energy. I had the morning shift with Max and we had one customer in the store, Will, a bartender at New Rouse who'd given up studying physics for his "true love," alcohol, and who didn't have anything better to do before he went down to the bar.[4] I was working on inventory, and we could hear "The Ghost of Tom Joad" over the store sound system. It was the version from Bruce Springsteen's Magic Tour, with both Springsteen and Tom Morello.

---

4 Ed.: New Rouse's Tavern, a dive bar about two miles from the UNCW campus.

"What a sad song," Max sad. "I remember it sounding a lot angrier."

"You're probably thinking of the cover by Rage Against the Machine," I said. "It's basically crap."

"What do you have against Rage Against the Machine?" Will asked. "Their version kills."

"It's the wrong way to interpret the song," I said. "It *ought* to be sad. It's about the Great Depression."

"How can you hear a line like 'wherever the police are beatin' a guy' and think, 'how sad'?" Will said. "Springsteen's reeks with sentimentalism."

"Why do you think it's sentimental?" I said.

"It ought to have more hope," he said.

"Really?" I said, surprised.

Will laughed. "Hope of giving the idiots in charge what they deserve, good and hard."

"Do you mean vote them out of office?" I said. "Beating them up? Revolution? What?"

"Revolution," he said, "but I'm not opposed to the others, too."

"That will fix the problems of the Depression?" I said.

"It'll get rid of some of it," said Will.

"And it will get rid of the evil that produced it, too?" I said.

"It will get rid of enough," he said.

"You're a big fan of the insurrection of '98, then?"

"What?" he said "No, I'm not a fan of that gang of white supremacists."

"But isn't that what you said you liked?" I said. "They were weak and out of power, and they overthrew those in power to get what they wanted."

"Don't be absurd," said Will. "You're twisting my words, and you know it. That's not the right kind of revolution."

"I was having a bit of fun, I admit," I said. "But there is something serious to it, too. Aren't the people who fought to overthrow our city leaders in 1898 the children of those who seceded rather than submit to President Lincoln in the 1861, when they feared for their rights? And aren't *they* the children of the revolutionaries of 1776, who fought to overthrow King George, when they feared for theirs?" I said. "One people's rights are another people's wrongs." I thought this was clever until I said it.

Will shook his head. "Don't be absurd. You're using 'rights' too expansively," he said. "One's rights never include the right to wrong others. I don't think the colonial revolutionaries were in the wrong, and far as this city goes, I stand with Abraham Galloway rather than the coup of '98. He didn't think his rights included the right to another person's life or liberty—except, of course, when they threatened his."[5]

"Well, that's an interesting qualification," I said. "Perhaps we're all threats to each other's rights, though, and then what? No, don't answer that, I know I'm pushing a specious line of argument. Here's my question. Are these revolutions any good at making people good? Jefferson and Madison didn't think that they had the right to own slaves, but that belief didn't give them the strength to act on their convictions, and the revolution sure didn't give that conviction to other slave-owners. They took it just the way *I* meant: they took this as a vindication of their right to be miniature King Georges themselves. I mean this in all honesty: what condition of goodness does revolution secure or make more readily available?"

"So you think the revolution will just put another bunch of jerks in charge, who'll also do their worst?" he said.

"Unless you're a skeptic about induction, so should you," I said. "As soon as people have any sort of power, they get their hands dirty."

"So you think we should just suffer and go on suffering?" Will asked.

---

5 Ed.: Will is referring to the Wilmington native son and Civil War hero who escaped the city a slave but returned as one of its most influential political leaders.

"Come on, guys," Max said, "let's not talk politics. Besides, the world can be a sad place, but that doesn't mean life is totally hopeless."

"You think that the ways of the world can be fixed?" I asked.

"Of course there's hope," he said. "I mean, everything happens for a reason, right?"

"I suppose," I said. "What do you mean by that?"

"I mean when bad things happen, they let good things happen," said Max. "Or anyway God will repay anything bad that happened to you if it didn't turn good."

Max, besides confusing two different ideas with each other, did not seem to grasp the problem I had originally started with. "Well, what if I refuse to let God repay what went wrong in my life?" I asked.

"Why would you do that?" said Max.

"Perhaps if you thought that what was wrong with your life could never be paid back," I said.

"What do you mean?" he said.

"I mean, don't you think that some things are beyond price?" I said. "So much so, that no one could ever offer you enough money, or power, or pleasure, or anything else, to compensate for it?"

"You mean, like how parents think about their children?" he said.

"Sure," I said. "But not only that."

"God is infinite," he said. "I think he could repay even the worst."

"What do you mean, 'infinite'?"

"God's power and wisdom are so great that there is nothing he can't do," Max said, "and he can achieve it by means that appear totally unlikely to us, but which he can work out. He can use anything, even the terrible things that you guys think make this world so harsh, and use them for good."

"So, he's so wise and powerful that we just can't expect him to use the same kind of means we would expect?" I said. "I guess that's fair enough, but it must make him rather confusing."

"Right," Max said. "That why people talk about faith. You need to have faith that it will turn out okay."

"And is this faith required for us to benefit from the bad things?" I asked. "Or, anyway, what if we refuse to let him do that?"

There was some discussion here that willy-nilly led to Max somehow affirming that God gives everyone infinite chances to love him, and that with these infinite chances and infinite resources, God inevitably succeeds in getting each person. "If God loves this person, he'll give him as many chances as possible—only, since we are speaking of God, that's infinitely many chances, until the person accepts his love."

"So, no matter what I do, or what happens to me, it will turn out fine in the end?" I asked.

"Yes," said Max.

"But look. Suppose I think that there's a 90% chance that you're right, and a 10% chance that some other view is correct. According to the other view, my life will be terrible unless I live a very particular way. What should I do? How should I live?" I asked.

"Well, go with my view," he said.

"The odds don't support that," I said. "On the 90% chance that you are right, everything is fine whether I live like your view is correct, or live as if the other view is correct. But on the 10% chance that the other view is right, it makes an enormous difference whether I live as if it is correct. So I ought, apparently, to live as if the other view is correct, even if I think your view is more likely to be correct."

"That seems…" Max trailed off. "That's not what I meant."

"Then you need to make your view much clearer," I said.

"Make it clearer!" said Will, leaping in. "What nonsense! This pablum about God's love for us is very hopeful, but if we examine the matter with a clear, *honest* gaze, our condition and circumstances all testify otherwise. Is there a loving God? I hardly think so, and, frankly, I hope not, because it would be pretty depressing to think that *this* is the best world he can fashion for us."

He was wearing his typical worn black jeans and a dark shirt with the faded logo of some heavy metal band. His dark hair was kept fairly short, but he hadn't shaved today. Earlier, he had been wandering around the store looking at comics, models, and games that he might buy, but wouldn't—"purposiveness without a purpose," to do violence to a phrase from Kant. The rusty Ford he drove was sitting outside beneath the large tree outside the store. He went on, saying, "Look, if you want to figure out the purpose of something, then examine its inbuilt tendencies. What way does it go—what's it got a drive toward doing? The task isn't too hard when you've got a simple machine to inspect, but it's harder if you've got a more complicated one; you need some time to sit down with it, to observe it and fiddle with it, to see what it's for. Or think of the organs of an animal. What's a heart for? Well, you've got to observe it, see what it tends to do. Not just what it does this one time or something—that might be a freak occurrence. Just like machines, some are easier to figure out, some harder. Ears, eyes, legs, we understand those easily. Hearts, though, were a challenge, and it took us a long time to reach the point where Harvey discovered that hearts were for circulating blood."[6]

"Suppose we accept this," I said. "Look for the inbuilt tendency of a thing to discern its purpose. Then what?"

"Let's turn to the relevant *datum*: the universe we live in," he said. "What's its purpose and what can we infer about God from its nature? In the not too distant past, we lacked the information

---

6 Ed.: It may seem surprising that an ex-physics student would show himself to believe in cosmic teleology. However, such striking juxtapositions are not uncommon around the periphery of the sciences, among those who are attracted to these disciplines without entirely belonging to them. In fact, such intellectual eccentrics are perhaps much more common than usually realized by those working inside academia proper. It may be that their striking divergences from common ideas are a mark of an overproud and individualistic intellect, but if one remembers that Descartes was one of these eccentrics in his own time, and he revolutionized philosophy and the sciences, one will not take them for granted. Never precisely scholars, they may yet be thinkers and real intellects, and one never knows what insights or nonsense might come from such outsiders.

necessary to answer a question like this. The universe is even more complicated and difficult to examine than the heart, but we've made great progress in understanding it over the past two hundred years. I won't say that we actually *know* what the purpose of the universe is, but we're not totally in the dark. We've got some idea of the big cosmic picture and the principles governing the whole, and we are able to examine our own little patch of it here on earth pretty closely, and these two can tell us a thing or two about what purposes the universe and the earth might have. In particular, there are two principles governing the universe that give us insight into God's purpose in forming the universe, and his attitude toward us: the primary law governing life, survival of the fittest, and the primary law governing all processes, the second law of thermodynamics.

"Now, the important thing about the first principle is that, as Spencer saw, the principle is broader in scope.[7] Survival of the fittest refers to the tendency of those better adapted to survive and reproduce in a given local environment to do so—more specifically it is currently used to refer to differential capacity for reproductive success. The biological principle is bound up with competitive environments where we are interested in comparative reproductive advantages, but the logical basis of the principle rests on facts simpler than these. Take anything whatsoever, and suppose it to possess stable existence of some kind; to ask why it exists again at a later time means going back to its stability—you are asking why the existence of such a thing is stable. Now, we could give this a truly absurd name, such as 'the principle of natural stability,' defined as the principle according to which stable structures tend to continue to exist, since that is just what it means for something to be stable, but here's the point—it's a logical truth that, if something has a stable structure or form, it will tend to continue to exist, at least in that form. That's what it means to possess stability. The question for science is the 'why' or 'how' question—why is it stable, how does it keep itself in existence? Is it because of its material composition, because of its arrangement, or what? A crystalline structure, for example, is very stable, and it's a scientist's job to find out why. Similarly for organisms: the job of the scientist is to explain how the organism, its lineage and type, have been successful and remained in existence."

"So your first principle is a kind of generalization of the law of natural selection, which according to you has the character of a logical law," I said. "What's your second principle?"

"Now, the second law of thermodynamics states that the entropy of an isolated system never decreases, it always increases or remains the same, tending over time toward maximum entropy or disorder. This is the second principle we see governing the universe, opposite the first, and giving our universe its peculiar charm."

"How do you mean that?" I asked. "Be clear about what you mean by the second law of thermodynamics, which is frequently spoken of, though not often well." I was again giving him a hard time, hoping to accelerate our motion toward the upshot.

"The definition of the second law isn't as well agreed upon as you might suppose," he said, "because of disagreements about the definition of 'entropy,' but we could state it as *entropy in a closed system can never decrease.*"

"Disagreements or not," I said, "tell me what you take to be 'entropy.'"

"'Entropy' refers to the dissipated potential for work, in a physical sense," said Will. "A system involving a water wheel, for example, where the water above the water wheel has greater potential for work than a system with the same water wheel where the water is below the wheel. The entropy of the latter system has increased."

"So entropy is a kind of anti-potential?" I asked.

"More or less, yes," said Will.

"I thought entropy was disorder," Max said, seeming troubled.

"Entropy has that meaning as well," said Will, "because systems with higher order also possess greater available potential for work. But here's the point: What does the second law *mean* for us? As the universe's entropy progressively increases toward a maximum value and all parts of the universe acquire a uniform temperature, it will gradually settle into a state of thermal equilibrium in which no heat can be converted into work. Lord Kelvin put it admirably: the ultimate consequence of the second law is the heat death of the universe."

"So how does the marriage of these two principles produce the dire progeny you proclaim?" I said. The vending machine deliveryman had arrived at the store a bit before this, to take the money from the machine and to restock it with drinks and snacks. His name, if I recall correctly, is Harper, a tall, white-haired older gentleman of the type who wears a cowboy hat without any irony, and, who knows if this is correct, but his weathered face strikes me as the face of person who lived most his life outdoors and outside of the city, until the erosion of rural jobs turned him into a deliveryman.

Will smiled. "Here is the answer. I said that we can discern an author's purpose for a thing by examining its tendencies, and God is the author of the universe; the relevant tendencies we discern in the universe are two, explained by the principle of natural selection and the second law of thermodynamics; the one of these states that whatever possesses a stable structure tends to remain in existence and is exemplified in the life- and reproductive processes of living things, the other that the universe as a whole is tending toward the dissolution of all structures and the cessation of all processes. There is then a kind of conflict between these principles: one preserves complexity and order and even beauty in the universe, eliminating the sway of chaos over events by inhibiting its ability to break down existing organized complexity and preserving every fruitful thing it gives birth to, and the other breaks down all complexity and order—though thermal entropy is not identical with logical entropy, maximal thermal entropy will bring about the other— and its end result is the elimination of everything natural selection serves to preserve."

"Many ancient cultures considered the cosmos to the riven by a fundamental conflict," I said. "You see it in the Babylonian *Enuma Elish*, when the storm god Marduk, embodiment of order, must defeat the goddess Tiamat, his mother, the embodiment of chaos, in order to create the heavens and the earth from her corpse. Or sometimes we see two gods eternally at war with each other, as in Zoroastrianism and Manichaeism. Plato's *Timaeus* is less grotesque, but there too the divine Demiurge must impose order upon preexisting and to some extent resistant matter."

"Those are all different," said Will, dismissing them with a wave of his hand. "Modern physics doesn't support fundamental conflict. Its laws are too intimately intertwined, too unified, too elegant. In any case, that is not how the matter stands between these two principles. Survival of the fittest, or natural selection, is a logical principle; it holds of the universe of necessity. It is not therefore imposed by God upon creation or a result of his creative work. But, in order to have application, it must first have suitable material. The principle will hold of anything bearing a suitable structure—but shall such structures exist, shall there exist material suitable for arrangement into such stable forms? The answer to this question is contingent, requiring God to have created a universe filled with a certain sort of matter, manifesting certain properties, following certain laws. Having done so, the principle applies of itself; and the answer is that the universe is filled with such matter."

"So on this cosmology, order is not imposed upon matter, as by a workman upon his material, but grows up necessarily if only the right materials are supplied," I said.

"Yes," said Will, "the spontaneous arising of order is one of the great discoveries of modern science."

"Then what of the second law of thermodynamics?" I asked. "You imply that its status differs from that of the principle of natural selection."

"Indeed it is," said Will. "The second law of thermodynamics does not seem to be a principle of logic, but a contingent law of physics describing the material universe as we know it. Just as the universe could have been made up of matter that would prevent order from arising, it could have been free from the second law. Now, God cannot be inferred to have intended a logical law, but he can be inferred to have intended contingent laws governing the universe he created. From its own internal tendencies, then, it is plain that the universe has two purposes: to allow the spontaneous arising of order and to finally destroy this order. We must therefore conclude as follows: God created a universe in which order, life, and beauty would be possible and would spontaneously arise, but in which that same life, order, and beauty, all of these, would necessarily be overcome by the power of the second law. I even once read a religious type who was honest enough to say, 'people who have to the end championed the eternal ideal die with human dignity but animal helplessness.'"[8]

"And this shows that God does not love us?" Max asked, unconvinced.

"Come on," said Will. "If you love someone you prize her life and you want her to get the things she longs for, unless they're bad for her; and of course all living beings, human beings included, long for life, and for their children's lives. But this universe is

---

8   Ed.: Vladimir Solovyov, *The Meaning of Love* (Aurora, CO: Lindisfarne Press, 1985), p. 101. This prompted editorial disagreement. Has Will actually memorized quotations from Russian religious philosophers, or has Elizabeth corrected this in her record of the conversation? Or is it perhaps rather that, haunting the intellectual realm without joining it, Will has simply acquired a large, eccentric store of knowledge, to which he has applied his own, idiosyncratic construction?

constructed so as to allow the spontaneous arising of life while simultaneously ensuring that the desire for life is systematically frustrated through the second law. So we get a material universe suitable for stability, but a material universe that cannot help but dissolve. In this sort of universe, most life lives upon life, fulfilling its constant need for new energy by taking it from other living beings. Constant predation is the cost of living a moment longer, and in the end, we all fall to the final enemy, both worm and wormkind, man and mankind, and not even our desire to perpetuate our species will be satisfied. All will finally die and all species will eventually go extinct."

"I see," I said. "So is your conclusion then that the purpose of the universe is to frustrate life?"

"That's right, darling," said Will. "The universe is designed to frustrate everything from the lowest to the highest, from the most humble to the most noble and admirable. It doesn't manifest an anthropic principle, as some people say, but a *misanthropic* principle."

"Then this is what you think we should take from an examination of the universe, that God's purpose for living beings is to frustrate their necessary desire for life, or any of these nobler ends you describe? This is the human condition?" I had taken a dry-erase marker, and was making some notes on one of the mirrors we had set up in the store to improve visibility. (We did not *wholly* trust our customers not to shoplift.) "If I understand your argument, it goes as follows." I had written the following on the mirror with my black dry-erase marker:

1. $\Box$NS
2. E & $\Diamond$-E
3. f
4. (NS & f) $\rightarrow$ l
5. $\therefore$ l
6. (l & E) $\rightarrow$ C
7. $\therefore$ C

"We have two principles, NS and E, natural selection or natural stability on the one hand, and the law of entropy on the other. And you indicated that NS was necessary, whereas E was contingent: it could have been otherwise. That's what those operators are on the outside—the square and the diamond."

"I understand logical notation," said Will peevishly.

"You're familiar with S4? That's a wonderful convenience. Next," I said, "we also have some facts that, conjoined with NS, entail the possible emergence of life through natural selection. Call these facts f, and for life, we'll use l. Finally, you have a conclusion, which is that the function or purpose of the universe is to frustrate life in all its dimensions. We can call this C for now. Do you agree so far?"

Will nodded.

"That describes our condition on your theory," I said. "Now, I am trying to understand your underlying strategy. Your view is, I take it, that human life is marked by so much unhappiness and suffering because the universe is ordered in such a way as to guarantee this?"

"More or less, yes," said Will.

"And it's not accidentally organized this way, because its fundamental organization is designed to produce this outcome, as its inherent tendency," I said.

"Yes, that's right," said Will.

"Which implies we can blame the designer for this state of affairs," I said.

"You've got it," said Will.

"Now I need to ask you a question—I need to know which of the following you endorse," and I wrote the following:

8. $(x)(\text{Responsible}(x, (f \;\&\; E)) \rightarrow \text{Blameworthy}(x))$

9. $(x)(\text{Responsible}(x, C) \rightarrow \text{Blameworthy}(x))$

"Number eight," said Will. "It was that God *chose* to create a world that would develop life, while also *choosing* to subject life to the second law. From this, you can ascertain that his will is opposed to ours."

"And from this we can understand how to respond to the evil and misery that we see?" I asked. "In terms of—resistance and solidarity?"

"You've got that right," said Will.

"Your argument looks almost as if it follows a cosmological strategy, like the Stoics—you begin by trying to discern some fundamental principle of organization to the universe itself, a *logos*, in virtue of which the universe is a truly ordered whole, a *cosmos*," I said. "Because it is a fundamental principle, it also describes our place in the universe, and explains how we should live, telling us our relation to everything else."

"Right," he said. "Except, I mean the opposite."

"Yes, and you're moving from the picture to the response so quickly, I can't quite see the transition," I said.

"What are you missing?" he asked.

"Why does the fact that God chose to create life and to subject it to frustration ground a response of resistance and solidarity?" I asked. "Why couldn't someone arrive at the theater of life, see that the only role he could audition for was Ozymandias, and refuse to play a part?" This question obviously had a personal angle, which Will had accidentally made painfully sharp.

"You mean, just drop out of the whole thing?" said Will. "Do you mean like suicide, or like one of those dudes who lives in a VW van and just goes from beach to beach to surf and hang out?"

A group of tourists suddenly entered the store, convinced that Pinnacles had been featured on "One Tree Hill" three years back. Comically, they took our disavowals to be the equivalent of polite modesty; we finally just allowed them to take their pictures and buy their mementos, cheerfully smiling at their jokes while we awaited their anticipated exit.

When they were gone, we returned to our discussion.

"Whichever," I said to Will. "It doesn't matter which form of dropping out is meant."

"Responses like that are failures," he said. "The ultimate rule for life is the same given by the principle of selection—to *live*. Striving to live and remain alive, to produce offspring, and to produce as enduring of a presence as possible."

"There aren't any moral norms or ethical ends besides life itself?" I said.

"I can't see anything that would support such norms," said Will. "There is only life and its will to survive and leave a footprint. Dropping out isn't a way of opposing God; it's a way of betraying yourself and everyone who depends on you." In which case, Sarah—well, let's stop here. Max's view made everything all too easy for me, in a rather different way, but I feel ashamed to have felt any relief at such thoughts. I do not desire to escape justice.

No lies.

"So the reason you focus on 8 is that by choosing to subject life to the law of entropy, God was setting his will against *our* will to live?" I said.

"That's right," said Will. "Since our wills are at cross-purposes, he made himself our enemy."

"We need to make a correction, then," I said. "It was a mistake to ask you to endorse either 8 or 9; you really have something else in mind." Having said this, I crossed out 8 and 9 and wrote the following on the mirror:

    10. $(x)(\text{Responsible}(x,(f \ \& \ E)) \rightarrow (\text{Opposed}(x,l))$

    11. $(x)(y)(\text{Opposed}(x,y) \rightarrow \text{Enemy}(x,y))$

    12. $(x)(\exists y)(\text{Enemy}(x,y) \rightarrow \text{OB}(x)\text{Resist}(y))$

"Yeah," said Will, "I think that captures what I want to say. God has opposed himself to us, and this makes him our enemy; and I take it you are using *OB* as a deontic operator of some kind, to indicate an obligation?"

"Yes," I said. There was really no need to formalize the argument to the extent I had, but I was in a mood.

"Then you've got that right, too," said Will. "The outcome is that we ought to resist him, because we ought to resist those who oppose our will to live."

"I suppose we could push the argument further, but it's unnecessary. We can see now how easy it would be, once we've assigned God responsibility for f and E, to draw all the entailments: that he is opposed to us, that he is our enemy, and so on. Now the question is what to say about the argument itself."

"What are you still wondering about?" asked Will.

"I mentioned the Stoics earlier," I said, "and that's because they encountered a problem with their system. They thought they could divide the world up into two factors, matter and reason. Matter is passive and inert; it's just material for the divine reason, which is active and organizing. Since human beings also have reason, they could identify with the divine reason, and embodying the divine reason was the best way to live, the way most fitting for us and best for us."

"Something I very much recommend against doing," said Will.

"You said that in modern physics there is no longer a distinction between form and matter," I said, "that is to say, both are combined into a single system of lawful mathematical relations."

"That's right," he said. "Matter can't be separated from its laws. For life, things are different, because life has will, or at least the analog of will in less complex creatures."

"But aren't you worried that the same thing could happen to you?" I asked.

Will looked puzzled. "What are you getting at?" he asked.

I answered, "Just as the Stoic system depended on the tension between their two principles, your argument depends upon keeping two things apart: f and E. I mean, what if $f = E$, or $f \rightarrow E$, or something similar?"

"What do you mean?" he asked.

"You said that the key was that God chose to create life by creating the kind of matter and the right conditions for life to emerge through natural selection, *and* that he chose, independently, to subject life to the law of entropy," I said. "This indicated that he opposed life and wanted to frustrate it."

"Right," said Will.

"But we also have here this admission that at least one extra factor is needed to create life," I said. "Natural selection so described governs second order properties of biological traits, but not their original appearance and formation."

"Yes," said Will, a bit impatiently. "I never denied that there were other physical laws, laws of gravity, electromagnetism, and so on, and that they, and factors like random mutation and genetic drift, play an integral part of the overall picture. The appearance of new traits is almost inevitably due to something falling outside of biology properly so-called, and governed by some other law."

"Okay," I said, "perhaps that's all so; and suppose we take everything necessary for the emergence of life through natural selection and the like, all these different principles, laws, and conditions, and we call it 'the life package,' as a way to lump them together without having to be too precise about what they are. Make sense?"

"Sure," said Will.

"Here's my question. What if the life package includes the second law?" I asked. "That's what I was getting at when I asked, what if $f = E$, or $f \rightarrow E$?"

Will was silent a moment, thinking. "Are you thinking of something like the view of Ilya Prigogine and that crew?" Will asked.

"I take it, then, that someone has already related the second law to the emergence of life in this way?" I asked.

"Yes," said Will. "According to their view, life is not just permitted by the second law, but favored whenever circumstances permit its emergence, because local order can be the most efficient way of increasing entropy overall. Swenson applied this to argue that if there is something like a 'law of maximum entropy production,' which some argue for, and which has an intuitive appeal, then life will emerge wherever it can, as the fastest way of dissipating the overall energy of a system."[9]

"Can you rule out a possibility like this?" I asked.

"It's not really proven," he said.

"That's not the question," I said. "As you've described it, it doesn't go all the way to showing that the conditions for life must include the law of entropy, but it would show that entropy, interestingly enough, *could* be one of those conditions. If this view, or a view like this, were true, then we might begin to wonder whether *f*, the life package, includes or entails *E*. For if it does, you'll have a sharp difficulty:" and I wrote the following:

13. $((f = E) \lor (f \rightarrow E)) \rightarrow ((x)(\text{Responsible}(x,l) \rightarrow \text{Responsible}(x,E))$

"For, if to create life is to also subject it to the second law, you'll now find it difficult to assess whether God *chose* to subject life to frustration; we could only know that he chose to create life, knowing it would be subject to frustration, which is a very different question—putting us back in the kind of territory covered by discussions of the ordinary problem of evil."

"Now, that's just a possibility," Will said, protesting.

No lies. For Will could not know this, but the very fact that this view would reduce my responsibility for what happened made me suspicious of it; for it was precisely in such matters that one tends to tell oneself lies and in which one loves to be deceived. "But if you can't rule this out, then we can't rule out that the second law might have a very different complexion. Besides, there is a different problem, a puzzle here I do not understand. You say that we should live in resistance and rebellion, something like that?"

---

9   Ed.: Will seems to be thinking of Ilya Prigogine, "Time, structure, and fluctuations," *Science* 201 (1977): pp. 777–785, and Rod Swenson, "Spontaneous Order, Evolution, and Autocatakinetics," in *Evolutionary Systems: Biological and Epistemological Perspectives on Selection and Self-Organization*, ed. Gertrudis Van de Vijver, et al. (Boston, MA: Kluwer Academic Publishers, 1998): pp. 155–180.

"Yes," said Will.

"But what are we resisting?" I asked.

"God," said Will.

"You mean, we're resisting his intention to create a universe suitable for life?" I asked.

"No, and don't play Socrates with me," said Will. "I mean we're resisting his intention to *frustrate* life."

"But according to what you said, aren't *all* actions events in the physical universe?" I said.

"Of course," said Will.

"And aren't all events in the physical universe subject to the law of entropy?" I said.

He had to admit that they were.

"So all of our actions contribute to increased entropy of the universe?" I said.

He agreed to this as well.

"Including our acts of resistance and rebellion?" I asked. "These, too, conform to the law we are resisting and only further the goal we oppose?"

"Technically, yes," he said, "but they aim at enduring as much as possible."

"You mean, by securing an enduring legacy, something like that?" I asked.

"Something like that," he said.

"The most enduring legacy, I suppose, would be to contribute to something that would last as long as the universe," I said.

"Correct," he said.

"Then I guess what you're saying is, we should all help God bring the universe to heat death," I said, "since that would give us an enduring legacy—our contribution to an eternal state of affairs."

Will now looked quite irritated, but at this point the discussion took another unexpected turn. Harper, the deliveryman who had arrived some twenty minutes ago and was still listening, suddenly broke in, saying, "This may not be the best way to introduce myself, but in my opinion, this discussion is on the absolute wrong track." He was tall, as I mentioned earlier, wearing light blue jeans, bright white sneakers, and the dark blue uniform jacket over a white t-shirt. Though weathered, his face was still lively.

"Oh?" I said. "What do you think has been our mistake?"

"Well, everybody's liable to changing their minds," said Harper, "and doing one thing at one time and another thing at another time, but look, on this view, God's mind is all made up. He's not allowed to change it, and think to do something different at one time than at another."

"And what difference would that make?" I asked.

"If you say that, then you're deciding ahead of time that whoever God is, he ain't the God of the Bible," said Harper, "because even though the Biblical God spends a lot of time keeping things running just the same way, from time to time he likes nothing better than coming in and mucking around in the mess we've made of things to set things heading one way or another. You especially notice two big changes he's already made, and another he says he's gonna make. It's the Bible that announces this curse you're talking about, Will, the Bible says that creation is groaning, 'subjected to futility'—but he ain't done this for nothing, it's God's judgment on sin. The Bible also says that the same God who cursed the world also promised to send a day of judgment when things will be turned upside down and creation set on a new course and put an end to the rule of death. In your terms, that means the end of your second law, which you admit is not a law that has to be followed all the time. So I don't see as God has to follow this law that he's imposed on creation or let it continue forever if he doesn't want it to. But if he doesn't have to, then I don't see why all those things you say have to follow."

"I think that I'll set my trust in science rather than antique folklore," Will said. Max was watching Harper curiously.

"Don't start a new debate about faith, and reason, and science," I said. "That is an important debate, and I would like to get to the bottom of it, some day. But right now I want to hear what our new friend Harper has to say about the question, and since he is a stranger here, the rights of hospitality demand that we let him speak his piece before subjecting him to cross-examination. But, Harper, first I want to clarify what you're saying, since Max here was just making a long speech about God and God's love for us." I summarized the gist of Max's view for Harper.

Harper said, as far as he could tell, his view was as different from Max's as it was from Will's. "I think you each have got something right, an' yet both of you are missing the big point. Max, you're right—if God is God, you can't go right from all the evil of life to saying it's impossible that God loves us; God can use even the worst things for achieving his good goals, no matter how bad things seem. To keep all of this straight, you've got to get straight on God's will—that's what you were right to focus on, Will, but you didn't understand what you meant."

I didn't immediately see what he was getting at. "How does that relate to the question at hand?"

"Well, there's a way that something's the will of God, when it's got to do with how he's arranged the world, like how you'd stock your shelves; you might shelve things one way, you might set them up another way, but you choose one way to do it with this product over here and that product over there. That might be your plan for the store, and that'd be a kind of your will. That'd be the laws of nature and such, the ones that could be one way or another, like gravity or that second law."

"Okay, I think that I understand you, then," I said. "There's a way in which something is said to be 'God's will' which indicates that the world is organized a certain way, and God's will (in this sense) is chiefly expressed in the laws of nature?"

"Anywhere you see a long, unchanging way of things working out a certain way, that's what I mean," said Harper. "And it's just this that testifies to what Will was just saying here about the second law—even though it looks like God wants things to live, it also sure looks like it's God's will to subject his creation to death."

"Because everything we do increases the entropy of the universe and contributes to the ultimate cancelation of life, this has to be accepted as God's will?" I said.

"Yep, that's it," said Harper. "I'm not going to say that the purpose of the universe is to frustrate life, but you can't avoid the conclusion that it is hostile to us—not each of us, maybe, but all of us, if you know what I mean. The way of things shows us that the Almighty is not working on our behalf, but, in some big way, he's working against us, throwing up all kinds of opposition to us getting what we want. So, yeah, I know that we want God to love us. We want our lives to make sense and we know, somehow, they won't unless they are part of a story that's bigger than us, part of God's big story; and yeah, sure, God can still bring it about that it happens this way. He can do just about anything. But isn't it kind of reckless to throw everything on this hope without wondering why the world has been, you know, bent against us in this way?"

"Oh? What is the conclusion you draw, then?" I asked. "How is it if God loves us that he has created such a dark universe for us to dwell in?"

"Well, hmm. God *created* the universe good and whole, but because of sin the world was cursed. This is another way of talking about God's will. There's a way of talking about his will that is talking about what *he's* doing, but there's another way of talking about it, where we're talking about what he wants *us* to be doing. Sin is us not doing his will, and that's why his will is now against us, because we're against him. We're the ones that started the opposition and made ourselves the enemies of God. As the Bible says, 'the creation has been subjected to futility' because of sin, because every human being that's ever lived, that's you and me brothers and sisters, because every human being is a sinner. And the Bible says the penalty for sin is death. So why shouldn't the world be bent toward destruction? If creation is turned against man, who is man to complain? We have no right to demand God's love. You shoot a man's dog, and you ask him to love you? You want him to hug you and say, 'That's all right, that's fine, maybe it was just his time'—I mean, that's crazy. That's what we want, but it wasn't some dog we shot, it was God's own son. That's what we all did, we were all there when Christ was here on earth and showed who God was, in all his love, and we all, Jew and Gentile, we all shot him. I mean, he got crucified, he didn't literally get shot, we nailed him on a cross, and that's, getting shot, that's just a way of putting it. A way of putting it: we all had our fingers on that trigger and not one of us pulled back, we all pulled down, and we shot him, shot God's son. Ask him to *love* us? It's a miracle he hasn't put us all in the ground already, that anyone even gets a chance to get born, since we're all born to torment one another. We're under judgment, brothers and sisters, we're under judgment, and the wonder isn't that creation is bent against us, but that he still gives us time to fix things and get it right with him again. Will is right: creation *is* turned against us and it's not an accident, it's God's will. God's hand is still raised against us."

Harper was close to running off the rails here, so I brought him back toward the main question. I didn't know what to make of his claim that we were all implicated in a death that occurred before we were born, but I didn't need any imaginary guilt, since I had real guilt; and at least here there was an admission of that truth and I was willing to hear Harper out on how to respond to it. "And is this wrath the end of the story?" I said. "What's next, or is the death of all now God's will?"

"Well, now we've got to introduce a third way of talking about God's will, the will not to set things up one way or another, or to direct us one way or another, but the will for something to get done," said Harper. "That's where the Bible disagrees with Will. He said that the whole universe is bent toward death, and then that the end of all things will be this universal kingdom of death, so to speak. But what we see about the biblical God is that he can even use evil for good, that's a bit like what Max said, so this needn't be the end."

"Can you explain that?" I said.

"Well, imagine this. A man gets on the bad side of the boys in charge. They don't want him around anymore and they put him on trial on some made up charge. The trial's no good; it's rotten straight through. They beat him and spit on him and give false evidence. The governor is the judge, and he can see they're up to no good, but he's scared, and he goes along with it. There's a mob outside the courthouse chanting for the man to die, and the governor's made some mistakes in the past, and made himself some enemies too, and he knows that if he messes things up here, it could go real bad for him. So the man is sentenced to die, and they don't waste any time, they get 'm dead that very day. That's evil; you might ask, what good can come from that, an innocent man killed, and the killers on the right side of the law? Why, they used the law to kill him. They ain't going to pay nothing for what they've done. Man's friends can't do a thing, they're all scared stiff, hiding in their houses, hoping everyone'll just forget they knew him. But that's Jesus, that's his story: that's what happened to him! Purely innocent man, never did a thing wrong, God himself in human flesh, and *bam* we killed him. But God never brought about more good from anything than he brought out of that, the greatest evil ever done. Third day, God brought him right back to life, comes see his friends, let 'em know it's gonna be alright, better than alright in fact; if they follow him, then when they die, none of 'em are gonna stay dead either, but they'll be back—and those who wanted to kill him? They're free now, but judgment's coming, and a day's coming when there'll be hell for 'em to pay. What I'm saying is, what the Bible's saying is that evil, the death of God on a cross, God was bringing about the greatest good; Jesus was getting punished in place of you and me, so we could have a chance to stand on the day of judgment. You can look at that day, and you'd say, *nothing* is going this man's way—everything was bent against Jesus. Betrayed by a friend. False witnesses. The angry crowd. The weak governor. But now Jesus is sitting in glory at his Father's hand, and his friends got his promise that they'll live with him forever. With God's power, even the worst evil can become the greatest of goods. God arranged all things to bring about Jesus' death and he didn't stop it, but that wasn't the end of the story. And now death doesn't have to be the end of our story, either."

I said, "So what you're saying is that, first of all, the reason the world is bent toward death is God's judgment on sin, and second, we can't infer from that that death is the end—he might relent and send things in a different direction or, even if he brings the whole house tumbling down, so to speak, he can turn even the worst outcome into something good. Even if you've made what seem to be irreversible, ruinous mistakes in your life, God can make that turn out for good."

"Yeah," he said.

"So...why would God do that?" I said.

"You need to become God's friend, like Abraham," said Harper. "God has promised that everyone who trusts him like Abraham did can be his friend. 'But to the one who does not work but trusts him who justifies the ungodly, his faith is credited as righteousness'—that's, uh, that's Romans 4:5."

"Even if you're under his judgment?" I asked.

"This whole line of questioning is ludicrous," Will objected.

I persisted, "But God helps even those under just judgment?"

He laughed. "There ain't any others."

"But why think he *did* make this promise?" I asked.

"Because the Bible tells us so," said Harper.

"And why trust the Bible?" I persisted.

"'Cause it's the Bible?" he asked. "Trust it and see."

I saw Will smirking again. "Trust and obey!" he said. "Don't think or reason, just do as you're told!" In my mind's eye, all I could see was Sarah's eyes staring straight through me, up at heaven beyond.

I shook my head, trying to clear my mind. "I don't know. That sounds, ah—well, why would God do such a thing?"

"If God is such a lover, why does he judge people at all?" Max asked.

"Or, if people deserve judgment, and it's obvious that they do—I'm not talking about Hitler, either, I'm perfectly aware that people deserve judgment—why should he forgive them this way?" I asked.

"He forgives them on account of he loves 'em," Harper answered.

"That's the most absurd thing of all!" I said. "Why would he love the wicked?" I knew that my outburst was out of place, but I could not escape the memory of Sarah's eyes.

Harper shrugged his shoulders slightly, giving the hint of a sympathetic smile. "A mystery beyond mysteries, that! Wish I could say I know, but I reckon it will all be revealed in the end when the game is up."

Max shook his head. "In the end, it always comes down to faith."

"Oh, you can say that again," Will said.

A spirited discussion grew between the three at this point, but I was silent for a long time, thinking about what had been said, so I don't recall exactly what was said. It is hard to explain what happened next. I became preoccupied by the conversation from last March, with her—it was all in my head. And I could hear her saying, *Re-dime me, re-dime me, re-dime me*, although I knew very well she hadn't said this at that time, and had never said it so plaintively, asking *where were you, where were you, where were you, when I was right here?* I strove to clear my head of her voice.

You hated my guts, didn't you, M... The others were arguing among themselves but the conversation felt dreary to me now. I was full of thoughts like the following: Has God never learned what a vicious, nasty insect he has set himself to loving? What kind of God would adopt such a project? One so dim and unobservant that he knew less of humanity than a girl of twenty-one? At least Harper's God noticed what kind of people we are, but in the end, he loves the sinner anyway, just like Max's. One mustn't lie: isn't this all a bit obscene? "I know what you did, I know how devastating it was for her, all the pain she suffered—but really, it's alright, I forgive you on her behalf! Let me give you all happiness." Thus although I was tempted by the thought of receiving such love and forgiveness, I was also disgusted at it, and disgusted at myself for being tempted by it. I would rather be dissolved in hellfire than avoid justice. *Even then, even then, I will remind you; we'll burn together, you and I, I'll burn right side up, but they'll hang you from your heels...*

I did not even believe in hell, so I did not know where such fearful images came from. Or have I started to believe in it, and simply not admitted this to myself? I've been losing my mind recently. A certain strange idea had fixed itself in my mind, which I found it difficult to dislodge. Perhaps the cruelty of creation was this—not that God had created a universe "bent" toward self-destruction, but had created one that would deserve its destruction? What if God, in creating beings of freedom and love and conscience, also planted a seed of evil in the heart of every being he created, an insect which would grow in darkness only to awaken and reveal itself at the right moment, so that it would become manifest that although he had sentenced this being to death, it certainly deserved the death he had destined for it—deserved that death, and more, deserved the torment of life, life with that insect that had revealed itself and would certainly never leave him be. Yes, and mustn't life be a torment for any creature to whom is given both seed and conscience? To look in the mirror and every time to see the hideous insect poking its head up over one's shoulder? Knowing, of course, the most pertinent fact—that by no means was this creature separable from oneself, that no matter how much one hated it, it would by no means leave one alone? No, one is sentenced to live with the insect, because one must, and this *is* a logical law, one must live with oneself. Mustn't such a being necessarily either tear itself apart or find a way to hide from itself? And I was transfixed by this idea of the cruel God who created beings who would deserve punishment, beings who even left to themselves would find methods of self-torture, who did this because of nothing but the purest sort of sadism. Isn't righteousness a sort of sadism? That was how I thought. *Quid iustum, soror?* she was laughing, or crying, saying *I learned that from you.*[10]

I regretted not speaking further with Sal. I should have examined him over that "Ahab happy" remark. I wonder what it could have meant? It reminded me of the one party I attended during my whole time at UNCW, the very strange party at Sal's house—or rather, one of his mother's houses, south of the city out on a tip of land that juts out with a spectacular view of the sea; I cannot forget that view. I went only because of our connection through the chess team and the argumentative rapport we had during the *Moby-Dick* seminar freshman year. He was quite sharp, if a bit too clever, and had an enigmatic manner; blond, with heart-shaped face and dark, gray eyes, strongly but slenderly built, wide shoulders, not graceful enough to be a dancer. I could not say that I liked him, yet somehow, I was sufficiently intrigued to accept his invitation. When I arrived, he was wearing black slacks and a gray shirt, out of keeping with the general atmosphere. He smiled when he saw me. He spent most of the party in the kitchen with his girlfriend Sibley, and rather than enjoying himself, he seemed preoccupied with taking on

---

10 Ed.: "What is just, sister?"

the role of a bartender of sorts, providing drinks and *hor d'oeuvres* and speaking with or listening to each person who came. It was October, so most were in beachwear, though a few were dressed up as pirates; the date of the party fell during the ridiculous Wilmington Pirate Festival. Soon after arriving, he motioned that he wanted to talk to me. Dropping his voice to a conspiratorial whisper, he said, "There's hardly anyone here with a brain. I'm wearing myself out trying to keep them all entertained." The lightness of his words concealed something angry and pained in his voice.

"What's the point?" I asked. "If they are so brainless, I mean."

"Science," he said. "Knowledge."

Indeed, however, the party was very strange, and the house had been arranged in a thoroughly strange way. There was a room of all mirrors, for example; every wall was a mirror, and the ceiling was a checkerboard of mirrors and dark tiles from which plants and dark metal discs hung, while the room was filled with settees, potted plants, and smaller upright mirrors, the type that can be rotated to face either direction. The reverse of these featured the face of the Green Man of European mythology, as if the mirrors were intended to be in a garden.

Another room, with queer acoustics, featured a complex music system that allowed individuals standing in different parts of the room to listen to completely different music without, however, being in any way aware of what else was playing in the room. The room was twice as long as it was wide, with a door on either end, and each long, curved wall featured several different sound systems, each supplying sound to a particular, unspecified part of the room. Thus someone could be talking with someone next to him, and yet be hearing completely different music.

Sometime during this party, I ran into him as he was walking through the house, and he remarked to me, "You know, they are really very complicated beings—they are—but, you see, they are so tightly wound, you hardly see them as they are."

"What do you mean?" I asked.

"People have so many desires and fears and things, and when they act, these get knotted together somehow in the act—excepting, you know, the ones that don't. The business is very complex, much more complex than anyone admits. Thus it is, even with these animals we call our neighbors. Or did I mean, these neighbors we call animals? Well, it doesn't matter really, although the second is what I want to insist on. They are brutes, it's true, and may seem to have no more than animal instincts in them, that's what you see here at UNCW—just gluttony, lust, sloth, irascibility channeled into sports. And their tastes! But tangled up with the base motives we deplore as 'immature,' 'undeveloped,' 'philistine,' 'bourgeois,' and so on, are much nobler motives, too—I can't think of anything more brutish than listening to popular music."

"Oh?" I said.

"You're bored, I can tell," he said. "Answer one question. Name one thing you would never part with."

"Myself."

He smiled. "Now, there's an answer. I think you mean it, too. Do you think that someone can lose his self?"

"I don't know exactly what that would mean," I said.

"Then why is your self the one thing you'd never wish to lose?"

"Well, look at these pirates here," I said, pointing at some of the other students.

"What do you mean?" he said.

"Have they kept themselves? Or lost themselves?" I asked.

"This is your game, perhaps you'd better answer," he said.

"They are losing themselves in an imaginary identity," I said. "But I doubt it will go very far. They'll return home to whatever they were before they came."

"Well, maybe," he said. "What about *real* pirates?"

"Well, that is different," I said. "There might even be something profound there, I suppose, about human nature. Perhaps there is something in all of us that yearns for the open skies and the unlimited horizon, something drawn to water, as Melville said, and this yearning strives to get away from the defined world of the land, with its pre-given roles, interpretations, laws, and customs. When that seed of yearning is fully grown it becomes Alexandrian *pothos*—wanderlust, adventurelust; in bad soil, it becomes something else. You see, in the pirate, that lust for adventure is dominated by brutish desires. When he pursues it, he distorts his ordinary human relationships to the point he cannot belong to society any longer—but society is a necessary aspect of his existence, no man can live at sea—in Melville's sense—all the time, because he hasn't the necessary self-sufficiency; the pirate's brutishness rules that out in any case, so now he becomes something perverse and broken."

"Oh, now that's good," said Sal, smiling, or perhaps grimacing. "You agree with my idea that we are knotted beings, then. You think the pirate has knotted together his yearning for the horizon with his animalistic desires, and this produces a trajectory he can't hope to succeed in. Is that it?"

"I suppose we do agree so far," I said. "They grotesquely emphasized one side of themselves, and twisted it up with another, until finally their desires became so confused they lost their self-mastery. Reaching the point you can't discern yourself any longer, and are enslaved by a single aspect of your being, this is what I mean by losing oneself."

(Sarah and I searched Wrightsville Beach and the surrounding islands for Kidd's treasure many times. I wonder if that desire for adventure left her in the end, or what happened, once I grew to find it all rather low and ridiculous?)

"Hmmm," said Sal, tapping his fingers while thinking. "What do you say about Edward Low, King of the Pirates?"

"Nothing but a sadistic murderer. What about him?"

"Well, he lived an ordinary life in the beginning, excepting some petty theft, but what's that to take account of?" said Sal. "No one knows what made him such a monster, but according to one tradition, he was broken by grief over the death of his family, and that grief transformed him from an ordinary man into a maniac hell-bent on finding new ways to inflict suffering and destruction on others."

"What are you getting at?" I asked.

"Can grief really transform someone so utterly? Grief doesn't replace what we are with something else."

"No, it doesn't," I agreed.

"Then how did grief give Low this new self? Mustn't it have reached into Low's own dark places, and found Low's new self already prepared by past events and the unspoken, secret contemplations in the dark corners of his mind? Didn't the grief only *make him himself*? Didn't events merely reveal a self that he had come up with all by himself?"

"I don't know," I said. "That's a dark thought. That's Bizet's idea in *Carmen*, that it was a kind of fate—that what Carmen drew from Don Jose must have been there in the beginning. But I've always rejected that idea. Surely freedom was involved."

"Freedom!" Sal snapped. "The self is nothing but freely unfolded necessity, that's freedom for you. When grief removes every constraint, every finite reason, every ambiguity, every 'to a certain extent,' every 'I suppose,' and leaves you with only that what you have in your guts—then you're free."

"So you think that grief brings freedom?" I said.

"Of course," he said, "if it's deep enough. Look, do you believe the legend about his disappearance?"

"No," I said, "I don't believe the story that a hurricane destroyed his ship and all hands, while he himself survived, in South America or anywhere else.

"Right," said Sal. "Why not?"

"Because surely he would continue to be a psychopath, sadist, and murderer," I said.

"Of course," he said. "He wouldn't lose himself, in your sense, just by being shipwrecked." His face had a strange glow, evincing fevered excitement, but his words sounded uncertain. "So isn't this his true and permanent self?"

"Well, maybe," I said. "But haven't you oversimplified? How can a vicious self take a decent self as its material? It's simple: the more innocent self always has more freedom. Self-mastery and freedom both exist at that point. Entwine and strangle the material of that self through acts that enlarge and engorge malice, greed, hatred, and selfish ambition. A self is drawn out from someone by single, repeated free actions, that gradually let that self—that interpretation of who the person is—a self is like a portrait that gradually becomes one's real face, by repeated single actions that transform what is ambiguous into something definite. But how could he make the reverse movement? There is no new 'decent interpretation' of hardened sadistic misanthropy, no ambiguity to fill in as one shade or another. Self-mastery is gone, now. It may not have been his original self, but it became his self. Losing self-mastery like this is what I mean by losing myself."

Sal seemed disappointed, and merely sighed. I would sigh myself, now, at so naïve an argument.

When I left the party, I remember Sibley clinging to Sal, him smiling, and I wondered how he could stand her. I think she wanted him to tell her what he had been talking to me about. I hated jealous girls and was quite cold to her myself. I heard that she died a few days ago of a drug overdose, and I am ashamed of this coldness now. I wonder if they were still together?

&

"Harper," I said, "I want to return to the main question. You began with the idea that creation has been turned against us because of sin. Very well: I accept this. I, at least, cannot gainsay the only part of it I have privileged knowledge of, and for all I know, it is because of such things that the world has been corrupted. But then you followed this up with the message of forgiveness."

"That's the gospel," said Harper.

"And so we can be forgiven if we believe?" I asked.

"That's right," said Harper.

"If we believe—what?" I said. "That God exists?"

"Nah, 'the devils believe, and they shudder.' You've also got to believe you're a sinner and believe that God forgives you in Christ," said Harper.

"And how did you come to know this?" I asked.

"Well, it's what I grew up with," said Harper, "so I guess I've always known it."

"And if I'd grown up with it, then I'd have known it also?" I said.

"Yes, of course," said Harper.

"Just as if I'd grown up with an Islamic background I would now perhaps know that Mohammad was the Prophet, and other things of that sort?" I said.

"Well," he said, "I suppose you'd think so."

"And the same if I had grown up in a Buddhist household," I said, "then I would know—or think I knew—that the Buddha's teachings provided the true path of salvation?"

"Yes, I suppose you would," he said, shrugging.

"Then why should I believe your claim, that it is Christ who answers the human need to escape our condition of well-merited misery?" I said.

"Well, I'm telling you, this is the truth," said Harper, "Christ says he is the Way, the Truth, and the Life—that's the way."

"And I am to believe this on your authority?" I said.

"No," said Harper, "on the authority of the Bible."

"Because it is the word of God?" I said.

"Yes," said Harper.

"And God *is* authoritative," I said.

"Yes," said Harper.

"Even when his pronouncement appears absurd?" I asked.

"Yes, even then," he said, smiling a little.

"Because God is all knowing, all powerful, and morally perfect, and therefore even if an event appears most unlikely, this probability cannot be compared with the authority of God?" I said.

"That's it exactly," said Harper.

"But upon what basis am I to accept that the Bible is the Word of God?" I said.

"Faith," said Harper.

"And what is this faith?" I asked. "What is it more than believing?"

"Trusting, I guess," said Harper.

"What *kind* of trust?" I asked. "Trusting someone's word? Trusting someone's good will? I mean, you might trust even a liar with some things, like feeding your dog, even if he lies all the time."

"Well, I'm not sure what to say, right away," said Harper, "but faith involves a special kind of trust. The kind of trust Abraham had."

"That's what you said before," I said. "Tell me, what is the significance of Abraham's example?"

"It goes like this," said Harper. "Abraham was a typical pagan living in the city of Ur with his father and the rest of his family— his father Terah and his brother Haran. Then he heard the call of God, who told him to leave everything he knew and go to a land he'd never seen and there God would make him into a great nation. Although he was already old, and his wife Sarah was both barren and old, he went, and he trusted God when he did this."

I asked, "So is that the kind of trust faith requires?"

"Well, yes," said Harper, "but—let me go on, because there is more. So Abraham goes to the place that God has called him to and unlike Ur it's not a great city, it's hardly inhabited at all. He lives here with Sarah for decades and they do not have any children. How will God make them into a great nation, then? Repeatedly, they are tempted to try to take things into their own hands, and God is patient with them, God puts up with their mistakes and lack of trust, and shows them repeatedly that he can be trusted and that they need to wait—that he will fulfill his promise to

Abraham but will fulfill it on his time, in his way, for his glory. When they are threatened, Abraham lies and deceives, but God always cares for him and eventually Abraham accepts that God will always fulfill his promise. When the promise seems impossible, Sarah dreams up a scheme for Abraham to have a child by her handmaid, but God says no, that is not the way either—Abraham will have a son *by Sarah*, though they are both old and Sarah is barren. Again and again, God brings them back to the point by telling them to trust him and to stop trying to work it out themselves as if he hadn't already made them the promise and as if he didn't have the power to accomplish it."

"Now, that *is* interesting," I said.

"What do you mean?" he asked, a little surprised by my interest.

I said, "It sounds as if, even though Abraham had faith, this period of waiting is like when a wood carver has found the right piece of wood and knows what he is making from it, but needs to carve it first, and remove all the things that *aren't* the thing he's looking for before the work can become visible and real."

"Right," said Harper. "Abraham is learning to give up all the things that faith ain't and he's coming around to trust God more and more. Some theologian said—what is it? He said, faith is the removal of every ground of confidence except confidence in God alone. Something like that, and that sounds pretty good to me."[11]

"What happens then?" I asked. For, it now seemed that Harper would actually give me something to work with, a principle of life and action I could test in a serious way; yet I was also suspicious of it, suspicious of hope, because hope is the principal means by which someone is caught by a lie.

---

11 Ed.: Harper seems to be thinking of Karl Barth's *The Epistle to the Romans* (see *The Epistle to the Romans*, trans. Edwyn C. Hoskyns (Oxford, UK: Oxford University Press, 1975, p. 88), which he slightly misquotes: "religion is the possibility of the removal of every ground of confidence except confidence in God alone."

"God does fulfill his promise, and Sarah becomes pregnant, and bears the son they name 'Isaac,'" said Harper, "and then God renews his promise that Abraham will have offspring and become a blessing to the world."

"This shows us what trusting God is?" I said.

"Yeah," said Harper. "And what Paul says is 'bout this, 'bout Abraham believing God's promise. One day in the middle of this wandering, Abraham is wondering about whether it will happen, and asks God to reassure him. So God takes him outside and says, Look at the stars—that's how many offspring you will have, and you'll have them through your very own son. Abraham believes him then and this is what is 'credited to him as righteousness.' And then God did what he said."

"So faith involves believing what God said when it seems hard to believe it," I said. "Abraham felt uncertainty because circumstances and expectations pointed the opposite way, but when God reassured him, he believed him, even when he couldn't see how the promise could be fulfilled."

"That's it," said Harper.

"So Abraham believes what God says but, moreover, he trusts that God will *do* what he has said he will do."

"Well, I think it's still something more than that," said Harper. "It's like, like holding onto something."

"Like a commitment to something?" I said.

"Abraham continues believing because he keeps going back to God's promise," said Harper.

"So faith is a kind of steady trust in the faithfulness of another person," I said. "But Isn't Abraham usually described as having faith for another thing as well?"

"What do you mean?" asked Harper.

"Even I know the story about God calling Abraham to sacrifice Isaac," I said.

"What?" Max said. "How could he?"

THE HURRICANE NOTEBOOK 49

"Yeah," Harper said. "That's one of the main examples of his faith. God called to Abraham, 'Take Isaac, your only son, whom you love, and travel three days to the land of Moriah to offer him as a burnt offering.' Abraham did so, taking Isaac with him to the mountain God pointed out to him, and there he bound Isaac and laid him upon the wood, and he drew the knife to kill him."

"Your religion is really friendly, isn't it?" Will said.

"You had your turn, and I didn't interrupt you, though you had a long speech to make, and a lot of it nonsense!" Harper responded heatedly before collecting himself. "So Abraham drew the knife and got ready to make the sacrifice. Then, just as he was getting ready, God stops him—he calls out to him, 'Abraham, Abraham!' and tells him not to lay a hand on Isaac or to do anything to him."

"Thank God! That was creepy." (Max again.)

"Well, it was frightening, that's for sure, because God's ways ain't our ways," said Harper.

"And that was faith?" I asked.

"Yeah, but in a bigger form," said Harper.

"So in this example Abraham is still showing a steady trust that God will be faithful to his promise?" I asked.

"Yeah," said Harper. "He still believes that God will fulfill his promise that he will have offspring through Isaac, but now he ain't bothering with trying to do this himself."

"You mean, Abraham is done with those schemes you mentioned earlier, which he used to try to make the promise come off by himself?" I said.

"That's it," said Harper. "He's completely given up on trying to make it come true by himself, and he believes it will be fulfilled even if he acts in ways that seem to prevent its coming true. And, if you think about it, that's always how it was. 'Hey, Abraham, what are ya doing?' 'Going to father a great nation.' 'Really, how are ya going do that?' 'Oh, going to leave town with Sarah and go somewhere I don't know anyone or anything and can't rely on any family or friends for help.' 'You going to take some more wives at least? That might help with the whole fathering business.' 'No, I think I'll just stick with the barren one.'"

"In that case, we could say that faith always included an aspect of giving up control," I said, "but that aspect looms larger here at the end."

"You could say that again," said Harper, laughing.

"That might well be right," Will said. "But the binding of Isaac shows that faith goes *far* beyond simply believing someone's promise to you. It's a demonstration of the irrational bankruptcy of faith."

"Oh?" I said.

"Look," said Will, "you know what my view is. Faith is submitting to the very divine power who wants to harm you and willingly being gulled into giving up your dearest hopes to destruction. In reality, God does exactly what he does in this story, except, instead of preventing Abraham from killing him, he lets Isaac die. But even if you don't accept my perspective, you still have to reject Abraham's obedience.

"If you're in Abraham's situation, what do you know? One, you know that murder is wrong. Two, you know some voice or vision is telling you to go murder your son. Three, you know—let's pretend—that God is trustworthy. But if you know these things, you know you have to disobey the command. You can infer from the first that you shouldn't obey, but you can infer from three that if God tells you to do this, then it wouldn't be wrong to kill your son. So how do you decide? As a matter of fact, a little reflection shows that this dilemma can only be a *real* problem for fools, scoundrels, and madmen. It is true that you can infer from point number three that you should kill your son *if* God commands it. But now we come to the crux of the matter: even if you are sure that you should obey God, you can never be so sure that the command has come from God. *That* you should not murder your son is certain; *that* you should obey God I am granting as certain; but *that* God commands you, right now, in this instance, to do this very thing, is never certain. The conclusion, that you should kill your son, is always subverted by the uncertainty of the minor premise. The conflicting conclusion, that you should not murder your son, is directly derived from its certain and universal parent, that you should never murder anyone. When one conclusion is certain and the other uncertain, the uncertain conclusion must give way; and so it can never happen that a sane and decent person will experience the horror of Abraham's dilemma. This absurd drama could only fall upon fools, who are too stupid to recognize the truth, or madmen, who think the voice in their head is Truth itself, or by scoundrels, who think it is sometimes acceptable to murder."

"So this demonstrates what you term the intellectual bankruptcy of faith?" I asked.

"Yes," said Will, "because faith is doing just what Abraham did, sacrificing what is certain to what is uncertain, that is to say, sacrificing reason for the sake of something that cannot even be proved to be divine revelation."

"Hold on now," Harper said. "What you said still ain't clear to me."

"Oh, heaven forbid," Will said.

"Well, you kept talking about there being a principle not to murder, but then comparing this with the command to kill. And killing and murdering ain't the same thing," said Harper.

"Does it really matter here?" I asked.

"Well, suppose your son has some terrible disease and the only way for the doctors to help him is to stop his heart and then revive him later, when they've done the thing," said Harper. "Isn't that the same as letting your son killed? But it ain't the same as letting him be murdered."

I said, "You are thinking of instances when a doctor might decide to induce clinical death but preserve the patient by reducing his temperature?"

"You say 'clinical death,' but ain't death just death?" said Harper.

"It's the cessation of blood circulation and breathing," I said.

"So, it's being dead," said Harper. "If the doctors do what they say, then they'll be killing your son, and you'll be there telling them they can do it." He directed this to Will.

"Yes," said Will.

"But they won't be murdering him," said Harper.

Will had to agree.

"And if you were one of the doctors," said Harper, "then you'd be there killing your very own son."

Will again agreed.

"But not murdering him," said Harper.

"I guess not," said Will.

"Then why ain't it murder?" Harper asked.

"Because he's not going to stay dead," said Will, "or, at least, you're only doing this because you think it will make him better, not worse, and you have some reason for thinking that's true."

"So it ain't murder because you think it'll turn out okay," said Harper.

"On the basis of your medical expertise," said Will.

"But if you're the parent and not a doctor, then you ain't got that medical knowledge, and it still ain't murder," said Harper. "You trust the doctors."

"Because you have rational confidence in *their* expertise," said Will.

"Well," said Harper, "Abraham thought God was kind of like an expert, and he trusted him. Even if he had to kill Isaac then he knew it wouldn't be murder because God would make it turn out okay. And he didn't have to be a fool, a madman, or a scoundrel. He just had to trust God knew what he was doing."

"Oh, this is impossible," Will said, but before he could make another argument, I interrupted.

"Now surely your example is right about one thing, but it is also leaving something out."

"What do you mean?" said Harper.

"I agree that trust is an effective 'wedge' between the act being a 'killing' and its being 'murder.' But, the example of the doctors also leaves something out."

"Which is?…" asked Harper.

"It leaves out the horror," I said, "which is what makes the original action so repellent to us."

"What do you mean?" said Harper.

"The example of the doctors illustrates the role of trust in Abraham's example, but there is also something lacking in it—the depth of the uncertainty and agony is rendered thoroughly mundane. Doctors are familiar figures that we are accustomed to trusting."

"And Abraham trusted in God's faithfulness when he obeyed him," said Harper, "and was accustomed to seeing his trust rewarded."

"But God had never tested him, or anyone else, in this way," I said. "There was no prior history of God doing such things, just as there have been no future instances of his doing so. No one put to such a test could fall back upon habitual trust or accustomed practice. Even Abraham's earlier obedience does not go this far."

He agreed that was true, and I went on.

"On the contrary, however, doctors are everyday figures, and medical science is something human, knowable: they explain themselves in a way that is accessible to us and provide reasons that we understand. If I were the child's mother, I would understand what sickness is, and I would understand that my child was sick, and that he needed this operation. I would understand the point of it all and understand the connection between the operation and the result—the cure of my son. I could, in principle, reassure myself that the procedure is practicable. Even if I do not investigate it myself, it is an entirely human thing, and I can reassure myself by the testimony of other human beings, those who have done the same or those with the expertise themselves, and who therefore know the matter. Everything terminates within the human realm, among things I am familiar with, within the knowledge and practices of other people just like myself, and any concern I have can also be assuaged within this realm on the basis of reasons accessible to anyone. I cannot expect divine reasons, based upon a knowledge and wisdom that entirely outstrips my own, to be accessible in the same way. I am not God's equal, nor can I consult with God's peers to see if they agree with his reasons; there is nothing but the singular divine reason to reckon with here and I am not its equal."

"Well, you know, I brought up all this about God's using infinitely unlikely methods to achieve his ends," said Max. "But it didn't seem so horrible."

"No, this is different," I said.

"How is it different?" said Harper.

"Think about how Abraham's testing begins," I said. "God says, 'take Isaac, your only son, whom you love'—Abraham's love for Isaac is *immediately* emphasized. If he did not love Isaac, it would be no test at all. This love is the ground upon which the test occurs, and it is why the act must horrify and repel him. Full of fierce love for his son, this unique child born of a miracle, he is repelled by what he is called to do and views it with horror, while at the same time he lacks any of the means by which he might soften his repulsion. He is being asked to trust God in a situation for which there is no precedent in his own life or in the lives of others; he cannot discern what the reasons for this could possibly be, because they are not given to him, and there is no rational connection he can trace between what he is doing and God's call upon him. He is forced to trust in an absolute way, without reason or custom or experience to buttress his will as he reaches for the knife."

"So," Will asked, "you think the difficulty is Abraham's love, not the act's wrongness?"

"Yes, because it is his love for Isaac that makes the test so hard," I said. "He is pinning everything upon God's faithfulness, and this trust is pitted against the most powerful passion in his heart—his love for Isaac."

"I don't think that would cancel my argument," said Will.

"You mean Kant's argument?" I said. For it came from Kant's *The Conflict of the Faculties*.[12]

"Yes, Kant's the source," said Will, peevishly.

"I don't think your argument can be right," said Harper.

"Oh?" asked Will. "Because it overturns your cherished beliefs?"

"There's something right strange about an argument that says we could never find out how faithful God actually is," said Harper. "Your fancy reasoning has led you astray—or it led Kant astray, it doesn't matter."

"Don't worry about this," I said. "Didn't we begin with the idea that Abraham's faith is the same kind of faith, or the model of the faith, that secures God's forgiveness?"

"Yeah, that's right," said Harper. "'And to the one who does not work but believes in him who justifies the ungodly it is credited to him as righteousness.' That's saving faith."

"So this saving faith is equivalent to Abraham's faith," I said.

"Yes," said Harper.

"So people are forgiven for their sins if they have faith like Abraham's," I said, "that is very interesting."

"What do you mean?" he asked.

"Abraham's trust in God was not premised upon any rational explanation he could fall back upon, nor upon any custom of God doing just the thing he was doing with Abraham, nor any testimony from other people about their own experience of trusting God

---

12 Ed.: See Immanuel Kant, *The Conflict of the Faculties* (Lincoln, NE: University of Nebraska Press, 1979; originally published 1798), p. 115.

in this way," I said. "The story is driving toward this point by constantly peeling back Abraham's trust in anything other than God. The pure figure of faith emerges only when all these other factors are carved away. Perhaps wishful thinking is believing something because you want it to be true. But if faith is what Abraham had, then it's too complex to be wishful thinking. That's just a response to the impingement of circumstances upon our hopes. But it is not circumstances that impinge upon Abraham's hopes—it is his own action, commanded by God to be sure, but freely undertaken by him. When Abraham obeys, he obeys without the clarity of reason, without the comfort of experience, without the support of other men, and *against* the inclination of his own heart. Faith stands alone, turning the whole affair over to God—so that even as Abraham carries out a course of action seemingly designed to void the promise, he still trusts that God will bring it off.

"And now we are saying that saving faith is like this: a kind of trust without external support and in opposition to the instincts of the heart."

"Well, you are trusting God to forgive you," said Harper, "and you ain't trying to earn that favor from him."

"And you also see no reason that would require God to forgive you," I said.

"Just the opposite," said Harper.

"But wouldn't there be others testifying to such forgiveness, as you are?" I asked.

"Yeah, so maybe our faith is less impressive than his," said Harper. "But you still have to trust that *your* sins are forgiven, too, not just mine or some other person's. You might feel you don't know how anyone could be forgiven for the sins that you did."

"I see," I said. "So those enter into determining the degree of faith, but not whether there *is* faith. That may indeed follow from our discussion of Abraham's progression in faith. Then what about the heart? What passion must faith run contrary to?"

"Well, there'd be pride," said Harper.

"Wouldn't it be strange to compare a father's love for his son with a sinner's pride in himself?" I asked. "Besides, Abraham's faith was also contrary to pride, as it meant giving up all control and allowing God to run the show. So we need another passion of the heart for saving faith to run contrary to."

"Clearly, you have some sort of answer already dreamed up," said Will.

"I was thinking of conscience," I said.

"What do you mean?" Harper asked.

"To express saving faith requires that one know oneself to be a sinner," I said.

"Of course," said Harper.

"But do you mean someone should just mouth the words, 'I am a sinner,' or know this?" I said.

"It has to be sincere," said Harper. "Not just an act."

"Do you think that all actors act for the sake of convincing others?" I asked.

"What do you mean?" he said.

"Suppose I feel bad about hurting someone else's feelings," I said. "Mightn't I say something to myself to make myself feel better about it all? Something like, 'Well, she had it coming, after all,' or 'It wasn't that bad, others do much worse than I did, what I did was really not so bad at all,' so that finally, after putting on an act for ourselves this way, we very nearly end up blaming the person we harmed for having the gall to have been harmed by us?"

"I guess we do do that sometimes," said Harper.

"So not only do we enjoy lying to others, we like telling stories to ourselves as well," I said. "And maybe those are the stories that are especially dear to us."

"Yes, you ain't far from the truth," said Harper.

"So suppose that you feel guilty about what you've done, and now someone tells you that if you 'have faith' you can 'be saved' and have all your sins 'canceled' and your guilt 'washed away.' Under those conditions might you not mouth those words and put on an act, maybe for others, but primarily, essentially, for yourself—so as to finally quiet the accusations of conscience?" I asked. "Although to tell the truth there are other stories you could tell that would work just as well; there are all kinds of stories about yourself, or about the world, or about God, that would erase your wrongs from the beginning or quiet your conscience in other ways."

"I guess you could," said Harper.

"Exactly so, what could be more commonplace?" I asked. "But if someone is thinking about faith this way, just trying to quiet conscience, would I be expressing trust in God?"

"I'm not sure," he said. "I'm not sure that person is trusting God the right way, so it might not be faith."

"I think it would be like setting out to sacrifice Isaac in order to avoid having to deal with fatherhood. Such a person would not be imitating Abraham at all. If I say, 'I know I am a sinner,' except under the power of a bad conscience, I do not know what I am saying—I am putting on a kind of act, producing the words without the conviction that they depend upon."

"I guess that follows," said Harper.

"Now, the reason for Abraham's horror is that, as a father, he loves his son, but he is asked to sacrifice him. His love requires satisfaction: is this act compatible with loving Isaac? Genuine love rebels against unloving actions. Or would you say that a father loves his son if he is willing to harm him for just any excuse?"

"No, I wouldn't say he loves him much," said Harper.

"No," I said, "he needs a good reason, doesn't he? Just like a parent who is faced with the decision you mentioned earlier—when the doctors are planning on putting the boy to death in order ultimately to heal him. In that example, the parent would have a good reason on hand: if I am the mother, I know that my son is already dying, and that this is the only serious chance for him to survive his disease. So he is already dying (and therefore the potential cost is less) and may become well if I allow them to do this (which would be a tremendous gain). Love would be satisfied with the action, and may even require it."

"That's right," he said.

"If I didn't have this answer," I asked, "would I ever agree to the procedure?"

"No, of course not," said Harper.

"Not unless I were a cold or cruel mother," I said. "But conscience is just like love in this way."

"What do you mean?" he asked.

"I mean, it demands an answer. If someone who feels guilt over a wrong is satisfied by just any excuse, then should we call him a man of strong conscience? For example, if someone feels guilty about murder, but feels fine as soon as he reflects upon the fact that all people eventually die, we wouldn't think that the man had much of a conscience to begin with."

"No," said Harper.

"Someone whose conscience is easily satisfied, then, is either vicious or ignorant and doesn't understand what he's done," I said. "If it's the latter, of course, then we can try to teach him what he doesn't know. But maybe he doesn't want to know, and his conscience is easily calmed because he is good at lying to himself. And the more clever he is, the better his lies will be."

"If you're right, then what?" said Harper.

"Conscience needs satisfaction as much as love does," I said. "Why exactly did Abraham go ahead with the sacrifice?"

"Because he trusted God," said Harper.

"And he had a promise from God, didn't he?" I asked.

"Yes," he said.

"Being God's promise meant it was completely sure," I said.

"Right," said Harper.

"By trusting the promise Abraham showed faith," I said.

"That's what I've been saying," said Harper.

"Bear with me a little longer," I said. "Conscience needs its answer, too, right?"

"Yes," said Harper.

"And the stronger the conscience the harder it will be to satisfy it," I said.

"That's right too. But the Son of God—" Harper began.

"Hold on, hold on, just one minute before we start on that," I said. "So if I am well and truly listening to my conscience I am not going to let just any answer quiet its accusations."

"No, 'course not," said Harper.

"So if someone tells me a story that would quiet my conscience, should I believe him?" I asked.

"Well, if it's from God, then you should," he said, looking perturbed.

"Surely—now that would be faith, and that would be just like Abraham. But surely you see the problem," I said.

"What's that?" he asked.

"God has not told me my guilt has been atoned for," I said. "Only you have."

"But the Bible says this, which is the Word of God," he said.

"So you say; but does God say so?" I said.

"Yes, of course," he said.

"Where?" I asked. "In the Bible?"

"Uh, yes," said Harper.

"You must see the difference, here," I said. "Think about Abraham again; when a command comes from God, the air is immediately charged with possibility, precisely because God's infinite power and knowledge and goodness provide the atmosphere in which obedience takes place; but erase that, and we are left with a purely ordinary action.[13] Abraham demonstrates faith because he recognized that although the command and the promise appear to contradict each other, the contradiction obtains

---

13 Ed.: Elizabeth seems to use "charged with possibility" in place of the more ordinary "filled with possibility," as if she envisioned possibility as akin to electricity, a kind of potential waiting to be actualized by the presence of an activating object.

only on the assumption that typical assumptions hold. When we decide to cut a tomato with a knife we do so with this presupposition in place: we hold down the tomato, we take the knife, and we plunge it in, acting as if it were assured to us that the ordinary rules are all in play. Yet God's involvement in any affair charges the air, I said, and possibility opens a wedge between the command and the promise and keeps them from canceling each other: this wedge may be infinitesimally narrow but it exists, and the secret of faith is its power to find and follow this path. Thus Abraham both loves Isaac and obeys God, and Abraham unites them in the 'absurd' of faith."

"Alright," he said. "Now what do you mean?"

"Our situation is the mirror image of Abraham's," I said. "He is faced by a prospective horror, the command to go and sacrifice his son; we are filled with retrospective horror at our own past. He is pained by the thought of raising the knife against his son; we are pained by the blood of the past, by memory of the knife we brought down. In faith, he conquers the future by following the infinitesimal thread of possibility that only God can draw him through. In faith, we would be even greater than Abraham, for we would conquer the past and redeem what we have done and who we have become, if, that is, there is some possibility by which we can accomplish so great a task: for we face an even more demanding claim, the claim of conscience, and if faith means anything, it must mean accepting God's forgiveness while simultaneously being crushed by the weight of conscience, and accepting God's forgiveness not to escape from conscience, any more than Abraham obeyed the command in order to escape the responsibility of fatherhood, but because somehow it will fulfill conscience all the more."

"Well, that's nicely put," said Harper, "but what's the problem?"

"Abraham showed faith because he trusted God," I said. "The horror of raising the knife against his son was mediated by the power of the promise that God had given him that his line would go though Isaac. The command and the promise would somehow be reconciled by the power of the God who gave both. Conscience, we may say, also comes from God. When we transgress the moral law it inflicts us with the horror of who we have become, that is, transgressors, sinners, and so on. The offer of forgiveness also comes from God, you say. But everything hinges upon that: without God's assurance of forgiveness, is it not premature to leap at any old offer that would coddle my conscience? Is it not rather more honest to reject a false comfort and instead accept the verdict handed down by conscience?

"So, since conscience is authoritative, and on the supposition that God exists the power of conscience is given by God, we should only accept this kind of total forgiveness if we can be assured the offer really comes from God. Anything short of this and we shall be accused of wishful thinking and worse."

"But look, you're going too fast," said Harper. "I can forgive a man who has sinned against me."

"So you can," I said. "But we are talking about erasing your status as a sinner. It would be impious to accept that without God's own command. Even one of the vermin in the cellar may, in a dreaming mood, imagine a different life as an honest creature, as a cat or a dog for example, but that is only a dream, and it is not safe for a rat to imagine such a thing unless the rat knows it is, after all, vermin, and will remain vermin. Otherwise will it not venture aboveground like one of the beings of its dream, and there be expelled or killed? It seems more in accord with conscience to say that sinners we are, and sinners we shall remain. At least, that is, for those of us who are sinners, and who *do* feel the accusations of a bad conscience. Those whose consciences are numb or innocent may, of course, judge differently."

Thus it ended with no one happy. Harper seemed flustered, and wanted another chance to convince me, but had to go on to his other deliveries. Will invited me to come to New Rouse for drinks "where we could continue to discuss this more appropriately." He was even more embarrassed when I declined, and withdrew awkwardly, leaving the store and throwing his parking ticket in the street before getting into his rusted Pinto and driving away. Max just wanted to move on to something else, making several attempts at finding something of interest.

The letter from yesterday weighed on my mind, and I went home more uncertain, but more resolute: No lies.

೧

There was a smuggler's tunnel beneath Sal's mother's house, the one where he had the party.[14] He hated her and resented her "constant spying," as he put it. He mocked her for being afraid to go down in the tunnel. "A psychologist, and she can't manage her own phobias!" he said. He was angry, and happy in his anger. "Her books are useless. Like Freud's, they're all lies, they need the lies to make their theories true. But the theories are also lies, the *true* lies."

"What is truth?" I said.

"Sin," he said. "Sin is truth!"

"Sin!" I said.

"Sin," he said. "It's universal and reliable."

"But what *is* it?" I said. There was a concept of "sin" in my system at that time, but it was to be misaligned—to have an extraneous factor interfere with the ability of the soul to mirror the ideal. Leonardo da Vinci said that the soul of a painter must be a mirror, and this was also my principle: that the soul must be a mirror in which the ideal is reflected and then, through a process of character formation—"painting"—made permanent, into iron.[15] Sin was

---

14 Ed.: Is this a flashback to the episode described pp. 39-44, or is Elizabeth describing a meeting with Sal following her work at Pinnacles? Later remarks in the journal strongly suggest the first option: that this conversation took place at the same party described earlier.

15 Ed.: See Leonardo da Vinci, *Leonardo's Notebooks* (New York: Black Dog and Leventhal Publishers, Inc., 2005), p. 11: "The mind of a painter must resemble a mirror, which always takes the color of the object it reflects and is completely occupied by the images of as many objects as are in front of it."

an error in this process, arising from allowing whim, desire, fear, convention, etc., to shroud or grime the mirror, so that the ideal was obscured and it was this extraneous factor that became iron in the soul.

"Sin is the self in its first graspings after its own validity, its assertion of distinction. But—no, perhaps not..." he said, trailing off strangely. "One needs something more than that, one needs something more, an—objection. Hmmm. But perhaps it's something still more desperate?" He did not seem to be embarrassed or nonplussed by having to reverse himself in the middle of conversation, and for a moment seemed to have forgotten I was there. When he noticed me, he began to talk of the tunnel again, and admitted that he used to be scared of it, too. He would go in a few steps but there was a sharp twist of some kind and then it grew extremely dark. "It was too dark," he said, "even though there was no one there but me. I would race right back out of there. Now I go there whenever I want to avoid her." This was why he permitted himself to use this house, though he did not stay in any of the other properties his mother owned, on principle. When I asked him what he did down there, he said, "Sometimes, I go swimming, though the old dock has completely disintegrated. Mostly, though, I go there to read... and write, if I feel like it."

"You read in a dark tunnel?" I said.

"I had some work done," he said, laughing. "Installed a little bookcase, put a desk and chair down there. And I got lighting put in, of course. Still, my mother's not a total fool. It floods in bad weather, so it's not precisely safe."

"And still you use it?"

"I wouldn't want to, otherwise. It makes it almost a wild place."

I suppose I understand that.

☙

As expected, allowing Joshua into my mind has produced a series of fluttering afterimages, little images of Joshua I can't let go of or figure out what to do with. I remember Joshua leaping, he's leaping ever so high, we're in the studio, but it excites me so much—I remember the surge of excitement and the desire—for what? To rise, surge upward myself? I don't know, but like a child with a favorite video, I keep replaying this in my mind, useless though it is, and I almost fear wearing the memory out, losing its vividness. Other images flit through my mind, too—a little shrine we stood in together, the sea sweeping out before us, the limitless horizon; Joshua and Sarah, and a bonfire, Joshua is leaping and Sarah smiling like a Cheshire cat; and a bagel, we're eating together, but I see a bagel, and crumbs—and then the whole thing is swept away, and I'm overwhelmed with claustrophobia.

I need to get out. Tomorrow. I should return Pete's books. They haven't been as useful as I hoped. I don't comprehend this stuff about wandering priests and desert fathers and etc. Perhaps if Dash is out, I could talk with him. That wouldn't be useless.

DIAPSALMATA

two figures upon the beach below
walking hand in hand
waves washing over their feet
drifting in and out of time
*

the stars soar out from their hiding place
sweeping east to west atop the sky
giddy, they dream
until they fall beneath the sea
*

ἀναμίμνῃσκε, ὦ ἀδελφή, δ'ἐγέρου[16]

Sometimes the dreams are different.

Yesterday, I dreamed I was walking down the beach again, not Kure or Wrightsville Beach, but the one by Duck in the Outer Banks, where we used to go when we were girls. The beach house

---

16 Ed.: "Remember, sister, and awake!"

was one of those places with a shower outdoors beneath the raised deck, so you didn't bring the sand inside, and there were spiders, but you didn't care. The sky was still bright and the sun was only just beginning to slip down toward the horizon. I was alone, except for those in the distance. A child flew a kite somewhere up ahead and a couple walked a quarter mile behind me, hand in hand. I skipped down the beach just like I used to, filled with the wonder and sublime playfulness of the sea. I danced and leapt along the shore, weaving in and out of the waves. I ran up and down the embankment, tickled by the loose grass. I picked up a shell with more swirls and sparkles than any shell you'd deserve to find and, not knowing what to do with it, tried to put it in my pocket, but it slipped away in my running. I danced over to a tide pool that was filled with tiny fish and lay down on the sand to watch them. I dipped one finger into the water and laughed as they darted this way and that. I felt a playfulness that's almost too big for a child, far too big for a grown up, a giddy hope found on the edge of infinity. I didn't remember forgetting it.

Then, when I looked up, I saw her, halfway to the horizon and hazy like a mirage, lively and wild like the sea. She was running into the ocean, waiting for a great wave to come toward her, and then dashing back to dry land in an attempt to outrace the wave. Back and forth she ran, sometimes beating the wave, sometimes having it crash over her, laughing when it soaked her. In the dream I forgot adulthood and I did not think the thoughts of adulthood, did not think, *Don't you know how dangerous that is? The under-tow—*. Instead, I ran toward her, disoriented, almost dizzy with a happiness I couldn't understand, like the wordless joy one feels when one almost remembers something wonderful and doesn't know what it is, and is happy with the happiness of existence. She did not see me, but when I was halfway there she darted in toward the foot of the bluff, where she disappeared. When I arrived her footprints were just visible in the sand, but I could not find her.

∽

Is despair this: to not find among all one's future possibilities even one possibility to console oneself with? Is the essence of despair the future? Pascal said: "Man's nature is not to go forward all the time. It has its toings and froings."[17] Just as despair works forward to empty the future of hope, so it also works backwards, foreclosing the future even within the past. So that the future will not be alone in lacking joy, despair strips it from the past as well. And this is half its pleasure.

ɛ/ɔ

I was listening to Sarah's record. When he says, "God's dead," the singer replies, "That's alright with me," not "That's true" or "I agree." This is, if one will forgive the expression, a deep wisdom. None of those the madman met in the marketplace made this response.[18] Despair has a sweetness, the sweetness of ongoing decay, when the loss of outward power is compensated for by a rapid, unstable increase of internal power.

ɛ/ɔ

There is a darkness inside me that strangles my attempts to get to the bottom of things, figure out who I am, why I did what I did, no matter how many times I tell myself I am done with lies. "Know yourself," we are told, and so we embark, and the further we proceed, the more incomprehensible we seem in our own eyes; the more intermediate questions we solve, the further the ultimate solution recedes into the distance, until we recognize that all our questions have succeeded only in making us more and more a question, a problem, an untraceable thread whose strands grow ever finer before our eyes, and we suddenly recognize that the minute, vibrating strings of this monstrous knot are our own exposed nerves.

---

17 Ed.: See Blaise Pascal, *Pensées and Other Writings*, trans. Honor Levi (Oxford, UK: Oxford University Press, 2008), frag. 61.
18 Elizabeth means the "madman" of Nietzsche's parable, who arrives in the marketplace searching for God. See *The Gay Science*, section 125.

So the pain of self-consciousness always becomes too much, and I flinch. No, Sammy, no to Kill Devil Hills, and no to Nag's Head. "It would have taken me from my studies"—pretense. "I hate crowds"—all the better if one wants isolation, for who is more isolated than an individual surrounded by a crowd, I mean an individual really turned in upon herself? A crowd perfects the inwardness of one whose secret cannot be shared. "I hate being surrounded by the surfers"—yes, there's a chance that they'd all be there, Freddy, Bessy, Tess, etc., perhaps in those interactions I would have found the thread that would carry me back into myself and discover the truth and allow me, once and for all, to repeal a lie.

ↄ

Even in saying all of this, I am still just avoiding the necessary thing, to think *myself* clearly. I do not know how to repent what I cannot recollect. When I think of who you were becoming, I immediately return to my old revulsion, and the disappointment I felt at your friends, your activities, etc., your life.

ↄ

During the moment, one hardly ever knows what will turn out to hold significance, whereas the retrospective glance finds it in all the most trivial places.

I found this note when I was cleaning behind my desk today:

> Going to KDH this weekend.
> PARTAY with Bruce and Sammy etc.
> You wanna come?
> No HW! Gonna go kill those waves.
> -S-

I wonder if you ever understood me, if we ever knew one another. Didn't you know how petty and absurd all those friends of yours were? They revolt me still. I threw this note away when I found it, but it fell behind the bin, and now it returns to me.

I despised what you loved, but perhaps it was you who were in the right. The veil upon reality is like the skin of a human being. What lies beneath that covering is fit only for a surgeon's eyes, and perhaps not even for them. The philosopher is like Oedipus, who does not know to stop asking questions—until it is too late.

℘

The light of the setting sun is falling on the apartment across the street from mine. Its rays are just visible in the mist that fills the air. I'm reminded of that morning—the yesterday of all my tomorrows. The phone ringing, it rings and rings, finally I answer it; the sun is streaming in the window, glowing with warm and overflowing life; its rays, caught in the steam from the expired shower, hover in my memory eternally: in that frozen moment the rays of the sun are always hovering there in the air, but I can't remember feeling their warmth. I answer the phone. It's mom. We're done, and I am standing there, the sun is blazing, everything is bright except the orange sitting on the counter. It's in the shade by the serrated knife. I step back. I am staring at my hands and can't lift my eyes to look at the mirror. The rays of the sun are hovering in the air in the eternal silence.

τὸν φρονεῖν βροτοὺς ὁδώ-
σαντα, τὸν πάθει μάθος
θέντα κυρίως ἔχειν[19]

---

19 Ed.: Elizabeth quotes the Greek tragic poet Aeschylus, drawing this from *Agamemnon*, the first part of his *Oresteia* trilogy of tragedies about the House of Atreus. One contemporary English translation puts it thus: "Zeus has led us on to know / the Helmsman lays it down as law / that we must suffer, suffer unto truth" (*The Oresteia: Agamemnon; The Libation Bearers; The Eumenides*, trans. Robert Fagles, ed. by W. B. Stanford (New York: Penguin Classics, 1984), p. 109, lines 177–179).

THE ANALYSTS

Trop et trop peu de vin. Ne lui en donnez pas: il ne peut trou-
ver la vérité. Donnez-lui en trop: de même.[20]

Pascal, *Pensées* 72

---

20   Ed.: "Too much and too little wine. He does not drink: he cannot find the truth.
He drinks too much: the same."

Sept 1

When I dream, I see your hair streaming out in the current, undulating in the lapping waters. Once, I'd envied it, wished for your curling blonde tresses in place of my mousy brown curtain. I remember the day you came in from the water, laughing, your blue and black wetsuit hugging your limbs, gleaming in the light of the glittering, too bright sun. This was two summers ago in Nag's Head, not far from Farm Dog, and you'd just wiped out while surfing. The others were there, the people you were hanging out with that year, you were talking and laughing. I was sitting on my beach towel. I'd tried practicing the Lilac Fairy's steps but I found the sand too slippery and kept losing my footing. I was now reading *The Rebel* instead. You came running over to me.

"Sis!"

"What?"

"You've gotta come to Kill Devil Hills tonight, M." You were wringing the water from your hair with your hands.

"Why?"

"Party. Fred's place tonight. We'll all be there. We might have a bonfire."

Your brown eyes were looking into mine, searchingly. I met them for a moment, squinting because the sun stood behind your head. "Bonfires are illegal in Kill Devil Hills, Sarah."

‿

It's been raining like a fury, so I haven't been able to get to Pete's place. In my determination to stop forgetting, I have started rereading Noverre. I haven't read his *Letters* in ages, but I still feel a connection. It reminded me of those old nicknames Joshua and I used, Pylades and Bathyllus. I was Pylades, of course, and with his laughs, Joshua had to be Bathyllus. I wonder which of us came up with these? I can't recall. Remembering this has made me more miserable than I expected.

‿

Chess and ballet are importantly alike, though I've never heard anyone remark on their affinity with one another. Each consists in an idealized dance of geometrically perfect movements in which chance and accidental features are reduced as much as possible to nothing. Like most of the great classical ballets, chess also generally ends only with the death of one of principals. Perhaps the Russians are the only people who grasp this affinity, and perhaps this is the secret reason why, despite so many efforts to brutalize and demolish their culture, they excel all others in both arts. To the dismay of the Bolsheviks, after the Revolution the workers demanded, "Give us ballet!" The party officials clucked and shook their heads disapprovingly, but they gave them ballet. One wants to applaud workers like that.

I can see Joshua in my mind, disapproving of this comparison with chess. He would have laughed at it, scorning to respond, but his scorn would have meant: "No dance can be reduced to a script, the dance is that which is contained in the physical memory of a living dancer." That is the dancer's view of truth, and I admit the point. Despite heroic efforts by Beauchamps, Feuillet, etc. to construct a system of notation, ballet companies rely almost solely upon memory. Ancient pantomime is completely lost to us, and so extreme is the problem that by the end of Louis XIV's reign they could not remember how to perform the most popular dances from its beginning. Even Vaganova's system of stage directions has failed to obtain universal usage! Every once in awhile, where there is some kind of notation kept, you see something like the attempt to recover the original steps of *The Sleeping Beauty*, but one must wonder if this could ever work if there were not already so much remembered—all the main content, in fact.

Joshua, you would smile and shake your head, regarding all this talk as so much distraction from the central thing, which is dancing itself. Chess pieces, of course, have no choice in the matter. They submit to the system of algebraic notation, and everywhere in the world, 1. d4 d5 2. c4 signifies the Queen's Gambit, 2. ... e5 is the Albine Countergambit, 2. ... c6 takes one into the Slav Defense, etc. So whereas oblivion has swallowed whole centuries of dance—how I wonder, my friend, what those dances in Louis's days were like—in chess even the smallest facts can become immortal.

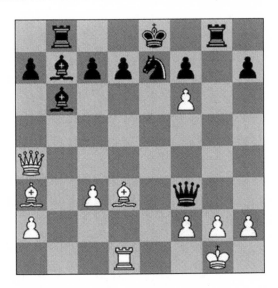

Thus we know that in 1852 Adolf Anderssen, playing as White against Jean Dufresne, was one move away from being mated by Black's queen, but won the match by playing 21.Qxd7+ Kxd7 22.Bf5+ Ke8 23.Bd7+ Kf8 24.Bxe7#, sacrificing his own queen in order to expose the Black king so he could, with surgical precision, be cornered and be defeated.

℘

In the dream, your hands are held out to either side, Ophelia-like. The dead eyes, surrounded by lapping water, stare up at heaven, asking. *Was this, then, my life?* There is an explosion of greens, blues, and light. The news anchor is saying a body was found in the Cape Fear River early this morning, as they cut to a shot of an unspecified part of the river. It's a part I know well. I have already been to the morgue, but I cannot look away and I watch numbly as the anchor speaks. A moment later, it's time to discuss UNCW's loss to Drexel, the end of another losing season. In the dream, you always die in the spring. Summer never comes. But in my mind I can see nothing but those eyes. I never did see you when you were still in the water, only when I came in to verify the body, but in the dream, I always find you in the river. "Wake up" I say, "wake up," but on your face I see only your unanswered question, the water lapping in and out of your nose, pouring in and out of your mouth, mocking its appearance of life. In the real world, there are no fairy enchantments, and even after a hundred years of waiting no prince arrives whose kiss wakes you from sleep. The river's waters swallow us, carrying us out, out, into the ocean, into oblivion.

ↀ

Is philosophy like chess? like dance? These are all idealizing activities—of thought, of war, and of embodied motion. Like chess, in logic philosophy has its perfect system of notation, describing a perfectly idealized set of movements; they enthrone rationality above the chaos and passion of life and transform argument into calculation. Despite this, philosophy shares something even more important with ballet: a superlative debt to the Platonists, the school that labored so much at the birth of each art to elevate humanity by subjecting first the mind and then the body to the ideal. (This was before philosophy began its long march toward the more purely dialectical idealism of chess and away from the old idealism of truth and beauty.) But has anyone ever succeeded in this art of idealizing human life? If it were successful, would Plato have had Socrates describe philosophy as preparation for death?[21]

In chess, however, they did succeed; they built the computer, and are idealizing human players right out of existence.

So, either way, idealization is annihilation. You cannot drink the ocean.

---

21 Plato, *Phaedo* 64a

Sept 2

Weather remains poor. I wonder when I shall be able to get to Pete's house? I feel frantic with energy.

⋯

Those summers we spent in the Outer Banks—Nothing was so good as having a secret in those days and when we didn't have any to keep we made them up, just to keep them between ourselves. We shared knowing looks and giggled over the misunderstandings of others, whispering to each other, *arcanum arcanandum.*[22]

I was all skinny limbs and sharp elbows, and my acid tongue defended us both against meddling adults. I now understand that a child's intelligence terrifies adults; it operates by knight's leaps and turns up in unexpected corners. Your sense of mischief and adventure must have equally terrified our parents, for you found every hiding place in and outside of the house, ruining half your dresses with soot, thorns, thistles, and dirt in the process, taking to the park with hair spray and matches to set teddy bears on fire.

Together, we had a world to ourselves. We were Anne Bonny and Mary Read on Halloween, with Popo the cat our jealous Calico Jack. We spent weeks that summer surveying the woods of Ocracoke, in preparation for the pirate fortress we'd construct one day, the hideout from which we could defy the whole world. I wonder what happened to the plans we drew up? Everything was written in code, "just in case."

⋯

A danseur stands upon the floor in fifth position; his head moves ever so slightly, cocking it to one side as if to catch the music—the left leg moves out in a glissade, the right leg lifts, just—and then he is leaping, leaping over the stage, a grande jeté, he is coming down, his feet barely touch the ground, and he is leaping again—a

---

22   Ed.: While the sisters' "twig Latin" often follows the rules of Latin, it sometimes develops idiosyncratically. Here the second has happened. The meaning *seems* to be something like "the secret that must be kept secret."

switch leap, he has reversed his position, and is now leaping again in a barrel roll, once, twice, three times, and he pauses again in fifth position—is he smiling? The music suddenly lifts, but he has already moved with it, leaving fifth position again for another grande jeté, and another—the whole stage in two leaps. In the thrilling moment when he soared over it all, he declared independence from the earth, asserted a citizenship in the heavens. Should you take your place among the stars, I will make all my wishes by you.

To act requires adopting a position from which the act is possible; but to act well, one needs a position from which the act is easy and natural; especially if the point is to do the act gracefully, that is, without hesitation, resistance, and wasted movement; above all, without wasted passion, energy. The positions of dance have been studied. Beyond the five positions, Vaganova says "There are no others possible."[23] But have the positions of spirit been so studied? Perhaps this is what Aristotle thought to do in studying virtue? But there is something over-hydraulic in his conception of the human spirit; it lacks agility, dynamism. He lacks a position for the movement out of despair, a position for the inward act of recoiling the spirit's spring, enabling it again to leap into action.

☙

I remember a double date we did with Chris and that boy from band. You were 14 and I was about to turn 16, the last summer of our shared secrets. I'd just begun dying my hair auburn, after Judit Polgár, whom I idolized terribly. We were sitting in some little coffee shop or bistro and things were going terribly, and you handed me a dime. Your eyes were somehow playful, earnest, trusting, all at once. I looked at it quizzically, but you just held out your hand with the palm open and said, "Re-dime me, M."

I tried to keep a straight face, but we both collapsed in laughter.

---

23 Ed.: Agrippina Vaganova, *Basic Principles of Classical Ballet*, New York: Dover Publications 1946, p. 17.

You ran out the door, and I tossed the poor boys a five dollar bill before running out after you into the shining summer outside.

℘

Six months ago in March, on a day that seems only yesterday, we argued by the Kenan Memorial Fountain.

"I won't get to go to Greece," you said.

"Oh."

"Do you even know what I'm talking about?"

"No...Um. Did you apply to go?"

"I told everyone over Christmas break! You were there with mom and dad and everyone."

"Why did you want to go to Greece, anyway?"

"God! Why do you hate me so much?"

"I don't hate you. We just don't—"

You walked away, and I didn't know what to say. As you turned away from me, the slanting rays of the setting sun shone in the sparkling spray of the fountain's bitter cold water. That moment is now frozen in my mind, twisting and turning, and it is always that cold March day, the sun is always sparkling in that water, and you are always turning away while I stare at your back, not knowing what to say.

℘

Petipa sometimes used a chessboard to plan out his choreography.[24] This suggests how different the view of the choreographer and the dancer are; just imagine if the choreographer designed the whole dance with the idea that no dancer would ever step upon some single square he had selected—say, g4. Would any dancer know that the choreographer had this in mind? Wouldn't the dancer, rather, be wholly focused on the steps he was intended to perform, and not much notice the missing square? For how could he notice it? In just the same way, I feel that there was something

---

24 Marius Ivanovich Petipa, 1818–1910, leading choreographer of ballet's Romantic period.

not quite honest about the argument yesterday, as if we performed such a dance designed to avoid the crucial matter. What would we have found the other day at the store if we'd stepped upon the forbidden checkerboard square? But only the choreographer knew which square that was, and we dancers merely knew the steps by instinct. Nothing is harder than to move by instinct and to observe oneself moving at the same time; reflection and immersion in action exclude one another. It is never a compliment to tell a dancer that her movements appeared calculated, rather than free! So we never stepped upon the predestined square. The dancer will discover the omission only if it forces her to act ungracefully and do something unnatural from the standpoint of the music, the dance itself, or her partners. What was ungraceful in the argument yesterday, then?

Or, it was as if a chess teacher set up a student's chessboard with an end game between the white king and white bishop and the black king and black knight. "Choose either White or Black: which one leads to the earlier mate?" No matter how this student wracks his brain, no degree of cunning will suffice. What is wanted was ruled out by the beginning.

I assume that this is why the Oracle said we must begin by seeking to know ourselves, and Socrates was wise to make this principle central to philosophy. I have nothing but respect for Socrates; he followed the examined life right down to the grave, so he knew he was recommending no easy task, a task harder than the professors make it out to be. But I am sure he underestimated the challenge. It is interesting that Socrates never despaired, even though he fully believed he would never know what he needed to know. He never even understood the nature or cause of his ignorance. He knew all this, but goes to death cheerfully. Yet what if his ethical inquiries had revealed him to be complicit in a monstrous crime? I don't mean *ignorantly* complicit! As if that was what complicity meant. What then?

☙

There were twigs, leaves, and bits of branches in your hair. You had just fallen into the tree house, after having climbed around it, over it, above it. I was kneeling with a big book to one side, writing on a pad of lined paper. You fell with a crash, but had a wicked grin and cunning glance in your eyes. You turned to me with a grim and conspiratorial look. The sunlight fell through the leaves of the tree on the tree house floor in dappled blotches. "Don't tell the pirates I'm here," you said. "They've been chasing me ever since I stole Blackbeard's peg leg." You held out a table leg you'd taken from the basement.

"We need a code language," I said.

"Yes! Then the pirates couldn't understand us."

"I'm basing it on Latin."

"You know Latin?" You sounded awed.

"I know enough," I said. "I've been reading about it."

"Wow."

"Say, 'redime me.'" I pronounced "-dime" like the coin, and "me" as it is said in English.

"Re-dime me."

"That means, 'Save me!' If you need my help, say that. I'll say it if I need your help."

"And then we'll help each other, but no one will know."

That was the beginning of "twig Latin," a hodgepodge of Latin, English, and misunderstandings. You were seven, and this was our first and best secret.

Sept 3/4

I finally walked down to Pete's house yesterday (the beach house off of Wrightsville Beach, past the Causeway Café). When I let myself in, I was surprised to find Simon instead. He was sitting in the kitchen checking his email on his phone, and barely looked up when I arrived. He was wearing a smart black suit, polished black shoes, and a red tie; his hair was black, cut short and close to his head. Simon used to work with Dad in the Pitt County DA's office, but I hadn't seen him in years.

"You still playing chess?" he asked.

It was Simon who had taught me to play chess all those years ago, during free moments working all those cases with Dad. He was blunt, hard-driven, and preferred argument to small-talk. I always imagined he must be hard drinking, too, but I had never seen him drink. For a long time he supplied my stereotype of a New Yorker. He was not actually from New York, but had only gone to school there. "Not much recently," I said.

"Oh," he said. "You were so promising, I didn't expect you to end up just a café player."

"That's what they called Polgár, too," I said.

"Touché," said Simon. He sounded bored. He continued scrolling and tapping his phone, grimacing at something he saw, furrowing his narrow, laser-like eyebrows. His face seemed pale, almost skeletal, next to his dark clothing.

"What are you doing these days?" I asked.

"Putting people in jail," said Simon.

"Guilty people, or innocent people?" A lame attempt at a joke.

He laughed. "Everyone is guilty."

"Do you know Pete?" I asked.

"No," he said.

"Then how is it you're here in his house?" I said.

"Perhaps I am breaking and entering, or seeking to cover up a crime," he said.

"That would be absurd," I said.

Simon shrugged, as if to suggest he found absurdity irrelevant. "I'm here because a certain friend of mine needs my help. I believe you know him—Professor Rufus Rushnevsky?"

"Oh, yes, of course," I said. "But now I'm more confused than before."

"Just so," he said. "Rufus had an uncle of sorts, an artist who lived in Ontario, and when this uncle passed away this year, everything came, willy nilly, to Rufus."

"But I thought Professor Rufus had no family," I said.

"Is that what you, his students, call him? How interesting," said Simon. "Yes, he took himself to be without a family in the world, and yet, here was this inheritance, landing right on his doorstep, so to speak. Your professor had no interest in most of what he'd inherited, and you know his fondness for grand gestures. Well, looking over all this artistic apparatus and accoutrement, he recalled he had a student with an interest and talent for such things. This would be your Pete. The next matter became how to pass this on and, if possible, avoid paying taxes, and so on and so forth. He was at his wits' end, perplexed by the legal technicalities, whereas I know just enough tax law to show the way—that is, I know the prosecutor's side of it, and so—here I am."

"Oh," I said. That seemed reasonable, at least if you knew the professor. "How do you happen to know Rufus?" I asked.

"We sometimes discuss legal and political philosophy," said Simon, waving this aside as no matter of importance.

"I didn't know you read philosophy," I said. "Are you one of those philosophy majors who went to law school?"

"Eventually one has to stop reading and get on with living," said Simon. "Perhaps some people should spend their lives reading books, but I can't believe that there are many like that. People should do what they're good at. I'm good at finding out what people are hiding."

"Oh," I said. There was an awkward silence. Finally, I asked, "What do you know about the Delacroix case?"

"What do you mean?" he asked, with a sharp gaze.

"I recently came upon an essay that referred to it," I said, "but I couldn't make out what the author meant, because he—I think the author is a 'he'—referred to the case at a crucial point without explaining its details."

"Your author made a sloppy mistake," said Simon. "Do you know anything about him?"

"No, not a thing," I said. "The essay is very obscure, but I think that understanding the Delacroix case would at least make the content clearer."

"I do know the case," said Simon. "Why don't you show me this 'essay'?"

I pulled out the letter I'd received the other day from my purse, and laid it upon the kitchen table where he was seated. The envelope had contained just two things: a small slip of paper, recently typed and printed, paper-clipped to a document written by hand in a neat, almost spidery cursive script much earlier, a decade or more in the past. The slip of paper read:

> Dear Elizabeth:
> Perhaps you will find this useful, if you are not yet too far gone.
>
> Yours
> *Niakani*

I kept this slip of paper to myself, and provided Simon with only the main part. It was not really a letter, but more like an extended philosophical analysis; but that's not quite right either, because it also seemed like a self-analysis, an attempt by the author to work upon a purely private problem, which, however, is only presented obliquely.

Simon picked it up and looked it over carefully. "I wonder what handwriting analysis would show?" he said, more to himself than to me.

I attach the letter below:

NIAKANI

I need a point of stability, a diamond of order that can resist the chaos of my swirling thoughts. I need a fortress to which I can retreat, in which I can vouchsafe truth and from whence I can sally to regain sovereignty of my mind. I keep asking, can evil be answered, atoned for, redeemed? Can what is twisted be made straight again? Can sin be expiated? I must know. For months on end, my head has been swirling with thoughts, unable to follow a logical sequence for more than a few seconds, but that misery has settled down into a steady, throbbing pain, now. Thought is again possible, and necessary. Writing is painful, speaking is worse, but keeping silent is most painful of all. So I will put my thoughts to paper. Perhaps I will even discover something; a single point will suffice. With a single point I can build my diamond and within this diamond I will be reborn.

I've been reading Kierkegaard and Dostoevsky like mad, and I feel I am on the edge of working out a solution. Dostoevsky is closer to the truth than Kierkegaard, though…it is one thing to grow bitter in old age, another to grow old before one is even forty. Others can say what they will, I am sure this is because he got the essential thing wrong in his relationship with Regine. Besides, what would infinite resignation be for someone who understood so much but a way of trying to escape responsibility?... Yet Dostoevsky is so ambiguous in everything, and leaves so many questions to us. I have to begin with two questions. This will give me the order I need, and then I can look at the main thing—is there hope for evil to be redeemed?

I need to focus. My question resolves into this: Why does Dostoevsky's Prince Myshkin fail as a savior? But that's not quite it—it's not about him, in particular, it's a general question. The general question is: Why doesn't his sort of love save anyone, least of all himself?

I think that this gets wrapped up with another question: If there's an answer to evil, it must surely be God's grace! How the stricken sinner longs for such grace! For forgiveness of wrong, for transformation, redemption! To be bought out from sin and brought in a member of the heavenly host! But isn't it obscene to reach for this too soon? Bonhoeffer said, of justification by faith, that "as the answer to a sum it is perfectly true" that salvation is an act of grace on God's part, "but as the initial data it is a piece of self-deception." The only person who has a right to say that he knows that he was saved by faith in God is the one who has arrived at this truth after a long trial. Someone who approaches the idea of grace as an initial starting point, rather than as a conclusion, can never avoid the suspicion of not having genuinely grasped the idea.[25]

Let's get to the point. Here's what I take as a fact: The world is full of evil. I don't mean suffering, though God knows there's enough of that. I mean it is filled with evil, our evil. We stand in horror at the plain hypocrisies and compromised integrity of past generations and fail to apply the lesson to ourselves. We think,

---

25 Ed.: This idea can be found in Dietrich Bonhoeffer, *The Cost of Discipleship* (New York: Simon & Schuster, 1995), p. 51.

somehow, we are immune to their blindness, without reflecting upon the fact that nothing is more common than for evil to be blind to itself—and that we therefore will find our hands stained with blood we never imagined to find there. The best causes we support may turn out (frequently do turn out!) to involve us, not accidentally, but essentially, in evil. We've turned a blind eye to these things, even turned a blind eye to turning the blind eye; but eventually, won't this all be found out? Not only that we were involved in evil, but that our ignorance was culpable? How much work, how many stratagems and mental machinery, it takes not to know. But once the machinery is in place, it runs and runs... Therefore to know oneself is to be either crushed in one's conscience or to sear the conscience so as to go on living.

I hate all these authors who make evil into some kind of external thing, something to be fought against. I despise Camus's *The Plague.* He wants us to imagine human life as a kind of dark story in which many are oppressed, many despair, and a few fight for the sake of humanity, but what he leaves out is the principal thing, complicity! In a more accurate story the doctor would try to heal those with the disease, but not only would he come back infected, he would later, when it is too late, discover himself to be one of those spreading the disease, even while he healed. Oh, contemporaries can make believe that there are heroes, but historians know that even those who have fought for justice have turned out to have been far from pure, and to have been complicit in far more evils than they knew ... if indeed they did not know.

To say that God saves us—that he forgives sins and washes away the corruption of sinfulness—means that God, whom we say is holy and just, reconciles himself with sinners, beings who are opposed to his holiness and justice, beings who will avail themselves of his grace and then enslave or murder others just like themselves, who will trample upon their fellows and sing hymns of forgiveness on Sunday. I do not understand how God could reconcile himself with such creatures.

That is the fundamental problem associated with understanding Christian love. To get to its root one must simply get down to what such love is, why it looks past sin and reconciles sinners. How can a perfectly holy God stand to love, redeem, and reconcile himself with sinners? How can this be a standard of human life? For won't it make us into Myshkins, and Prince Myshkin was unable to save anyone, wasn't he swallowed up himself in the evil of human life, in loving those he couldn't save, whose love only humiliated those he loved more and more?...

A sinner who is becoming really conscious of his sin can become offended at forgiveness, offended, as it were, for righteousness' sake. For the sinner who has become conscious in this way, who sees himself in a mirror for the first time, what offends him is not the 'third-person' question; he doesn't view God's love for sinners theatrically, as an observer. The question is how he can bring his own sin into the presence of a holy God, or what God could want with a being like himself, a cockroach, that is, the repulsive insect he has found himself to be—in such a state one may well drive oneself mad and flee God for the sake, again as it were, of righteousness, for the sake of God's righteousness. When the prodigal son returns and his father offers him the ring and roasts the fattened calf he must wonder, or he is not really repentant, at the propriety of accepting his father's gifts. Is his father not doing something, not just unconventional or against the tide of custom, but isn't he doing something really quite scandalous in accepting him back? So the sinner too asks, 'How can God love me? How can I accept such love, would not associating with him, knowing what this means, mean besmirching his honor?'

I feel my mind is beginning to swirl again. I have to begin with love. This is what we always come to: *For God so loved...* God loves, and we, too, are to love, but what does such love—agapic love, I mean, not romantic love of friendship or whatever other types of love there are—come to? The Biblical dictionaries are of surprisingly little use, and the theologians so often seem to regard landing a glancing blow at the thing as some kind of great triumph. They frequently treat love entirely as a matter of the will. This is really just a sign that, having given up comprehending the concrete content, they have found it necessary to make the concept entirely abstract. In this way agapic love is represented as being effected through the bare will acting alone as a kind of pure volitional act detached from the rest of a man's soul. If some wretch, feeling the call of God and hoping to escape his sinful lifestyle, came into a church to discover what it was to love—for he knew this, that Christ's disciples 'shall be known by their love,' and that this was the place to come to become a follower of Christ and find such love. The sermon probably doesn't explicitly answer his question, it only alludes to it, so imagine that such a wretch gets the opportunity to talk to the pastor alone. 'Ah!' he'd say to himself. 'Now I shall find something out.' He asks what this love is that God provides to sinners and how it changes sinners. The pastor, who is studied in books and theological dictionaries, displays confidence in answering. I expect that the original man would now be quite excited. But then the pastor informs him that love is something to engage the will only, not the sentiments, and it performs actions without a corresponding affective state in man's soul. That is what these compendia all declare: love is nothing but the will to a man's good. What can this mean, but that love means something like pretending to care? 'Well do you Christians deserve your reputation as hypocrites!' the man might say to himself angrily as he walks away. 'Whatever this love business is, you know nothing of it, it's just something you do to keep up appearances, or something!' He knows, besides, that without the right sort of heart, one shouldn't be able to do the thing properly, so Christian love becomes an absurd vanity. And so he walks away disappointed; he'd wished to discover what God's love is like and what sort of love he ought to practice and found out merely that it was a way of behaving, even a sort of aping.

There are real priests and real pastors, I know, ones who really do love. But can they explain it? They live it. The authors, however, are trying to guard against sloppy sentimentality and the idea that God's love is called forth by the admirable qualities of the beloved—if God's love is willing to die for sinners, it can't depend upon the antecedent merit of its object to call it forth. How much more beautiful would it be if the visitor found someone who simply practiced love, and who showed it to him! A Myshkin. But, that has its own problems, doesn't it? Myshkin is a failed savior, but I can't see how to avoid beginning here; his love is presented so vividly and accurately, and if he fails, well, still, this is a better starting point than those compendia.

Prince Myshkin is supposed to represent a "truly beautiful soul," but also to have suffered from a kind of "idiocy," an inability to engage the world or speak with others. Dostoevsky represented this very beautifully in one particular passage:

One bright, sunny day he went for a walk in the mountains and walked a long time, tormented by a thought that, try as he might, seemed to be eluding him. Before him was the brilliant sky, below—the lake, and around, the bright horizon, stretching away into infinity. He looked a long time in agony. He remembered now how he had stretched out his arms towards that bright and limitless expanse of blue and had wept. What tormented him was that he was a complete stranger to all this. What banquet was it, what grand everlasting festival, to which he had long felt drawn, always—ever since he was a child, and which he could never join? Every morning the same bright sun rises; every morning there is a rainbow on the waterfall; every evening the highest snowcapped mountain, far, far away, on the very edge of the sky, shows with a purple flame; every 'tiny gnat' buzzing round him in the hot sunshine plays its part in that chorus: it knows its place, it loves it and is happy;

every blade of grass grows and is happy! Everything has its
path, and everything knows it path; it departs with a song
and it comes back with a song; only he knows nothing,
understands nothing, neither men nor sounds, a stranger
to everything and an outcast.[26]

I treasure this passage and pray that I never forget it. How vividly it highlights the two aspects of love: what love *grows from* and
what love *grows into*. What is so helpful is Dostoevsky's separating
the two through Myshkin's illness, because he has the first and not
the second, and this clarifies so much.

What he *has* is the aspect from which love grows. It emerges from
our openness to the world and from our capacity to respond to the life
of other living beings in empathy, compassion, and joy. It is a mistake
to emphasize the side of human nature that responds to the suffering
of others over that which responds to their happiness. If we focus all
of our attention on compassion, for example, then we are left with a
picture of love in which love is relegated to the sphere of suffering, as if
love would have nothing to do in a world without it. But as Myshkin
says in another place, 'I don't understand how it's possible to pass by
a tree and not be happy to see it.'[27] I understand this, I understand it
profoundly! He says this because it is a joyful thing to *experience* the
joy of another, or even to experience the much lesser 'happiness' of the
tree or fly as it fulfills its nature. There is in human nature the ability
to attentively 'enter' the life of another, insofar as this other has a life
and history of its own, and to experience joy and happiness and pain
and grief along with it. Myshkin, although still an "idiot" and unable
to interact with the world in any substantial way, felt the ongoing life
all around him—the way that even flies or grass may be spoken of as
'happy'—he felt this in a deep way.

---

26   Ed.: Fyodor Dostoevsky, *The Idiot*, trans. David Magarshack (New York: Penguin,
1955), p. 406.
27   Ed.: *The Idiot*, p. 531.

Love grows from this capacity to respond to the life of another, but what it grows *toward* is actually *joining* in the life of another, becoming involved in it somehow. To have one's awareness wrapped up in another person's life and yet to be cut off from interacting with the person and becoming part of his or her life— this is the agony Myshkin expresses in the passage, in which he can sense that there is a world of life outside of him, a world of life which he cannot join. He can feel the concerns of others but cannot form any kind of relationship with them.

Aquinas somewhere in the *Summa* refers to these two aspects as 'formal union' and 'real union' or a 'union of affections' and then a 'union in life.'[28] That's not bad, but a bit formal. I will say that love involves both *openness* and *involvement*.

To return to the question above: how is it that God may love sinners? The answer is that when we consider the essence of love, responsiveness to the life of another and the wish to become involved in the life of the other, the question becomes quite strange, and we realize that the opposition of sin and love is not as straightforward as it seemed. For what is it about sin that could prevent such responsiveness from operating? Or what is it about sin that could prevent someone from seeking to become involved in someone's life as a result of such a response? Might not sin actually drive someone to become involved in someone's life—to help a person escape its slavery and guilt?

It now becomes hard to see where the question finds purchase. Suppose it's true, *God is love*; now what shall we say could prevent him from loving someone, sinner though he be? I know that they say that this statement refers to God's trinitarian existence of mutual love, and let's say that's true; but have they really eluded the force of the point? Are we going to say that God is *not* radically

---

28 Ed.: See Thomas Aquinas, *Summa Theologiae*, I-II, Q. 28, A.1; and I-II, Q. 26, A. 2, Reply Obj. 2.

aware of and open to the lives of his creatures? And surely it is always open to him to become involved? What they mean when they want to insist on this is something else entirely—they are thinking about *actual* involvement.

That's a good point. Could a being prevent God from getting involved? Is that what sin is? I need to understand this. Here is what I think, here is the second facet of my diamond: It is only an infinite hatred or infinite pride that can really disqualify someone from receiving God's love; that is sin raised to the highest power. This is what Smerdyakov was up to in that mysterious passage of *Brothers Karamazov* where he commits suicide. In my view, that act is infinite hatred, or it's meaningless. Hatred of this type is hatred of a quite different order from ordinary hates—hatred taken to the level of an existential stance, a concrete way of understanding one's identity and approaching life.

What is an existential stance, though? The first manifestation of freedom. It is first in the sense that Aristotle would say that an animal's life, or soul, is the first entelechy of the potentialities embodied in its tissues and organs. Kierkegaard calls it "positing the synthesis," an astonishingly abstract way of speaking about this.[29] What it means is that our identities are a complex of factors, historical, biological, and social factors on the one hand (necessity, temporality, finitude), and, on the other hand, we are freedom, thought, and soul (possibility, eternity, infinitude). We include, as constituent elements, the fact of our embodiment, various physical features, a biological inheritance, personality, talents, capacities, historical relationships governed by when and where we were born, relationships with others, what we have done, what we have suffered, and the social world in which we find ourselves, our language, etc. We may wish to have been born with this trait rather

---

29 Ed.: See Søren Kierkegaard, *The Concept of Anxiety*, ed. and trans. by Reidar Thomte in collaboration with Albert B. Anderson (Princeton, NJ: Princeton University Press, 1980), p. 49 (and elsewhere).

than that trait, or in this family rather than that family, to have had this father rather than that father, or to be born in this time rather than that time, but these are part of us without any choosing on our part. So, too, our past... although we may wish we had done one thing rather than another, we are now the person who chose to do X, and that, too, is who we are. We may regret and repent of X, but that is not the same as not having done it. It belongs to us now as one of our necessary, temporal constituent elements.

What brings everything to a point, though, is that we're not just this—we contain thought and freedom as well. We can consider our identities and evaluate what we are and, finally, take a side on what we find there. I am so-and-so's father?[30] But I will not be like him. And so on. But, it's not all just positive and negative evaluations. It's a messy business trying to work out your identity, and a lot comes down to the "how" of it. We sense that there are many possible ways of cooking up the ingredients, many ways of mixing them together, more recipes than we can imagine, and yet, in life, we get to cook up one of these only. Now, which shall it be? To make that decision is to take an existential stance.

The obvious difficulty is, if you've got multiple factors, you've got a potential for conflict. In fact it seems not just possible, but actually true that everyone has conflicts. Dostoevsky is wonderful at showing this, especially in *Brothers*, which also shows a variety of ways in which individuals can take such a stance; each Karamazov has one, but so do the other characters, and in fact each Karamazov is matched by a female character with similar stuff, and, often, a similar stance. E.g.: you're passionate for wine and women, but you're passionate about honor, too, and there are difficulties in your life that keep making you have to turn one of these against the other—that's Dmitry. He takes a stance: pursue the base thing, but pursue it honorably! Is that

---

30   Ed.: One expects the son to be the one who declares he will not be like is father. Niakani has reversed this.

a good way to combine those factors? It takes all the novel's resources, but Dostoevsky gets Dmitry to recognize that this recipe won't cook up and, what's more, there is another, better way to combine these together. The characters all have conflicts like this.

Taking the wrong stance leads to suffering. Well, I get that, too. We have lots of factors in us, too many factors, and it's not easy to get them together. Having them wrong means being at odds with yourself, and in a very bad way, too. If something is part of you and can't be gotten rid of it, then trying to put yourself together as if you were a mix that didn't include this part will mean something's always left out. A comic author would know what to do with this by always having the missing element on the verge of popping out again, placing the character in the position of constantly needing, by ever more absurd attempts, to keep the piece out of view. A tragic author could do the same, except here, the contradiction between what the character is, and what the character wishes to be, is a gradually growing threat that chases the hero until the last moment, when he drowns in the open conflict with truth.

What is the first sin? It is the incorrect use of freedom, to posit the self in defiance, to cook up the recipe the wrong way. It's a stance on how one should be that won't work, it's contrary to what one is. This first use of freedom has a binding power that is difficult to escape. Once we've got ourselves set out a certain way, something we do when we are young, thirteen or fourteen, we have a devil of a time getting ourselves any other way. There's too much resistance, and too much stuff, and too much that just doesn't get along with other elements inside of us. What's a Myshkin missing? Love us how he may, he can't do a thing to get the mix fixed, because what's wrong in us can't be corrected without a more powerful medicine, and he can't save himself, either, because by loving, he gets himself dragged right down into perdition with those he loves; being open to others and involved in their lives exposes him to their own sin and madness without providing the power to change them by getting them back to a point "before" this misuse of freedom.

How do we get this mix of material right? For this, we need what I'd call a "self-making passion," what Kierkegaard sometimes calls an "infinite passion." He did not use this phrase to refer to the intensity of such a passion, but rather to its inner, dynamic potential and scope. It possesses the power to define, shape, or realign every aspect of the person, thereby giving a single concrete form to the person's will and inner being. It assigns other passions and concerns their function, direction, and meaning, and they allow it the right to condition their role within the individual's overall subjective life. It gets into everything a person is and draws this together into a combination that makes sense. It holds this dynamic power within it at all times, and so is a power whereby a person can attain unity, if only he can be found by such a passion.

It is remarkable that the ancients, whose lives are testaments to such remarkable passions, have so little to say about this topic. Even when it is obvious that we are in the presence of self-making passion, it is obscured and wiped off the map. Just consider Plato's Socratic dialogues. Anyone can see that the remarkable hold of his beloved teacher is just as significant to Plato as Beatrice's was upon Dante, yet Platonic love can't capture what was most significant about this love. Plato imagines that the reformation of the individual must proceed from a redirection of the person's energies (so far, so good), but he envisions this in the manner of ends and means; what a person really needs is a new end, the Good itself, the Beautiful itself, which he'll now pursue all his life. But why must the self-making passion treat everything else instrumentally in this way? Was that the significance of his love for his great teacher? The significance of Socrates for Plato was, on the contrary, that he showed him how to put all his being to use at once ... for Plato the artist and Plato the philosopher could not have been one individual without the power of a Socrates to draw his whole mental equipment into coherent function. Second, he always envisions this transition to the dominant passion as leaving the original object behind, which is entirely contrary not only to our moral instincts—a common charge, I don't give a fig for it—but more importantly false to the love itself, false to Plato's own instincts, and false to Socrates. For it is clear that Socrates did nothing but concern himself with individuals, and Plato the same, above all with his beloved master. The beloved is no mere occasion for growth but something deeper than this.

So the self-making passion is not a "dominant love" or some such thing, in virtue of which a person *just* loves this one, big thing that everything else is a means toward. Instead, its unity is a function of its power to perfect the individual through bringing him into coherent functional unity. Nor is it an *ideal* standing outside the world; rather, it has a different sort of power. If Myshkin represents love, and what is, in its way, a perfect state of soul, then the self-making passion should be understood as a power that draws someone back from himself into the world *via* the passion. It makes the person coherent with himself, but also gives him a relation to the world of which he is a part, and from which he receives some part of his identity. It opens him up to that world in the way that Plato's love for Socrates made him aware not just of Socrates, but of the whole project Socrates was engaged in—meaning, the drive to draw people into thirsting for wisdom. The self-making passion harmonizes the personality and corrects a person *toward* loving, in the particular way that makes use of all his being in a coherent way.

This is what I believe, what I must believe, from myself. That I find anyone else talking about such singularities is remarkable for me, but one doesn't learn about such things from books. Just as Arkady was thrilled to find another who knew what idea-passion was, so I was thrilled to find that others knew what this passion was ... but, but, but ... if only perhaps I had found this all out earlier.[31] I thought I knew everything, that I needed no teacher, that no one could tell me what I knew in every particle of my being

---

31 Ed.: See Fyodor Dostoevsky, *The Adolescent*, trans. Richard Pevear and Larissa Volkonosky (New York: Vintage Books, 2004), p. 63.

without any instruction at all. I've observed the whole matter as carefully as possible from the inside, and this is what I've found. But it is too much pride to say I need no teacher. I think without finding some others I would have gone mad.

So it follows that if we are meant to be beings who love, like Myshkin, like Christ, but we are in a state of contradiction and defiance due to our misuse of our own freedom to posit a self that cannot make sense of who we are, and that makes us unlovable and unloving ... for no one who wills more than one thing can love properly, there is always something kept back, a something that emerges always at the wrong time.

I don't know what kind of limits there are regarding such passions. Maybe there are many different types of self-making passions—passions generated by a person's relationship with a place, a people, a family, a person, for example (Kierkegaard says: "any other interest in which an individual has concentrated the whole reality of actuality" can provide this role.)[32] Otherwise, what are we to make of David Livingstone's being haunted by those words, "I have sometimes seen, in the morning sun, the smoke of a thousand villages, where no missionary has ever been."[33] Those words burned in his heart and animated the whole remainder of his life, and when he had sacrificed everything—health, child, wife, comfort, etc.— to spend his life in the African bush, he counted that not a sacrifice, but a privilege. In each case the relationship generating this self-making passion is God's intermediary to us, drawing us together and drawing us into the world, into the mission he has called us to. Alyosha and Zosima exemplify this in their relationship with each other. Some people think that Dostoevsky's friendship with the philosopher Vladimir Solovyov was the reason this idea became so

---

32   Ed.: Søren Kierkegaard, *Fear and Trembling*, trans. Howard V. Hong and Edna H. Hong (Princeton: Princeton University Press, 1983), p. 43.
33   Ed.: See, e.g., Sam Wellman, *David Livingstone: Missionary, Physician, Explorer* (North Newton, KS: Wild Centuries Press, 2013), p. 19.

important to him. Whatever we say, the fact is that both literature and history feature such relationships; one needs only consider the friendship between Gilgamesh and Enkidu, Plato's relationship with his teacher, Socrates. I believe we see it depicted in fiction in *Moby-Dick*, in the friendship of Queequeg and Ishmael, and we surely see it in *Brideshead Revisited*, where Waugh depicts it in the friendship of Charles Ryder and Sebastian Flyte. In the case of Gilgamesh and Plato, the relationships provided them with an understanding of what life was for and the ideals around which to organize it. Perhaps for Socrates it was his relationship with Athens, a city he would not leave alone and would never cease trying to reform, even while thinking this task impossible. For such, as he himself said, was his mission from the God. And perhaps every sort of love a person may have may also take the form of a self-making passion, one with an unlimited capacity to draw the person into interconnection with other beings, into the parade of life.

Then what can disqualify someone for God's love? Here is what I take to be my most disturbing discovery, infinite hatred. This is what I saw in that moment, and … It is not easy for someone to hold out indefinitely against God or to oppose oneself to him utterly and completely, but if it can be done, it can be done like this. Perhaps in the end it is always like this. Infinite hatred is a transformation of self-making passion, which inherits the latter's unlimited transformative power, its unlimited scope and duration, and uses this to make the person's emotional life, mental life, and embodied existence all serve his hated; whatever passions serve that hatred are reinforced and strengthened by its inexhaustible strength, while those indifferent to it are suffered to coexist so long as they do not oppose or weaken it, being allowed to operate only within a delimited scope.

But how can the self-making passion, God's grace to us, become infinite hatred? I have studied this to try to understand how this can happen, even in this life, and what I have found (and this is my discovery, I claim it for myself) is the decisive importance of *the crisis*.

Yes, Kierkegaard certainly knew it, and his writing certainly flows out entire from his crisis, but he did not understand the category. Everything hinges upon this moment, one's whole life will be shaped by it. This is the next facet of my diamond. It must be held in place by the others, or become everything, but it is the centerpiece, the cornerstone so to speak. Everything depends upon this point.

Infinite hatred arises out of self-making passion in something like the following way. Here is a typical case, if we can speak of such. Suppose the self-making passion occurs within a typical romantic relationship in its ordinary trappings. The lover surrenders to his love—he is not held back by the risk of commitment, but allows this passion to define his subjective life, to infiltrate every aspect of himself, and redraw the lines of his personality and to provide their true interpretation, and he does this without reservation or recourse. But in doing so of course he does so with some specific ideas about who she is and about the sort of relationship that they will have; without these his devotion would have no content. Yet these ideas might contain or entail a mistake about her, in fact they must contain a mistake, for no human being knows all that may be known about another human being; the heart of another is always to an important degree a mystery to us. He continues his devotion and walks in devotion and love and care for months and let us say even for years.

But then the crisis occurs. It is the crisis that undoes this activation and throws the lover back upon himself, now open to the ultimate and unthinkable commitment. Only someone who has surrendered to self-making passion can encounter the crisis. It is a moment when the person is thrown back upon himself by means of a blow that, because it strikes him through his passion, and strikes this *just so*, in just such a way, it strikes him in every aspect of his being and shatters the self.

A self-making passion involves two types of interconnection: interconnection with a specific *object*, firstly, and, secondly, a *pattern* of interconnection whereby this single connection becomes a general pattern for us through which we are now fitted to enter the pageant of life and engage with it in a certain manner. Someone who surrenders to the self-making passion allows each of these to hold as much sway as possible over himself, allows it to establish his identity. But because this identity is formed, not through the agency of the individual, but through the individual's interconnection with being, an interconnection channeled through a particular locus—a person, place—this leaves the individual peculiarly and precipitously open to influence from without. Quite unlike the sinner curved in upon himself, this person is radically open at the point of contact through which the self-making passion acts upon him. The crisis erupts when fundamental conflict arises within these elements.

From what was just said, it follows that the crisis can have two main valances: for if there is conflict it is between the pattern and oneself, or the pattern and the other person. So the crisis is a betrayal of some kind by one party.

I'll start with the second case, where the conflict arises between the pattern of interconnection the self-making passion is integrating into the person's self and the generative object of passion, that is, the other person. Then the individual through whom we discovered the mode of engagement and interconnection—this very individual, the one through whom we became connected to the world and through whom we discovered this mode of integrating the self—now appears to reject this mode of engagement.

Examples may help. Imagine that you are Gilgamesh—and Enkidu says that he participated in the adventures you shared only out of boredom. Would this Gilgamesh, his spirit indelibly marked by an obscure darkness, return to Ur to rebuild the city as the new man and new king we see at the end of his epic? No longer the boisterous boy-king whose passions and strength exhausted his subjects, he would return as something new—but what, we cannot know, for that lies on the other side of the crisis. Or imagine you are Plato, you are enamored, entranced, by the figure of Socrates, by his devotion to truth and to questioning every assertion of knowledge. Under his influence, the way of life practiced by your aristocratic Athenian family, a way of life devoted to power within the *polis*, seems misguided and irrelevant, and its hallmarks contemptible. But now suppose that one day Socrates disparages the examined life and claims it was nothing but elaborate political theater. He says his goal in practicing this way of life was the acquisition of power and influence in the city. From an external standpoint this may seem like nothing, because the external standpoint leaves out the crucial information—that what ties Plato to Socrates is nothing short of a self-making passion and therefore involves the whole of his being and identity, because the passion has unlimited authority over his internal constitution.

The duality of the passion, however—its being directed to a mode of engaging the world but only via a single individual—has left it open to the problematic condition in which the individual has crossed over to the new way of life but finds himself in conflict with the person devotion to whom made that way of life possible and desirable. And so now he faces the crisis.

How does this happen? The betrayal could arrive with an explicit repudiation, but can also come through a chance remark of some kind, a statement whose subject is something else entirely, which however has bearing on the essence of the relationship—all too much bearing. Such a chance statement exerts an hypnotic power over the individual's attention, like a screw from which one cannot turn one's gaze, a screw that drives itself ever deeper into the self as one gazes upon it. In fact, this casual remark is far more powerful than an explicit statement, since such a statement has the character of a free act that might be taken back again as easily as it was made, or that might have arisen from a fit of anger or transitory emotion. The casual remark emerges as if the whole thing were a matter of common understanding—that *of course* things stand in such-and-such a way, *of course* the pattern means nothing at all. It makes it impossible to speak, for you do not know what to ask the person, and you quickly seem to be speaking differently languages.

So to make sense of this I think we must say that the self-making passion has two parts: a content and a motor. The content of the passion is the way of configuring the self that unifies and actualizes the individual. The motor is the remarkable openness to the other person that gives this individual and our relationship with this individual the power to remake us. Our openness to the other individual remakes the self, or perhaps, just makes the self, the first entelechy of freedom. We experience wholeness and joy.

However, once the self has been remade (or is far enough along in being remade) so that our identity is configured to match the content, it is possible for the other person to turn against what we obtained only through them. But despite the change, our openness to this person stands, as absolute as ever before. The motor hums. The self is constituted by a mode of engagement but also by a relationship, in both cases, absolutely constituted, without limitation. In that first moment of joy, they work together, but in the crisis, they move against each other, yet in such a way that the individual through whom we learned seems to fight on both sides. The difficulty is memory. For (this is Plato's mistake) what we discover in the relationship is not separable from the individual through whom we find the mode of engagement that will configure and constitute the self. So the mode of engagement always bears the imprint, so to speak, of the person. If Socrates had revealed his indifference or antipathy to the examined life, Plato would not have been able to do what his *Symposium* suggests he should have done, and ascend from a love of a person to a love of the Beautiful itself, keeping himself whole all the while; no, he could not simply forget Socrates while pursuing the way of life he learned from Socrates.

Living the same way would constantly recall him to Socrates, whose influence he could not escape, and yet, if he tried to change his way of life, he still could not escape Socrates, since he had granted their relationship, their joint pursuit of the truth, unlimited sway. Since every part of the self was open to the influence of Socrates or his relationship with Socrates, there would have been no aspect of himself to turn to, no interior fortress to escape to.

He doesn't have some part of his life that he can escape to or some other goal he can now pursue, a dream that wouldn't have borne any of Socrates' influence, that wouldn't recall Socrates' memory in some way, no goal apart from Socrates that could be pursued without, in some way, being marked as an *escape* from Socrates.

The internal conflict brought on by the crisis breaks down both the individual's identity and the individual's interconnection with others. The inner state becomes what Kierkegaard would term 'dialectical'—it is impossible to pin down one interpretation of one's condition, it is always subject to yet further debate. Was it the other person who disappointed you, or was it you who disappointed yourself? With whom does the blame lie? One constantly finds oneself tied together with the other in a knot, from which there is no rest in trying to unravel. Every thread that seems to lead back to the self leads to the other, and every thread tying responsibility to the other brings it back to oneself. One question in particular stands out, and grows in importance: did the relationship ever exist in the sense one understood it? did it ever hold the significance one had thought it possessed? This crucial ambiguity appears impossible to resolve by thought.

So long as the crisis continues—this condition in which the individual and the mode of engagement remain in contradiction—the question of the relationship is inescapable. One might think that the relationship was genuine, but hold the other person now to be mistaken, perhaps out of some grief or despair he or she is suffering. Or one might think that it was oneself who was mistaken and mistaken all along. Between these two possibilities there lie all the variations, above all those which seek a definite point when the other party might have changed, or some definite evidence that the relationship had existed in the form one supposed, in the form that generated the self's identity. If the quest cannot be arrested by taking a new stance, the ongoing quest for one of these definite points causes the relationship to disintegrate both in the past and in the present, as the crisis reaches back further and further, until the crisis seems to date from the distant past, recognized only lately.

Soon one feels that one must be mad. For can anyone understand what is happening? One's friends will merely say, "Give it some time, you'll get over it," because they do not recognize how deeply one's suffering reaches—or, if they do, then their recommendation is truly horrifying. For they think that you can forget yourself and become someone else, and that this is salvation, to forget. If someone made a drama from this, it would be like Hitchcock's "The Lady Vanishes."

Suppose, however, that someone found a single memory that guaranteed the relationship in the past and arrested the crisis's backward looking disintegration. Then the focus would turn to discovering the other point: when the relationship changed, and whether this was because of oneself, or because of the other person. This, too, will lead only to despair, for every thought of the other contains two thoughts, the memory of the past and the ongoing torture of the crisis.

There is a dialectic to such unraveling that is as intricate as it is destructive, and it cannot be arrested by any of the ordinary means. That is what I mean to insist on. This dialectic is founded on the contradiction within the self between the individual, the mode of engagement constituting the self, and memory. These three combine to constantly drive the individual back upon himself in a process that unravels the self. Thus the result that there is no longer a principle of unity holding the person's identity in place. It is caught in a process sapping its integrity and coherence.

Finally, the individual reaches the point of ultimate despair, the anti-pinnacle of self-hood. For the dual action of self-making (which unified an identity that was lost in diffusion) and self-unraveling (which shattered the self, leaving it in a state of ruin) creates a new condition of maximum possibility. During the crisis an individual surveys a field of possibilities impossibly vast, not in terms of sheer number of meaningless variety, but in terms of the different types and degree of significance they hold. Like Jesus when he was tempted by the devil, the individual in this moment stands upon a 'very high mountain' from which he can survey 'all the kingdoms of the world,' but he is not offered all of them, oh no; he must select just one. This will become his being.

From the pinnacle it is not easy to see which of these would promise happiness or return him to a state of joy. It is possible that none will, that none can. Those with sharp sight will discern all kinds of possibilities, many never imagined. There is one, in the furthest distance and yet infinitely near to him, that would make him whole again, but at the greatest possible cost. That is infinite hatred. Of all the possibilities visible from that pinnacle, infinite hatred is by far the most dreadful. The individual knows that, in a sense, he is to blame somehow, at the very least for misjudging his beloved, perhaps for far more, but this is shrouded by the sense that his beloved has failed him, has failed his passion, not just by falling short, though this occupies his mind—not just for that, but for showing him the meaning of wonder and then draining all the color from the world. He cannot understand how it is that the other's life continues, as if life could continue, while for him life has become impossible to conceive. In agonizing contemplation of meaninglessness, he struggles desperately for a new *pointus certus*, a new place to stand and new anchor for his will. Infinite hatred arises when his attention focuses upon the infinite harm he has suffered. For hatred arises from bitterness, and bitterness from harm, and no harm could be greater than the harm that shatters every part of the soul, which is what happens to Plato when we imagine Socrates telling him—"It was just for power, a way of winning fame, no one *seriously* thinks the examined life is worth anything." When someone harms us and the harm goes unhealed, it may become the lingering distaste for the one who harmed us which is bitterness, the *resentiment* of anger and ill-will for harm. When that bitterness acquires a permanent place in our heart and weights our will against its object, it becomes hatred. The suffering one, then, finds no healing for the wound; perhaps he even immerses himself in suffering, for there is a kind of invigoration and meaning found in such swimming, a meaning found in the self-making passion's new status, in taking its shattered condition precisely as it is and fashioning from this the new meaning of one's life. Everything within him reverses itself, which is why this movement is so easy for him. In embracing the pain and making it the meaning of his life he needs only use the same infrastructure as before, take the defined form of his will and turn it on its head. Malice, which had before crept in fear about his soul, croaking suggestions from one soggy marsh or another without revealing itself, now marches for the capital no longer a frog, but a prince, a prince of demons. This prince of hatred enthrones himself in the suffering one's soul and from that moment his new identity is established. He is a hating one, the blackest of 'black knights,' whose thoughts never cease from spite—the Knight of Malice.

This is coming to my point—how can one make oneself ineligible to receive God's love? We are now very close indeed. Even the Knight of Malice can receive God's love and repent, he is not yet wholly lost, but he has completed the first stage. His doom is tied up with the fact that his relation to being in general is mediated by his relation to the hated one. Because his hatred is radical, and therefore without determinable limit, this hatred influences, checks, and modifies every other aspect of himself. A being whose movements occurred instantly could never be saved once he resolved the crisis in infinite hatred. The movement being instantaneous and complete, his whole being would have become directed to malice without reservation. Thus do I imagine the fall of a devil and the essence of the demonic (Kierkegaard's opinion notwithstanding; Anselm seems more nearly correct). But a being whose movements occur in time and for whom a change from one state to another requires a transition in which his parts rearrange themselves and the change reaches deep into his nerves, thoughts, and feelings—such a being, I say, still has time to repent. For though the hatred is lodged in every part of his soul, not every part has been irrevocably converted to malice—each part is only partially transformed and, though his malice grows every day, many days must pass before every part has been completely transformed.

One of the most common things in the world, though less commonly noticed and even less understood, is the multiplicity of motives with which we act. Myshkin's loving attitude toward others in *The Idiot* shows us a person who fully expresses Christ's love within a human scope, by a person lacking Christ's divinity but possessing the best of his humanity. He develops a significant insight in doing so, which concerns how it is that Myshkin manages to love in this way. In many ways, Myshkin is an innocent, but it's not just his innocence that makes him accept and forgive others so easily. He constantly reconciles others to himself because he perceives the multiplicity of their motives. As the narrator points out, "Don't let us forget that the causes of human actions are usually immeasurably more complex and varied than our subsequent explanations of them. And these can rarely be distinctly defined."[34] Thus someone might have a very nasty motive for doing something, they might have other motives as well, ones which are more agreeable—trying to see the best in someone need not, therefore, consist simply in fantasy or naïveté; it is a matter of discerning the better aspects of a person and engaging with him on the basis of those better aspects. Myshkin reports his discovery of this secret to Rogozhin with sad naïveté regarding its potential to annihilate

---

34 Ed.: *The Idiot*, p. 463.

him.[35] By this means Myshkin comes to surround himself with a most unlikely collection of friends, all of them visibly flawed sinners—though he also has his failures in this regard. Be that as it may, the point I wish to insist on is this, that it is human multiplicity that makes divine redemption and reconciliation possible, for it is the multiplicity that the divine love may call out to, reawaken, and draw to itself, strengthening and giving new life to them. It is these motives that provide purchase for the divine love whereby it may fasten its hooks within us and draw our hearts back into relation with God. Thus so long as the Knight of Malice has not yet completed his transformation, insofar as time drags out the perseverance required for his infinite hatred to become complete, he may relate himself to being in general, and God in particular, on the basis of motives other than those provided by his infinite hatred. Those motives remain in him and provide the channels by which redemption may proceed. Such multiplicity, then, although it is the source of so much of the evil we do to one another because of our ability to hide one motive behind another, is also the ground for God's redeeming us.

How does the Knight of Malice's infinite hatred, when fully developed, ultimately cut him off from God and make him incapable of receiving God's love? First, of course, there is the matter of the Knight's disagreement with God—that he hates one whom God loves. To the extent that the Knight recognizes this, he cannot accommodate himself to fellowship with God, for the friend of one's enemy is himself one's enemy. But then how can he receive God's love? God is not a Cyrano de Bergerac, offering love to one man merely—one who receives God's love knows his love is universal. So how can he not know that God loves the one he hates? But perhaps he can convince himself that God loves all but this

---

35   Ed. Niakani probably means *The Idiot*, II.4, pp. 210–212, where Myshkin tells four stories to Rogozhin about his encounters with Russians. Each story involves individuals acting from conflicting motives.

one, that the hated one is beyond God's love; he must constantly deceive himself, but that is not unusual. Still, insofar as all his affections come under the sway of his single hatred, so too he must be driven to hate God, and in the end it is hard to see how his self-deception will survive; for in the end he will lose even the need for it, when his hatred is complete and no affection remains to attract him to God.

Secondly, however, the Knight cannot but see everything in the hated one as twisted, flawed, evil, pathetic, and in need of extirpation from the world; in a word, as hateful. So if we imagine again a case of lovers, where a man suddenly sees his beloved turn the relationship on its ear, initially his hatred may fasten upon her betrayal, but the hate cannot end there. His whole being was involved in delighting in her. Now, however, he must reinterpret everything he admired in her or thought to be wonderful, discover the way that what he delighted in may be regarded as hateful instead. And yes, one sees this in Smerydakov's reproaches to Ivan, in his "you used to" statements—"you used to be brave once, sir, you used to say 'everything is permitted,' sir," and "what you taught me, sir"—see the bitterness, there—Smerdyakov returns to this because the contrast between the past and present is unbearable for him; his god has failed him.[36] This involves the disappointed one in a long process, at the end of which the one who was fairer than all in his eyes is now regarded with the blackest of visions. Entering this order involves passing through two stages. In the first stage it is the object of passion that absorbs his malice. There is nothing sound in him, but he regains his strength by refocusing himself in hatred upon the one he loved. He had already allowed her to define every aspect of himself, so that the wound she inflicted penetrated and exploded every bone and

---

36 Ed.: Fyodor Dostoevsky, *The Brothers Karamazov*, trans. Richard Pevear and Larissa Volokhonsky (New York: Farrar, Straus and Giroux, 1990), p. 632.

nerve—but there is something left of him yet, the subject of all this pain and disappointment. He takes the pain of this explosion, of this shattering, and returns it upon the object of his passion. In this way the broken bones become twisted but strong, and flayed nerves pulse with bitterness. All his will turns against the object of his passion with one consuming need—to destroy her, to find some fitting revenge to take against her.

Such a Knight could choose to express all his heart's bitterness and malice in murder; but should he succeed, this creates a problem for the Knight, since his malice does not free him from the object of his passion but rather solidifies the essential connection of the object to his identity. The Knight's most characteristic act is therefore not murder, but suicide.

As an act of malice, suicide allows one to pour out one's hatred all at once while at the same time affecting the Knight's target forever—to create an enduring memory or enduring effects for the life of the other person that are difficult to escape. This inverts the situation, so the Knight escapes the memory, while the once-loved one is trapped by it. Suicide has obvious power if the object still has some affection for the one who hates her, if she has a conscience and is conscious of how her actions affected the one whose will she broke. But even if there is no affection, there are ways to ensure that one's suicide haunts them in other ways—this is what Smerdyakov surely had in mind with his death, for example, since he couldn't have imagined that Ivan or anyone else would miss him.

Suicide also allows the Knight to avoid his most difficult quandary: if life's meaning is exhausted in malice toward the object of passion, then what is left to live for when the object is gone? Supposing the object of passion is thoroughly destroyed—even if not murdered, yet having been subjected to a suitable revenge? Or suppose that the Knight has no means at his disposal to take revenge on his object of passion—what then? Having to answer these questions would require the Knight to come to terms with the true meaning of infinite hatred.

Of course, there is much that is good in the hated one that he once loved—even a being with an evil will is a being made in the image of God and still glorifying him in its substance. Yet the infinite hatred cannot consistently regard as hateful in the hated one what is good elsewhere. The logic of the infinite therefore carries his despite of the hated one's qualities to despising those qualities wherever they are manifested elsewhere. Self-deception may keep him blind to this for a time, but in the end, his black vision must extend to the rest of creation. Step by step his malice must extend from the object of his passion to larger and larger commonalities—perhaps from her to womankind in general, then to humanity, then to life, and finally to being itself. He might take any number of paths but the end is always hatred of being. He must, that is, come to see the process of life in the hated one in a hateful light, and regard it as selfish, pathetic, mere grubbing after sustenance, and then come to see living things in general as hateful in the same way. So in the end he will come to hate life and wish life itself could be extirpated, to hate being and wish that the universe might be brought to nothing. He will concentrate himself, pour his whole will into one single wish for the annihilation of all things. It follows of course that he must regard God as hateful who created such things and who manifests all their properties with the greatest purity and power. The Knight of Malice will therefore never accept fellowship with God or willingly receive his love; he will war with God to the uttermost. That is the final stage.

That was all about one valence of the crisis: the crisis that feels like a betrayal. Of course, there's another kind, too—the kind of crisis faced by Kierkegaard, in which the incoherence appears to arise from oneself rather than the other. I don't know what to make of all the things that people say about Kierkegaard; I conclude only that they don't know self-making passion or the crisis, and if they've felt it, they hid it from themselves long ago... The only one who understands Kierkegaard is the one who has faced the crisis. He makes this clear himself, just see what he says about Mynster; Mynster can't understand him because he's never been "out over 70,000 fathoms," and that's Kierkegaard's way of getting at this.[37] For clearly the problem for him was that he saw that, to fulfill the passion, he had to marry Regine, but if he married her, he's to either hide himself from her or reveal himself to her. He says all of this in his journals, it's very straightforward. If he hid himself from her, then he's betraying the relationship, but if he reveals himself to her, he will destroy her. He saw clearly that he would be the one who broke the pattern, would every day find himself out of alignment with it, harming or hiding from the one he loved. Thus his dread over the whole thing and his determination somehow to save her through *recherche* gallantry ... a determination to save that was, however, faithless.[38]

Someone on this path, who faces a crisis in which it is his own lack of fitness for the relationship that crushes him, would face a different kind of disintegration, the decay brought on by enduring, unactivated possibility, where that possibility is a necessity for the self. In that case, the self is held together only by continually denying what it needs to be whole, and so, it gradually falls apart, and comes to hold more and more to itself, having denied its bridge to the rest of the world. Without that bridge, it gradually turns to pride, contempt, isolation....as indeed the case shows. Finally, of course, to malice, for the breakdown of the pattern always turns you against being. But anyone who wants to study this can better turn to Kierkegaard himself, and just read him with the idea of the crisis in mind. That will open up every door. He is fortunate not to have arrived at the ultimate stage, for he refused to blame God, but his bitterness at humanity is too great, and inconsistent with his own devotion. This all comes out in the Second Authorship, especially in the "attack on Christendom."

---

37   Ed.: Niakani probably means *The Journals of Kierkegaard*, ed. Alexander Dru (New York: Harper Torchbooks, 1959), p. 115.
38   Ed.: See the entry "My Relation to Her," dated 24 Aug. 1849, in *The Journals of Kierkegaard*.

Kierkegaard did not understand the crisis properly, or he did, but he couldn't apply it to his own case properly, because of the agony. This is why he misunderstands repetition. He does not grasp one of its most important dimensions. The Delacroix case is an example. How did Delacroix come to be standing there in the kitchen gibbering, "There was honey in the milk," except that the whole thing was a repetition, a repetition of the crisis he had failed to successfully resolve? For when the person finds the semblance of the crisis in his present circumstances, anxiety immediately constructs the whole past for him all over again, not as possibility, but as necessity. Now he sees the whole crisis rising up as an undefeatable enemy, he sees the future come before him to bind him with its iron chains, to draw him back through everything again. For how a person responds to the crisis is imprinted on his heart so deeply that every event that resembles the original brings back the whole panic, the anxiety, the anguish, and with it, the weight of inevitability attached to the response chosen long ago. Failure leaves this inescapable mark of freedom turned to necessity and appearing in the idiocy of repetition, as in other traumas. The fear of betrayal, the fear of oneself, the unraveling of one's world—your whole sense of yourself and your relation to the world breaks down in the experience of repetition, even when it is just the angle of a cocked finger, the sound of someone's laugh, or the honey in the milk. But, and this is key, just as no observer, or almost no observer, can understand a person in relation to his self-making passion, so too no one can understand what that person is repeating when the repetition arrives. Others will have sympathy for all kinds of trauma, but it is truly rare to find sympathy for the crisis. For who can understand what he is invested in not understanding? And so, on top of everything, the experience of repetition reinforces the isolation imposed by the crisis. Repetition is hell. That's the only word for it. Repetition is hell.

All this applies, too, to those who have the other types of

passion—I mean, Livingstone did not have a particular individual who could have disappointed him, or whom he feared he would betray, but the theoretical apparatus can be adapted. It would need more study to show how this is the case, and I feel I can't afford it, it would take me too far from my own problem. The same goes for the people who are passionately devoted to an idea or ideal—I mean someone like Martin Luther King or Tocqueville. No one understands Tocqueville because they do not see where his ideas come from, that is, from his devotion to a self-making passion for a free France, and his despair over its possibility. With King, though, they fail to grasp how easy it would have been to grow discouraged and become something very different ... how hard it must have been to remain faithful to such a demanding task, and yet, what it wrought!

To return to the larger point, though, when someone incurs God's wrath, this is not due to God changing his attitude to the person, but the person changing his attitude toward God. Whenever someone cannot receive God's love, the cause lies entirely inside the person. That is surely what is meant by saying that 'God so loved the world that he gave his only Son, that whoever believes in him should not perish, but have eternal life.'[39] Now all that is left to us is to decide to participate in that love or not. But just as important as recognizing why the Knight of Malice cannot receive God's love is recognizing what it would mean for the disappointed one to regather his will yet refuse the equipage and heraldry of that order.

Does my diamond hold firm? Are the facets in place? I hope to have shown that, given current circumstances, God's love is available to all, and there is nothing in the logic of love that is held back by the sinfulness of the recipient, even if through the logic of sin, as it were, the sinner holds himself or herself back from this love.

But besides malice, there is the question of the cockroach, which

---

39 Ed.: John 3:16.

can still keep the sinner back. Sin creates a barrier of separation between himself and God, and it is a neat problem whether this barrier is primarily due to God's holiness, or the self-barricading of sin, or some kind of combination of the two in relation to each other. Be that as it may, the sinner cannot approach God. His sin makes him unfit to enter the divine presence. One makes a mistake to think of sin as primarily an external reality. We sometimes, for example, consider the sinner's status to be like a legal status of some kind, the result of a legal sentence. Then what one receives is in salvation—'justification'—is a new legal status; the old one was wiped out, replaced by the new, pristine legal status. However, a change of externalities—which will not convince the cockroach that he after belongs in the presence of God—does not quite correspond to what is said in the scriptures. The surest sign of this is that in the scriptures what we hear of is not an ongoing tribunal, kept up by God, in which he issues a new judgment each time we sin, imputing another new 'guilty' status upon us. The idea of such a court is, of course, somewhat ridiculous; the court would have to be issuing new judgments constantly, and not even in the presence of the accused! But the scriptures don't speak of such a tribunal. Instead, they speak of a 'day of judgment,' that is, a specific time when judgment will be issued. That is when one will well and truly have a legal status, either 'justified' or 'condemned.' Prior to that one may only be said to be liable to judgment for a certain status, but not exactly having that status. This is what the cockroach knows: that he is liable to judgment, that in himself he is totally unfit for the divine presence. All his sins he holds in himself, so many more protruding growths inside him from which he groans, every one of them a blackening of the sun's fair light and blocking him from loving.

God faces the world as Myshkin did, with the situation turned all around: in his infinite love God holds within himself that pageantry of life, the eternal dance of the Holy Trinity, and the great chorus of the angels, with whom he holds a great and eternal festival, and he faces our world where everything is the opposite— the entire human world is composed of individuals curved in upon themselves, hunched over and unable to see the worlds of others or engage in them. Their capacity to respond lovingly to others is broken, but it isn't entirely lost yet either, so they keep it carefully in check, lest they be led out of themselves and pulled into the lives of others. If this unfortunate state were no fault of their own, this would be a piteous sight, and of course there is no challenge to God's love healing their spiritual sickness. But their blindness and perverse spirits are rooted in sin and hatred of each other as well as of God. Any spiritually healthy being, an angel perhaps, who came among them would have to do as a man does among a pit of venomous snakes, who greet him with hisses, rattling, and bites. They are as furious at his intrusion as they are at his health. He would enter only after taking every measure to protect himself and I do not know if he would bring himself to handle or touch such a being, except with a long stick that allowed him to keep it at a distance from himself, to keep himself as much as possible free from harm or contamination. If God himself were to come among them, the stick might be necessary for another reason, to avoid destroying them, since the touch of the divine essence would destroy them. A being who is curved in upon itself in selfish defi- ance cannot touch the being whose essence is loving openness to others, who brings all these others into relation with one another. To touch such a being would mean being snapped open by force; the spine, the entelechy created by the will, would break and the creature perish.

Only if we imagine the curved-in ones this way will we under- stand the difficulty that God faces in determining his own relation to the world. To reconcile such a world to himself means reconcil- ing hissing and biting vermin to the touch of a holy God whose very being burns away their self-isolation and forces them into a life of love that they hate in depths of their souls. It is sometimes said that God's wrath is a qualification within God's love, which is to say, it is love that is fundamental to God, not wrath; wrath is an accident. C. S. Lewis wrote, either a person comes to the point where they submit to God and say, 'Thy will be done,' and allow him to un-curve them, or God says, 'Thy will be done,' and they remain in that state.[40] Wrath is to allow the curved one to remain curved in upon himself and refuse to open him to the worlds around him, to finally cease to make the sun rise upon him and allow all in him to sink into death.

When God walks into the garden of life, so to speak, the crowd of hissing, scurrying hunchbacks flee, keep their distance, spitting and slinging filth at him whenever they can. 'God so loved the world'—it is this world that God loves! God is love, so God is infinitely responsive to the lives even of such beings. He sees the life his enemies lead for the pathetic debasement of human life that it is, pities them, and desires to rescue them from it. The cockroach says, 'But what could I, just such a hissing and scurrying one (and I was one of those who flung filth, I know it, and with what relish did I do it!)—how could I, that is, how could I ever be the recipient of such love?' In the brilliant light of such love, the cockroach is dazzled, and his question is a bit confused; it is in virtue of having a life of one's own that one becomes an apt recipient of such love. 'That is why you receive God's love, O cockroach! Because you too have a life of your own, which he perceives and feels pity for, just because it is a life, and because to be loving means to be responsive to life!' The cockroach doesn't lack a follow-up, of course—for even in degrading himself, the cockroach never fails to get the last word in. The cockroach is not yet wholly gone, his evil will still contains motives that are not wholly wicked; that is why he raises the question! 'But then what kind of life could I have with such a being? I mean, what kind of life could God have with me! How

---

40   Ed.: C. S. Lewis, *The Great Divorce* (London: Collins, 2012), p. 75.

could holiness and insecthood, my hissing-and-scurrying-ness, ever coexist together? Am I not far too vile even to come into contact with God?' 'Yes! Yes, cockroach, this is true. You are completely unable to enter God's presence or enjoy fellowship with him. You, after all, are a cockroach, and what man, even a gentle and kindly man, allows cockroaches into his kitchen or living room? But perhaps, cockroach, perhaps *you need not be a cockroach at all*. What if you were yourself instead!' With this answer the cockroach catches a glimpse of the swirling spheres, and his ears catch the strain of the music of heaven, the eternal festival and the dance of all the angels. This answer of course gets the cockroach thinking; he's a cockroach of course, so he has no single response, he has several! Above all, he is hopeful, but also frightened and despairing. He's hopeful to hear the prospect of becoming something else, something better than a cockroach—but frightened and despairing, frightened at the thought of being cracked open and despairing just because he is frightened, because he recognizes that he prefers after all to remain a cockroach. Frightened, too, because whereas it was easy to despair before, now freedom enters into it. Two destinies open before him, and which will he choose? He cannot even comprehend what life as something other than a cockroach would entail. He stalls for time, asks, 'But how? But how shall I become something other than I am?...' He is answered, 'Do not pry too much into the affairs of God,' and he cowers at this, resenting it too, but also listens to what comes next. 'He will become one with you, and you will become one with him. He will take all the darkness in you and you will take the light in him and since darkness is cast out by light and has no power over it, what remains will only be the light in him, shining in you, and the union of you and him abiding together.' Still stalling for time, the cockroach says, 'Surely that is a metaphor, and true on its own terms, but how can my evil be darkness or his goodness light? For evil is not mere privation, but something more ... something, dare I say, insectoid ...

an insectoid stance on insecthood, perhaps...' And the response is, 'No doubt, no doubt you are right, dear insect! All the evil in you will be straightened out, however, that curve in your spine will be gone forever. You shall stand straight and see the world around you, know it and delight in it! You will know the beings you share this world with and delight in them, besides, and God with all of us. We shall all delight together.' 'Ach, but there is this other business, you know,' the cockroach begins shyly, as if ashamed to bring it up—and indeed, perhaps he is ashamed, but he's ashamed out of pride, and calculation too—that's his cockroachness. 'What is that?' 'Oh ... well ... the business of punishment, you know. Retribution for what I've done wrong. For surely the nasty things I've done must be punished. If you only knew the things I've done! They couldn't possibly go without being avenged and I know it. I accept it. I accept the punishment. I know that I can't live with you.' Well, then, what do you think the response must be?

Here the letter ended, cutting off abruptly, as if Niakani were unable to answer the question, or perhaps did not dare to complete it.

When Simon read the letter, it was this abrupt ending that he first focused on. "I see why he ends here," he said. His face was dark a moment, then hard. "I more than suspect that the cockroach is in the right."

"Why do you say that?" I asked.

"Because it is a law of human nature that the guilty soul longs for punishment."

"Really?" I said. "I mean, you're the lawyer, but don't people try to escape punishment as much as they can?"

"These days, I am actually involved more in the investigation of crimes than in their prosecution. Of course, you are right, people do try to escape punishment, or my job would be incredibly easy," said Simon. "And the simpler, and more animalistic, a criminal is, the more he tries to escape. Animals perceive punishment only as injury, not as punishment. The difference is conscience, and it's this business mentioned in the letter about the 'multiplicity of desires' that does them in."

"You mean," I asked, "where the author invokes Dostoevsky's statement that we continuously act from a variety of motives, only a few of which we explicitly recognize?"

"Let me put it this way: As a matter of practical necessity, imposed by life or evolution or however you wish to put, it, we must act. At the same time, we possess a variety of motive factors: desires, anxieties, fears, hopes, and so on. Now, as a multiplicity, these factors may not be capable of being satisfied in the same act or course of action. Yet, no matter how that multiplicity of motive factors may war within itself, the animal needs to move in some one direction. Since desires aren't mathematical vectors, one can't just add them up and deduce the direction a creature will follow the way one would calculate the movement of a physical object subject to multiple forces. They do get wrapped up in the end, all these different motives, and somehow the person moves in some direction, moved by half a dozen motives or more, tied together into a thick rope of motive power.

"As they say, 'a threefold cord is not quickly broken,' and so people's wills are often more resilient than one expects; defeat or cast doubt on one motive for what they do, they will keep on at it, drawing on the reinforcements supplied by these other factors that were combined in the act. Even the simpler types, who at first seem to have no more than animal instincts in them have tangled up with these lower motives the nobler motives, present but hidden."

"That sounds like something Sal would say," I said.

"Yes, I am familiar with your Sal," said Simon. "He claimed that everyone has these undeveloped yearnings for transcendence."

"That sounds hopeful, I suppose," I said.

"Is that how you take it?" said Simon.

"It seems a very optimistic view to me," I said.

"I guarantee you, it was not. He wrote an article about this once, for some little journal of no consequence, where he discussed this idea in connection with watching a corpulent man, morbidly obese, eating pie *a la mode* in a restaurant. He claimed to observe a moment of hesitation in such a man—the man already knows he should not have ordered dessert, and the moment of hesitation is, Sal claims, the moment when he considers moving the ice cream to the side. He hesitates, according to Sal, because he has more than desire in him, he has other motives that tell him not to eat it, but—this is the key—he will anyway, and he will kill himself by doing this. He claimed to feel ill for such a man, not simply out of repulsion, but 'for his sake, out of concern for him.' So he put it, and his idea isn't bad. Apply it to punishment. As I said, one can't treat desires like mathematical vectors that get canceled out in the will's final movement; motives that aren't worked into the tangled cord, and aren't allowed expression are frequently invisible in the short term. Some are impatient and reappear inopportunely. Others are patient and await their chance. What is interesting is to see how they grow and develop when they are denied expression for a long time."

"Yes," I said, "those are ... interesting."

"They may emerge at any time, in a hidden way, so that one may even give opposite advice, or seek to love and harm someone at the same time," Simon went on. "Freud of course studied these, and the whole psychological profession is concerned with working out their problems. They frequently lead to exercises in disguise and self-deception, and secret attempts to undermine the main tangle. The longing for punishment is like this. It can be weak or strong, but it is a characteristic desire of human beings. It is produced by conscience. Conscience is a form of reflection, so its form and power varies with the degree of an individual's reflective power. Conscience is frequently purer in less reflective individuals—less refracted into various channels—but, when it is gathered together, it is more searching in the reflective individual. We live in a very reflective age, so the desire is often very refracted, but searching, and full of self-deception.

"I have a theory, which is unconfirmed, but which I hold to. What someone really wants is to be punished by God, but since the person is in the wrong, and therefore is in rebellion against God, and in rebellion one always takes from God and gives to someone else, what one does is find someone, *something*, to punish oneself with. One gives *it* the right to punish. Thus one remains in control, that is, in rebellion. I don't just mean masochists. That's not even an important case. This is seen everywhere, in all ages. Religious people, for example, often perform penances, pilgrimages, fasts, they flagellate themselves, and repulsively wallow in refined feelings of guilt. Many religious individuals are morbidly obsessed with finding fault in their lives and inflicting suffering upon themselves in the form of guilt. This is well-known, but non-religious individuals of our age possess a remarkable, almost insatiable sense of guilt. Many individuals with no religious beliefs to speak of are obsessed with finding things to be guilty of. It is trivially easy to find fault with oneself under the categories of racism, sexism, and environmental harm, since these encompass feelings, habits, institutions one interacts with, systems one benefits from (directly or indirectly), systems one supports (whether intentionally or only functionally, directly or indirectly), apparently innocent utterances, and so on. For the most part, they are right to do this, too; we are usually guilty. Our actions are always damaging in some respect or another; one needs only find the aspect under which they are destructive, and then guilt is ready at hand.

"The religious type detects failures to love God and to love neighbor everywhere, in intention even if not in deed, and the secular type puts social justice and ecology to the same functions. Both are reflective types and, as I said, my hypothesis is that reflection and conscience go hand in hand. Despite all the differences between the two types, they both love guilt, they positively need it, and will invent it if they cannot discover it. (Though this invention of guilt is itself a cause of guilt; for it is a distraction from rectifying the things they are actually guilty of.) Do you, see, then, why I said what I did at the beginning, about the desire for punishment?"

"I agree you have some suggestive evidence," I said. "Yet what does this have to do with the larger question? I don't see what this has to do with Niakani's question yet."

"Conscience lies at the root of problem. Punishment would allow someone to be free from guilt." He smiled. "Now perhaps you see how I understand my vocation. You see that I help people to lose their guilt by paying for it."

"Then do you reject Niakani's argument?" I asked.

Simon sighed. "I neither accept nor reject his argument. Rather, I see a problem for his argument, and it is possible that this lacuna can be filled in and the problem answered, but I do not see how. This 'self-making passion' makes everything much worse," he said. "Because it unifies the self, it therefore prevents one from finding some part of oneself to escape to after committing the wrong. If someone fell under guilt in such a situation, how could he ever recover?"

"What do you mean?" I asked.

"I mean that the judgment will seem to indict one's whole self, and the sense of fault will be omnipresent," he said. "The temptation to self-deception would be overpowering, to find a way to escape the feeling of guilt, unless the person forgave him. But that may not be possible. So the wrong will come to define him, and nothing outside himself will be able to free him from that sense ... except, of course, for self-deception, which, as I said, always stands at hand. But when he describes this moment of despair, when the individual must put himself back together, it seems to me he must assign blame for the mistake, and the blame must either lie with the other or with oneself. But if it lies with the other, then the answer is infinite hatred—inevitably, that is where one will end up. On the other hand, if the blame lies with oneself, how can someone avoid building guilt into his own identity? And then where has forgiveness gone?"

"Why not affirm both?" I asked. "Everyone is guilty, you said."

He smiled unhappily. "Then you should possess just as dark an outlook as mine. Perhaps that is best, but that is also not easy, and I cannot predict how it would come out."

Rufus and Pete were at this moment outside the house, trying to unload everything loaded on the truck, occasionally coming into the house. They noticed us inside, but did not engage with us at this point, being too focused on the task at hand.

Thinking of yesterday's discussion with Harper, I said, "Some people would say that someone else could pay the debt for you and release you from guilt."

"I understand the idea," he said. "That is what it is said that God himself did, in becoming incarnate as Jesus Christ, so that he could sacrifice himself for the sins of everyone else. If so, then that could release someone from guilt. But I will admit that I find the idea troubling and hard to accept."

"Do you think it would just be another wrong to allow someone else to be unjustly punished for what one did wrong oneself?" I asked.

"No, that is not quite it," he said. "When one person accepts the punishment due another this creates not a wrong, but a debt. Wrong and debt, however, are different concepts. Conscience is reflection, it is bringing oneself under one's own moral concepts. If I find that I fall short of those, it is not a debt I find, but a wrong. To be indebted is be to under obligation, but to be guilty of wrong is to stand under punishment."

"Then do you think it is wrong to refuse an offer like that?" I asked.

"I'm of two minds about that," said Simon. "On the one hand, what would it mean to receive this offer, and refuse to accept it?"

"What *would* it mean?" I said.

"Someone who insists upon standing in guilt rather than under obligation wishes to remain isolated and turned in upon himself. Under guilt one remains wholly one's own, whereas to be under obligation requires that one relate oneself to another and turn one's gaze away from oneself."

"Therefore?" I said.

"Therefore," said Simon, "to insist upon punishment is only pride. And that is in fact what one sees in all these self-flagellants, the ones I mentioned earlier, the stern, reflective individuals who punish themselves either with literal whips and cords or with merely metaphorical ones. Do you think, that for all their self-punishment, these individuals are less proud than their fellows? Do those who moan over their sins hold themselves below those who do not do these things? That is rarely the case. The one who detects his guilt, and even confesses and punishes himself for it, is set apart from, and above, the many who fail to do these things, whether this is the religious type or the non-religious type. Whether someone wallows in guilt over his appetites for the temporal or over buying a Styrofoam cup, this person always feels that he is superior to others, just because he knows his guilt, whereas the others do not know theirs."

"Then, why don't you accept the idea?" I said.

"In the first place," said Simon, "it is not so clear to me how this transfer is supposed to happen … if punishment itself *were* just like debt, there'd be no difficulty, it would be no more than accounting. Transfer the debt from one person to another as you do with money. But this is not what we are speaking of here. It shows too much innocence to think of guilt as being much like a monetary debt. Guilt concerns us as moral beings, not as economic beings—guilt concerns *my will* and what is owed me on account of it. Without retribution there is no moment when the soul is genuinely satisfied with its state. Thus I fulfill my vocation."

"That seems strange to me," I said. "You're right about debt, of course, but do you really think that someone must suffer punishment to be at peace with himself?"

He waved his hand. "That's not the important thing," he said. "Let's turn to the question you raised at the beginning, because it gets to the heart of things."

"Yes," I said. "Can you explain the Delacroix case?" Rufus and Pete were now moving things into the house. Simon and I remained in the kitchen, out of their way.

"I learned about this case from one of the lawyers who worked on the case for the prosecution," he said. "The Delacroix case occurred in 1972, and was both shocking and mysterious to its contemporaries. Henri Jean-Luc Delacroix was a successful New York businessman in his late 30's who had arrived in New York about ten years earlier, it was said from New Orleans. He hadn't been poor when he arrived, but not rich, either; however, within his first three years in New York he had made himself a millionaire several times over, and many expected he would end up far wealthier still. Moreover, he was charming, kind, charitable, and widely beloved. He moved in all the best social circles but also spent considerable time in Catholic parishes in the poorer parts of the city, not only giving his money, but being sure to be involved himself in serving the poor. There was much speculation about whom he might marry, and finally, after five years, he took a wife, Louise Braun. Everyone of course viewed her as fortunate in the extreme. Yet. a few days before the wedding, Delacroix handed a key to a safety deposit box to a friend, with instructions to open it 'if anything happens.' As to what might happen, he didn't say, and when the friend asked for him to be more specific, Delacroix said, 'It's probably nothing, but all the same, open it if something happens, you'll know if the time comes.'"

"This sounds very mysterious," I said.

"Yes," said Simon, "it was. Over the next five years Delacroix made even greater wealth, but not as much as in the previous five. He seemed blissfully happy to be married, and yet, three years later, one of his friends reportedly found him with such an expression of dread on his face that he became immediately concerned for his welfare. Delacroix, naturally, laughed and said nothing was the matter, nothing at all. But there were a very few others who saw similar signs over the next few years, when he seemed to be troubled by a dark secret, an unknown anxiety, that he refused to share. By highlighting these moments this way, I am creating a far different impression than he created at the time—after all, these were rare and isolated encounters, and seemed, even to those who witnessed them, entirely unimportant compared with the general impression he created of a man with a blessed life and even more blessed future, full of happiness, love, and success."

"Then what happened?" I said. Pete was continuing to go back and forth, carrying things in and returning to the van, but Rufus was standing near the kitchen, apparently catching his breath.

"The couple had a child in the third year of their marriage, and then, two years later, the housekeeper found him standing in the kitchen of their penthouse apartment one morning, gibbering, 'There was honey in the milk, there was honey in the milk,' repeating this again and again, broken up only by plaintive cries of 'Why, why, why'—and there was no sign of Louise Delacroix or the child."

"What happened to them?" I said.

"They were never found. But the safety deposit box contained a locket, with a picture of a woman and a child. Their identities were unknown."

"Didn't Delacroix himself know?" I asked.

"He must have, of course, but he hung himself the following day, so there was no way to ask him," said Simon. "Eventually, investigators discovered she was Olivia Evgeny of Montana, a murder victim. She had died two years before Delacroix arrived in New

York. She had a child but was unmarried, and engaged to a man named Patrick Laplace. The wedding had been scheduled. Then she was murdered. Police examination of the victim's injuries strongly suggested a crime of sudden passion, as might be prompted by jealousy, while the posing of the body with flowers in her hand indicated subsequent remorse. There were also rumors that she was seeing someone, or had seen someone, though this evidence was never more than rumor. So they strongly suspected Laplace. All of a sudden, however, another man came into the police office and confessed to the crime, John Manticourt. Manticourt was one of Laplace's oldest friends. He was also an alcoholic, a real heavy drinker. He knew the details of the case and even explained where they could find the murder weapon, something they had not known. And so he was thrown into jail. He claimed to have killed her in a state of drunken confusion, and was now wracked by remorse over what he had done. Two months later, however, he died from liver failure, and a little after that, Laplace himself disappeared, never to be seen again. But no one thought anything of that, since, after all, he had been devastated by the death of his fiancée at the hand of his own friend. Who would not want to pick up and begin again somewhere else?"

"*Can* someone simply begin again somewhere else?" I said.

"That is what I think one cannot do," said Simon. "As Pascal said, *He has not changed, he is still the same.*[41] It became clear that Laplace and Delacroix were the same man, and that Laplace had murdered his one-time fiancée, Olivia Evgeny, in a fit of jealous rage—or, rather, something deeper than this. For every-one—and this is partly why they so quickly accepted the story of Manticourt—everyone knew how perfectly devoted to Olivia he was. He practically worshiped her, regarded her as the best of all existence, he thanked God for her every day. His whole life

---

41 Ed.: See Pascal, *Pensées and Other Writings*, frag. 643.

had changed when he met her. A sullen and withdrawn man with few prospects, he became a better man, a transformed man, after meeting her, and he loved her with his whole heart. That is what everyone said. His love for Olivia Evgeny looks to me like one of this author's 'self-making passions.'"

"But the lover she took—" I said.

"Was there such a lover?" Simon asked. "I have studied this case carefully, and remain uncertain whether there was such a lover. The evidence in favor—of it being John Littleton or Denny Fuller or even John Manticourt, or any of the other names proposed—is ambiguous. There was no lover the second time, and yet, he seems to have murdered Louise all the same. Regardless, Laplace believed Olivia had taken a lover, and—now this is my theory, but I am sure of it, and certain it cannot be disproven—my idea is that the honey in the milk was something Laplace didn't want himself, and knew she didn't want for herself either. He believed it was for this lover. No doubt there were other such reminders, but association of the lover with the honey in the milk was so deeply inscribed in his mind that the reminder of it was sufficient to activate all the same jealous anxiety as before, so that he felt everything just as he had the first time, when he was thrown into the worst anxiety possible, that this woman he worshiped would cast him aside for another. His life, which had only become meaningful and whole in knowing her, would become what it had been before, sterile and empty, haunted by a memory he could never escape. He felt everything again, just the same way, because that's the nature of these passions our Niakani is talking about. Someone's response to the crisis, when it comes, is written so deep into who he is that, whenever there is a hint of its repetition, well, the whole thing is brought back. The crisis is the deepest—I mean, clearly, if Niakani is right, then it can produce the deepest trauma a person can know. An injury to the self. There is no escaping that, and no escaping such guilt. Perhaps Laplace acted in a fit of sudden jealous rage, and perhaps he only struck her, he didn't mean to kill her—and

so he believed what happened could be regarded as a tragic accident, an accident for which he was guilty, but not murder *per se.*
Manticourt must have thought the same, if he was moved to give
his friend another chance.

"But they didn't reckon on the depth of guilt. For if you resolve
the crisis wrongly, then you choose yourself in guilt, and that guilt,
that wrong, is written into your identity."

"And this is your answer to Niakani?" I said.

"Yes," said Simon. He spoke emphatically, but his face conveyed indecision, as if he hoped to be proven wrong, but could not
stop himself from speaking. "Even if someone makes offers to pay
our debt, as Manticourt did for Laplace—he knew he would die
soon, but went to prison for him and sacrificed whatever was left
of his life and his reputation to give his friend a chance to begin
his life again—then even so we remain who we are, we remember
who we are, and when the time comes, we show this again. There
is no escape from guilt, no redemption from evil short of paying
for it yourself. If Delacroix had any chance of resolving his guilt, it
would have rested in accepting the punishment he was due. There
is nothing else that could free him from the agony of conscience
over his having wronged one he loved as much as any man could."

BLOOD BROTHERS

Simon fell silent, apparently troubled by something. Rufus spoke. "I missed the beginning of this argument, I know," he said in a voice more suitable to a lecture hall than a kitchen gathering, "but our topic is, as I take it, evil? And what to do with it?"

"Yes, professor, that's it," I said. Rufus had taught several of my favorite classes at UNC Wilmington. He was a popular professor, albeit with an obscure role within the University—no one seemed to know what his home department was, and though he most commonly taught for Philosophy, he lectured on whatever topic interested him at the moment, whether that was Law, Economics, or Classics—and, although he stood on the wrong side of fifty, he was still a vigorous speaker and powerful personality.

"And you've been talking about a bunch of psychology and the essence of sin and all that?" he asked.

"Right again," I said.

"Of course, I won't wager which way he was arguing about it," said Rufus. "Half the time, he argues one way, half the time, the other. I suppose that's the lawyer in him. Whatever argument he gave you, he has another set of arguments for the other side."

Simon, looking displeased with this statement, stared at Rufus coldly.

"Well, I think these descents into psychology are always a mistake," said Rufus. "For others' evil, we have laws; for natural evil, we have the state; for everything else, we have *hesed*."

At this point, Pete was done carrying equipment in as well. "If we're going to discuss philosophy," he said, "we really should head to the living room."

Entering from the kitchen, one looked out wide picture windows facing the Atlantic Ocean. Although the sun lay behind us, through these windows we could see its dying light stretched out upon the ocean, dimly visible beneath its rays. The living room inside was furnished with a mismatched variety of large couches and armchairs. One felt dwarfed there by the ten foot tall ceiling and expansive, open floor plan. The seats were pulled together into a sort of circle facing each other. Rufus took an entire overstuffed loveseat for himself. He had somehow already filled a glass of whiskey in his right hand. Simon, initially hesitating, finally moved to a red couch to Rufus's right, looking small and dark against its bright red background. His hands held his head, rubbing his forehead, either from some pain or for another reason. I took the armchair opposite Rufus.

Simon remarked, "You have an impressive view of the ocean."

"It is, isn't it?" Pete called back from the kitchen. "You should see it during a storm! That's really something."

"I'm not sure I'd care to see that, actually," Rufus said quietly.

Pete then returned with the pot of coffee and mugs. The mugs were custom-made so that each was distinct, but all bore the same style, probably all made by some artist in Pigeon Forge or Ashville in the Smokey Mountains. "Now, let's begin," said Pete. "Dr. Rufus…"

"Laws, states, *hesed*," I said, trying out the word uncomfortably. "You're deliberately provoking us…"

"I am also over-generalizing, to the detriment of my professional interest in precision," he said. "Such is the cost of rhetoric."

"Spare us your bad conscience," said Pete. "Tell us what you meant."

"Surely it did not confuse you that I opposed laws to the evil of others," said Rufus.

"No," said Pete. "I grok that, and what you said about the state and natural evil. We use laws to minimize murder and other harms that one person inflicts on another. We use the state to help when natural disasters or other dangers affect us. We want you to explain *hesed.*"

"You'd have me skip my preface, then?" said Rufus.

"You can tell us your political philosophy some other time," said Pete.

"I suppose I must accede, then, with the wish," Rufus said. "Still, let me make a remark: the modern bureaucratic state governs life as much as possible by means of law and by the creation of an immense human artifice, 'the state,' which mediates each individual's experience of life by interposing itself as a barrier between the individual and life, constructing a new framework within which the individual lives and breathes and has his being—if possible, without ever noticing; and this is common to all modern states, whether it favors market capitalism, or state socialism, or some mixture of these. This is the opposite end of the spectrum from the original human societies, which were tribal, and which depended not on fear of the laws, but on familial attachments. In such a society, kinship ties perform the functions that our institutions and complicated legal mechanisms perform in ours. They are the means by which anything happens and the means therefore by which people protect themselves against the evils of the human condition. To restate my original *bon mot* a bit more perspicuously, the modern state is of course superior to the tribal society in its ability to deal with the vast majority of evils, but for everything it excludes, we still need the practices and modes of those earlier societies in which attitude-independent relationships provide an affective and normative structure, and acts of *hesed* performed by those sharing such a relationship, provide the means of action, for confronting and overcoming crises and evils that fall through the cracks of the state."

"That's better, but not by much," I said. I saw a pair of bright green lizards outside on the railing. I took them to be skinks. One was running along the railing toward the right, darting out of view where the picture window ended. The other kept still, sheltered in the dappled shadow of the foliage in front of the porch. It may have been sunning itself, but by a trick of perspective, it seemed to be staring into the house, watching us, judging or learning from our conversation as may be.

"Let me begin with the crisis," he said. "Then everything will emerge naturally. In any human situation, there are moments when an individual's essential interests are threatened in such a way as to make him need another's free assistance. Some of a man's needs he can meet using his own hands or resources, or by using the law to compel the assistance of others; but the time of crisis is a moment in which these are either unavailable or insufficient. He lacks the resources to meet his need by himself and faces circumstances in which the law is either silent or powerless to help him. Even in our big societies, such crises occur. Our society is full of institutions with carefully defined roles, regulated by rules and laws, and whenever that is the case, there is the possibility of a disaster that falls into a zone where they will not reach."

"So acts of *hesed* are, then, what? Free acts in response to another's crisis?" asked Pete.

"Exactly so," said Rufus. "I am not a religious man, but I will not disregard the biblical writers, and indeed, you will see that I respect them a great deal, for they understood the principal point—they knew what is required to face the crisis. What is required is *hesed*. An act of *hesed* is precisely action on behalf of someone in a moment of essential need, when the one called upon to act is in a unique or especially privileged position to provide the person's need but is free to refuse without suffering significant legal or other consequences. But upon what basis may someone call upon another to show them *hesed*? The Septuagint is no good on this point. Their translation of *hesed* as *eleos*, or mercy, terrifically obscures the nature of such appeals. When someone appeals to someone to show him *hesed*, he is not throwing himself upon their mercy or hoping upon their goodwill, but relying upon their faithfulness. Sakenfeld is particularly good on this.[42] He cannot compel the actor's assistance but he can remind him of the obligations he possesses toward him in virtue of the relationship that they share. This is why familial ties are especially important here, but not exclusively so."

"What do you mean?" said Pete.

"Everything hinges on the distinction made by Niko Kolodny between attitude-dependent, and attitude-independent, relationships," said Rufus.[43] "For example, someone may be another's father or son due solely to a biological tie, that is, an historical fact, regardless of how either individual feels about this or whether they care for one another at all, whereas relationships like friendship or a romantic relationship are 'attitude-dependent.' They depend upon those party to the relationship maintaining a certain 'pattern of concern' for each other, for the relationship, and for the pattern of concern itself. The *attitudes* of those in the relationship are irrelevant to whether the first type of relationships exist, but crucially important to assessing whether relationships of the second type exist."

"But isn't 'being born in the same hour' also an attitude-independent relationship I could have with someone?" Pete said.

---

42 Ed. Rushnevsky means Katharine Doob Sakenfeld, *Faithfulness in Action* (Philadelphia: Fortress Press, 1985). She presents an exhaustive collection of all instances of the word, with particular focus placed upon four stories of David (David and Jonathan, David and Hanun, David and Barzillai, and Hushai and David) and upon five other stories: of the Hebrew spies at Jericho and Bethel; of King Ahab and Ben-hadad; of Sarah and Abraham; of Joseph and Jacob; and of Ruth and Naomi.

43 Ed.: Niko Kolodny, "Love as Valuing a Relationship," *The Philosophical Review* 112 (2003): pp. 135-189.

"That's true," said Rufus, "and yet your birth-hour twin would have no special ties to you, nor you to him. That's because what's really key here is that some relationships make normative demands upon us, and some relationships are attitude-independent; and where a relationship has both qualities, it acquires a special status, insofar as it provides a whole normative pattern outside of our voluntary control in which we live and move and in which we can make requests for assistance, and expect to have them fulfilled. When we love someone in an attitude-dependent relationship, then we may well accept that the love is, in the manner of international treaties, authoritative merely *rebus sic stantibus*, so long as things remain as they are—so long as we share a common interest, for example, and not particularly concerning ourselves with preserving the relationship for its own sake. But if the relationship imposes normative claims outside our control, then we cannot so quickly dismiss it because our interest in it has flagged. Today, people appear tempted to consider even blood relationships optional, but a people who believes that it is up to them, individually, to determine whether or not their relationships with other people have a grip on their identity, will always find it difficult to face the crisis, no matter how big and sophisticated their big bureaucratic state is."

"So what does this come to?" asked Pete.

"If a relationship makes normative demands, then there is some minimal level of concern that it will require from us respecting the other person," said Rufus. "Now, Luther says somewhere, 'What kind of life would ours be if nobody could trust anybody else?'[44] For human life is such as to demand that we generally be able to rely upon others in a variety of circumstances. Anscombe

---

44   Ed.: Luther says this in his *Commentary on Galatians*, ed. Alister McGrath and J. I. Packer (Wheaton, Il: Crossway Books, 1998), p. 258.

said something similar about the human need for promise-keeping.[45] In the present age, when we largely rely upon each other via large and impersonal institutions such as 'the market' and 'the state,' we hardly feel the need that individuals felt in past ages for relationships with individuals of sufficient strength and reliability as to make life possible and worthwhile. For today we hardly feel the need to call upon others to show us *hesed*; we live among the great abundance provided by the market and when it does not meet our needs, we feel able to call upon the power of the law to act on our behalf. Thus we now hardly feel the difference between these types of relationship, and to the extent that we do, we frequently favor relationships of the latter sort, because while we do not need the greater reliability that attitude-independent relationships offer, attitude-dependent relationships offer us greater freedom."

"I understand," I said. "We want more freedom and more independence, and we feel less the different texture of our relationships with each other, and hope, perhaps, that somehow everything can become our own free act, even our most essential and defining relationships. So your answer is—what we need to face evil is, first, law, second, the state, and third, individuals who will show us *hesed*

---

45 Ed.: See G. E. M. Anscombe, "On Promising and Its Justice, and Whether It Needs to be Respected *In Foro Interno*," in *The Collected Philosophical Papers of G.E.M. Anscombe: Ethics, Religion and Politics* (Oxford: Basil Blackwell, 1981). For example, she describes promising in terms of a procedure for getting someone to do something without the use of force; see the following: "Now getting one another to do things without the application of physical force is a necessity for human life, and that far beyond what could be secured by those other means. Thus such a procedure as that language-game is an instrument whose use is part and parcel of an enormous amount of human activity and hence of human good; of the supplying both of human needs and of human wants so far as the satisfactions of these are compossible. It is scarcely possible to live in a society without encountering it and even actually being involved in it. Then not to 'go along with it', in the sense of accepting the necessity expressed by 'Now you've got to . . .' after one has given the sign, will tend to hamper the attainment of the advantages that the procedure serves," p. 18.

when a crisis arises that falls outside the generalized structures that the first two address; but the greater the strength and reliability of the former two powers, the more we exempt ourselves from, and the weaker the reliability of, the third factor. So the evil marking the human condition, it seems, is inescapable."

"Perhaps so," said Rufus. "But we face evil with the tools at hand, and construct the laws, institutions, and relationships that will make human life possible and as secure and happy as we may."

"Still, then, I wonder whether your view leaves a pretty significant problem," I said.

"Which is what?" he said.

"What do you take the evils of human life to be?" I said.

"Sin, death, misery," he said. "More or less."

"Not a bad list," I admitted. "I suppose that laws, social norms, and such are meant to cut down on sin—which is voluntary wrongdoing of some sort, I suppose?"

"Perhaps more, but at least that," he said.

"But is sin itself bad, apart from the death and misery it causes?" I asked.

"A difficult question," he said.

"Then here is a simpler one: is sin bad for the perpetrator as well as those who suffer from it directly?"

"Probably, yes," he said.

"Why so, in probability?" I asked.

"It distorts our relationships with others," he said.

"And those relationships are important for us?" I asked. "I mean, beyond some instrumental value we might get from them, they also have some intrinsic value?"

"Of course," he said. "Human beings need relationships with others. Love is also natural to us, and love makes us vulnerable in our relationships."

"Now, what do you mean by 'need'?" said Simon, interjecting himself into the discussion quite suddenly.

"*Need* expresses the relationship of one thing, A, to another thing, B," said Rufus. "It designates that B requires A, that A is necessary for B. But it also goes on to say something else: that B itself is necessary."

"Now, this is paradoxical," said Simon. "Are you saying that need is need's need for something?"

"That would be worse than paradoxical," Rufus said. "It would be no definition at all. But that is not what I said."

"You said that need expresses a relation between two things, in which A is necessary for B, and B is necessary also. So are we to take B to be necessary in the sense of, what?" said Simon. "Mathematical necessity?"

"You pile absurdity upon absurdity," said Rufus. "Not at all. B is necessary in the sense of being a pregiven end. For a living being, it is life that constitutes the pregiven, the end internal to its own definition, for to live is to strive to live."

"So *B* is life, and *A* is water?" asked Simon.

"Narrowly construed, yes," said Rufus.

"You suggest there is a wide construal," said Simon.

"Naturally," said Rufus. "The life that a living being strives to realize is the life characteristic of its species. The jellyfish strives for the life of a jellyfish, strives to maintain its internal organs in the manner of a jellyfish, strives to keep itself alive within its environment in the manner appropriate to a jellyfish. So *B* indicates the type of life characteristic of the species."

"The given is the species?" asked Simon.

"Yes," Rufus said.

"I see," said Simon. "And human beings need relationships, is that it?"

"Yes, does this bother you?" Rufus asked.

"No, no, carry on," said Simon, "Everything is now clear enough."

"Then everyone should understand now that *need* indicates that something is necessary for a living being (let us restrict ourselves to that, since that is our interest) in order for that being to live in the manner designated by its species, to carry out its characteristic way of life," said Rufus.

"So," I said, "a horse needs strong legs, a wolf needs a pack, and a sparrow needs a nest, although strictly speaking, an individual organism might live without those things, given enough luck and moxy."

"Do sparrows have *moxy?*" he said. "But, yes, human life depends upon the existence of relationships whose normative claims are inescapable and whose support is provided, not by coercion as in the case of law, but by an internal motive, which is love. Not the love of the storybooks, but a steady internal commitment to persons and relationships that make claims upon us. We need this both for instrumental reasons and for intrinsic reasons, as we seem unable to remain whole and happy without relationships in which to ground ourselves and find common understanding."

A mosquito hawk was drifting through the room, in the vast area above our heads and below the elevated ceiling. It finally left to hover through the hallway.

"Then what can we do when our own sin has damaged our essential relationships?" I said.

"Why, seek forgiveness, of course," he said. "This can itself be a way of requesting *hesed*. Such requests, remember, are requests for another person to provide something of essential importance that this person is in a privileged position to provide, but which you cannot require them to provide. If the relationship is important to you—as it should be, given its status—and you feel the pain of having distorted it, then the other party to the relationship stands in this position to you, and you may request forgiveness as a way of requesting *hesed*."

"But what if the other person can't, or won't, provide such forgiveness?" I asked.

"Have you noticed," Rufus said, "that we can create new

attitude-independent relationships from attitude-dependent relationships?"

"Yes, I suppose," I said, nonplussed. "What of it?"

"Thus in Lucian's *Toxaris*, a dialogue between a Scythian and a Greek about friendship, Lucian has the less civilized Scythian argue that 'we are more loyal friends than you, and we treat friendship more seriously.'[46] Toxaris says that the Greeks, who at this time were, like us, city-dwellers, form friendships 'over wine cups' or on the basis of 'considerations of age or neighborhood,' but Scythians view the matter as too important to be left to such casual factors.[47] For them, friendships follow only after something like courtship, during which two men might come to know one another, and involve performing a ritual that concludes with each person taking an oath 'to live and if necessary to die together' with the other. The Norse Sagas, which take place in circumstances even more dangerous than those faced by the Scythians, describe a similar practice, known as *fóstbræðralag*, whereby two men become as brothers to each other, vowing to avenge each other's death in the same way a brother would. In the Bible, we see the same kind of oath exchanged by David and Jonathan and perhaps by Ruth and Naomi."

"This is a fascinating history lesson," I said. "But…"

"I will return to your question," he said. "Such oaths demonstrate our power to transform attitude-dependent relationships into attitude-independent relationships. This is a power that human beings always discover whenever human life depends upon the creation of reliable human relationships. These rituals, along with marriage and adoption, are the primary means that

---

46 Ed.: Lucian, *Toxaris: A Dialogue on Friendship*, in *The Works of Lucian of Samosata: Complete with Exceptions Specified in the Preface*, trans. H. W. Fowler and F. G. Fowler (Oxford, UK: Clarendon Press, 1905), p. 40.

47 Ed.: Lucian, *The Works of Lucian of Samosata*, p. 56.

humanity has discovered for transforming the one type of relationship into the other, from attitude-dependent relationships to attitude-independent relationships. You see this?"

"Yes," I said.

"Yet, although marriage itself is created by a free act, and varies with the conditions, what does not vary is this: that a vow is a vow. This was Locke's mistake. For he thought that, since marriage basically exists for the sake of rearing children, the bond of marriage—the bond created by the vow—became dissolvable as soon as the children had been reared.[48] This is a simple-minded mistake, the kind of error someone falls into only through a weak head or a bad conscience."

"It doesn't seem quite as obvious to me as you say," said Pete.

"It is not difficult to see," said Rufus. "If a vow alters a relationship, so it is now attitude-independent rather than being attitude-dependent, then the basic nature of its claims is also altered. The purpose of the vow is to make those claims nearly inalterable or at any rate enduring. That's why Locke is mistaken. Just because the occasion of making the vow has passed doesn't mean the enduring normative effects of the vow are now also in the past."

"I think I get you," Pete said. "If you make someone into your brother, then he's your brother, whatever your reason was for doing so, because that's what a brother is—he's always your brother, no matter what, and he always has claims upon you."

"Correct," said Rufus. "If I am worried about personal enemies I have made, and I make a vow of mutual defense with another person, make that man my blood brother, the power of that

---

48 See John Locke, *Second Treatise of Civil Government*, Ch. VII, section 79: "For the end of conjunction, between male and female, being not barely procreation, but the continuation of the species; this conjunction betwixt male and female ought to last, even after procreation, so long as is necessary to the nourishment and support of the young ones, who are to be sustained by those that got them, till they are able to shift and provide for themselves."

vow does not dissolve when my enemies have disappeared or been defeated. Once it comes into being it remains in force by its own logic, for that was just what it is to make a vow: to create a normative claim where there was none before. The action of creation was free, but the obligation now has its own life. So the marriage vow will not dissolve simply because the occasion has passed, for it is nothing but sophistry to insist that a vow undertaken 'till death' could be dissolved prior to death because one no longer needs it. No, what one needed was a bond that could not be dissolved, that was the reason for the vow, and having made such a bond, one must accept its force, just as one must accept the claims of one's brother, whether one needs him or not."

"Okay, I grant you that," said Pete. "But I don't think you can say that *nothing* can cancel the power of an attitude-independent relationship to generate normative claims. I mean, most people accept that promises can be overridden."

"That is probably right," said Rufus, "although a vow is not a promise; it is far harder to 'cancel' or 'override' as you put it. Nor would anyone accept that the claims of brotherhood or family more generally can be 'canceled' in the way that a promise can. "

"I will agree to that," I said—oh, did I ever know that you cannot easily cancel those claims—"but I do have a question. Promises are different from vows because, as I take it, they belong to different categories. An attitude-independent relationship (like brotherhood, in your example, or motherhood) is an ongoing source of normative claims. As long as the relationship exists, it continues to generate various claims upon us. Its ongoing power to make these claims generally continues 'til death' as you put it—or even longer, since blood brothers were to avenge each other's death. Now this is different from a promise, in that a promise does not usually make something into a source of claims upon us. Instead, we would say that the promise itself represents a claim upon us, to do what we promised we would do. So, of course a promise can be overridden, but then, we have already agreed that particular circumstances can override the claims based in relationships. The exception was in the 'moment of crisis'—coincidentally, my discussion with Simon also revolved around this little phrase!—when we agreed that, in the moment of crisis at least, when one party to a relationship stands in essential need of something that the other party stands in a privileged or unique position to provide, then there was no escaping the normative claim; every escape clause is closed and canceled. The difference then is between a claim and a source of claims, and it is natural to expect that what can cancel a promise is different from what can cancel the power of an attitude-independent relationship to make claims upon us."

"I thought you had a question," said Rufus.

"So I did," I said. "What happens if the moment of crisis arrives and—the party called upon to act does not act?" That is, imagine *there were two voles, and the little one climbed a tree and said, 'I want to live on cheese and beer, like the squirrels,' but the other vole was disgusted. She turned her back, saying beneath her voice, 'Go then, I will not follow you,' and she left...* "Suppose a son grows up, somehow, despite being abandoned by his father, or a man survives a danger from which his blood brother ought to have defended him; have these failures broken the bond of the relationship, in the way we mentioned earlier regarding the historical claims of friendship? Does the relationship remain an attitude-independent source of normative claims?"

"As I said before: the relationship is attitude-independent, so it does not disappear just because the state of affairs has changed," said Rufus. "The new action does not cancel the source of the norm it violates. Rather, the violation is *added* to the normative structure of the relationship and reverberates through the relationship. The relationship of the blood-brothers you mentioned is not canceled—far from it! If that were so, then the two men would now stand before each other as indifferently as two strangers do to each other. Instead, they are now separated by betrayal, which stands between them and colors all the normative bonds connecting the one to the other. No matter what comes to pass, no matter which way one looks, the betrayal will be there, and will shape and color the norms of the relationship. For the offender, it becomes imperative to find a means of reconciliation, a way of correcting the wrong and restoring the relationship to the state it was in previous to the betrayal." Indeed, it is so. "But that does not mean that the relationship should not still provide reasons for the other to offer forgiveness, when honestly sought."

"But that's where we were, wasn't it?" I said. "What if the other doesn't, or cannot, offer forgiveness?"

"Yes, of course," said Rufus. "I have not lost sight of this. In fact, the evil in us is much greater than we realize, so that we probably discover much of it too late. Perhaps the true measure of the wickedness living within us is manifested in circumstances such as the plague afflicting Athens during the Peloponnesian War or the rise of Fascism, when ordinary people became ever more involved in highly compromising activities. The evil within us is constrained by things like laws and customs, but bursts out whenever these constraints are loosened or, worse, given positive approval by social and political forces—not to speak of those injustices, like slavery, in which the law itself stands among the culprits, bullying us into the crowd with all its threats and vehemence. A perfectly just judge would discover many forms of complicity in our lives that we have made ourselves blind to, and would judge us as much for the comfortable ease with which we have soothed our consciences as for the original outrages themselves in which we are complicit."

"Yes," I said, "and if we suppose life to have the kind of normative structure you have described then we must assume that we are guilty above all from our failures to act—for choosing to separate ourselves from each other and refuse responsibility for each other, saying to ourselves, 'What is it to me?,' 'Let another take care of it,' and other things like that, withdrawing ourselves as much as possible into our own projects and concerns."

"Yes, of course," he said, "and if we are generous with those closest to us, to friends and family members we enjoy, then we congratulate ourselves on this basis and make our consciences forgetful of all we do not do and all those we neglect. All this and more, I grant you. I grant that it is highly likely that Qoheleth is right, that 'What is crooked cannot be made straight and what is lacking cannot be counted,' and that Kant is right too, in saying that 'out of the crooked timber of humanity, no straight thing was ever made.'[49] The wrong in us is widespread and hard to fix. What else?"

"Well, consider your 'moment of crisis' again, the moment that calls for *hesed*—won't a wrong action performed at a such a moment be very likely to possess a very special property?" I asked.

"What property is that?" he said.

"Irreversibility," I said. "Clearly, if someone is in a unique or privileged position to provide what someone positively needs, and does not provide it, then the consequences for the person in crisis are likely to be very great."

"That is so," I said.

"And very often the harm done at that point will not be easy to correct; it may even be impossible to correct," I said.

"Yes, indeed," said Rufus.

"So conscience is often left perplexed at the impossibility of undoing what we have done, and of doing what we have left undone," I said.

"You have completely caught me out," he said. "But I am not without resources, as you shall see."

---

49   Ed.: Qoheleth is the name the biblical author of Ecclesiastes gives himself. The reference is to Ecclesiastes 1:15. Kant's remark about the "crooked timber of humanity" is found in his "Idea for a Universal History," found in Immanuel Kant, *Anthropology, History, and Education* in *The Cambridge Edition of the Works of Immanuel Kant in Translation*, Vol. 7 (Cambridge: Cambridge University Press, 2007), p. 113.

"Proceed, then, and show me," I said.

"So a person stands with an anguished conscience, occupying what we might call the moral crisis. Such a condition, such a crisis, surely meets the conditions for an 'essential need.' Humanity has spiritual as well as physical needs, this is what you draw out, for satisfying conscience is a human need. But whom may one call upon in the affliction of one's conscience? Who may answer this call and rescue one from punishment, corruption, and death? Clearly, if God exists, then God occupies not only a privileged position to answer one's need, but a unique one, for only a being privileged to stand as judge of the universe could answer the need for acquittal. Finally, he is certainly free to act or not to act, insofar as neither we nor any other possess means of compelling him to act. The whole human condition therefore constitutes a condition of crisis, and what the individual requires is for God to show him *hesed* when he calls upon it."

"But can we rely upon God to answer our calls for him to show us *hesed* in this way, to forgive us our debts and overlook our wickedness?" I asked. "Why should he do such a thing? Upon what basis could we make this demand of him? The nature of the human condition, as you specify it, militates against the conclusion that we can."

"I understand," he said. "Because sin stands between the sinner and God, you want to know whether we can, with Jacob, refer to him as 'the God who answers me in the day of my distress'?⁵⁰ Someone might think to call upon God as his Creator, but that is just the relationship that was disrupted by sin. Now the relationship between creature and Creator is replaced by a new, legal relationship, between Judge and accused. Can the criminal come before the judge and appeal for *hesed*, with the precise purpose of escaping the penalty of the law? Absurd."

---

50 Ed.: Genesis 35:3.

"You must be driving at something here," I said, "and not simply recommending calling on God's assistance in desperation."

"Surely you have not so quickly forgotten what I said about *covenantal* relationships," said Rufus. "Our past history stands in the way of relying upon God to meet our need out of either a general or a relational obligation to us; we cannot rely upon either law or a preexisting relationship or past history of merit that would constrain him to salve our anguished conscience. But we would have such a basis if God covenanted with us to create an attitude independent relationship with us, grounded in the covenant, and if this covenant included terms that obliged God to act on our behalf despite our status as sinners. When Jacob referred to Yahweh as 'the God who answers me in the day of my distress' he didn't say this because God had honored his past obedience—for there was little enough of that—but because of the covenant Yahweh made with him at Bethel. Similarly, Abraham and Isaac relied upon God because of his covenant, not because of their prior obedience, and Joseph was able to rely upon God to show him *hesed* because of the covenantal relationship the Patriarchal family shared with God, as it says in the prison narrative—'The Lord was with Joseph and showed him *hesed*.'[51] When human beings stand in great need of each other, they discover their power for transforming attitude-dependent relationships with more uncertain relational obligations into attitude-independent relationships with specific relational obligations. Human beings of course cannot simply offer to covenant with God in the same way. Rather, heaven must come down to earth, and God offer to make covenant with man, as he does for Abraham or at Sinai. Then, and only then, can someone call upon God to show him *hesed* in the perpetual hour of crisis known as the human condition. Only one who shares in a covenantal

---

51 Ed.: Genesis 39:21.

relationship with God could depend on calling upon God to show him *hesed* on the basis of the relational obligations created by the covenant."

"Is that all?" said Simon.

"Is something missing?" Rufus said.

"The most important thing of all," said Simon. "In law, we can never dispense with facts to support our arguments, while you philosophers are forever proving the conditional premise of *modus ponens*, and leaving us wanting for the other, without which there is no proof and no inference at all.[52] *Is* there such a covenant?"

Rufus sighed. "That is a good question," he said, "and all of my scholarly studies have been unable to satisfy me on this point—not only whether God exists (an obscure metaphysical question, which I regard as being more probable than not, perhaps with a probability of 0.62), but more importantly on this historical question whether God has, at some point, made a covenant with man, I must admit that I simply do not know the answer."

Simon had a kind of smile. "So you admit that your case depends upon two assumptions which you, at least, are uncertain of."

"Indeed, I must admit that," said Rufus. "Though I know what your smile means."

"Forget about me," said Simon. "Regarding your case—mustn't the verdict be: *not proven?*"

---

52 Ed.: Simon is speaking of the logic of conditional arguments. The principal conditional inference is known as "modus ponens," in which one can deduce, from the truth of "If X, then Y" and the truth of "X," the further conclusion, the truth of "Y." (Consider: If it is raining, then it is wet outside ("If X, then Y"); it is raining ("X"); therefore, it is wet outside ("Y").) If someone has established the truth of the conditional ("If X, then Y") but has not established the truth of "X," then nothing follows regarding "Y," which may or may not be true.

JOHNNIE WALKER BLUE

After deploying so much logical machinery and argument, the conclusion of Rufus' speech was disappointing. But no sooner had he finished then we noticed raucous noise from outside the house, and I realized that there was a large group of beachgoers just outside. People were talking, laughing, and shouting. I was instantly filled with loathing. Simon said something to me that I did not hear and Pete was talking with Rufus. The laughter outside rang in my ears, and I noticed a record player in the corner of the room, against the wall. My gaze lingered on it and I responded noncommittally to Simon before excusing myself and leaving the room.

When I was washing my hands in the bathroom, I was surprised to see a knife lying between the basin and the mirror. I shuddered. Gazing into the mirror awakened two memories, which were mixed together in confusion, succeeding one another again and again. That morning:

> The morning sunlight streamed in through the bathroom window a foot above me, its rays visible in the mirror, caught in the lingering steam. The transcendent aura appeared out of place in the dingy bathroom with its scarred

walls and out-of-date light fixtures. I was humming a bar from Tchaikovsky, caught up in the beauty and purity of the light. Surroundings mean nothing me when the world holds such glory. Beauty always has a visceral effect on me. I felt light-headed and my skin was tingling with delight at the joy of being alive. The existence of beauty, I thought, was theodicy enough, and more than enough.

The phone rang while I was cutting up oranges for breakfast. It was my mother. "What?" I said, irritated at the interruption of my reverie, holding the knife in my hand.

At first, I couldn't understand her, but finally, an emotionally choked voice said, "Sarah's dead."

Coolly, crisply, I asked, "How?" My head was full of thoughts like, *That fool, what did she think would happen?* I bitterly regret this, my first response.

"Her body was found in the Cape Fear River. She threw herself from a bridge."

"What did…?"

"A bridge. It was suicide. She killed herself. Suicide," she repeated, helplessly.

I didn't answer.

My eyes had returned to the mirror. I stared into my own eyes and it seemed to me that I had never known this person before. She was my sister, her neediness repelled me, my little sister. The sun was shining, its rays caught in the dissipating steam from the expired shower, but I do not remember feeling its warmth.

The second memory, that other morning, from the year I took off from school, when I woke up and I had the idea.

I immediately got up and went to that old playroom, which we had converted into a home dance studio, with mirrors along the north and west walls. It was very early, and still dark outside. I stood in the middle of the room, staring at those mirrors, and contemplating my object, assessing whether this would suffice. I often wrote out thoughts on these mirrors: chess strategies, paper ideas, idle perplexities—anything where it would benefit me to see everything before me all at once, and life-size, so speak, not miniaturized, as anything written down on paper seemed to me to be. The idea was big, but with two whole walls of mirrors? I thought I could. I got a black dry-erase marker and an eraser. Then I began.

I did not have any particular order of execution; I simply began writing in different spots, guessing how the whole pattern would fall together. It began with a handful of lines on the left panel of the north wall, then a dozen on the middle panel of the west wall, a single assertion on the right panel of the west wall, and then an increasingly complex pattern of assertions, assumptions, and coordinating functions written wherever there was room. I quickly escalated from the single black marker to three, then four, then seven different colors. I wrote in Latin or English as seemed appropriate for the thought. In later versions, once I had mastered Greek's superior article and verbal system, as well as various logical languages, the Arcanum developed into a kind of private language—sorry, Wittgenstein—of symbols and coordinating functions, but this is getting ahead of myself.

It wasn't long before I had to erase it all and begin anew. This was just as the sun began to rise, its light warming my back. The glare upon the mirrors of the west wall hurt my eyes, but I didn't pause. The second time I used only black, although I had worn out the first black marker, and I worked out carefully from the two central panels. On the west wall, I wrote out the thought as it pertained to the individual; and on the north wall, as it pertained to the ideal. Sarah, as usual running late for school, came in during the middle of this wearing shorts, a sweater, one rain boot, and a white sock, giving my creation a look of combined amazement, perplexity, and bemusement—as if, naturally, this was exactly the sort of insanity she expected from her sister. But it was not insanity, and still less was it a game. Nonetheless, I lost track of time, and I'm not sure whether I remembered to eat.

Finally, sometime in the afternoon, when the light seems directionless and one has no shadow, I stood in the middle of the room, contemplating the mirrored panels all around me, covered with all that seemingly incoherent script. At some point I had removed the barres to make it easier to get the idea down. The one on the west wall was just a portable model and easily moved to the window, but the one on the north wall had been bolted in place. Now, all that was visible was the idea, elegantly expressed. I knew it was not yet perfect. Many of the subsidiary relations had to be worked out more precisely, and who knows how many adjustments would have to be made here and there. But as for the whole? I was confident in it, entranced by this vision of script upon mirrors, expressing the relation between the human being and the ideal.

I don't know how long I had been standing there in reverie when I saw Sarah in the mirrored panels, staring into the room from the corner. "What is it?" she asked.

I didn't know what to say, so I just told her the name, "The Sacrum Arcanum."

"What—like, our arcanum?" she said.

I was confused. "The arcanum?" I said, questioningly. "Oh. No, that is, that was, just something, just make believe. This is real. This is everything."

"Oh," said Sarah. She was very pale, her eyes glancing

rapidly from panel to panel, trying to grasp what I had done. "Can you explain it to me?"

I was silent a moment. "I don't know. Maybe someday."

"Oh," she said again. And remaining a minute longer, she finally walked away. In fact, I was not eager to explain it to anyone until I had a better grasp of it, afraid that doing so would disturb its delicate strands in my mind.

There were numerous arbitrary assertions, but most of these were arbitrary in the sense of the arbitrary assertions made in logical proofs—their very arbitrariness was their strength. They were arbitrary stand-ins for any of a range of possible other assertions I could have made.

I made just two assumptions, properly so-called. I formulated these in various ways, and spent years refining them, but this is how they stood that day. One was that the idea, the ideal, was articulable. The second was that the individual was sufficient for her relation to the ideal. In this idea, I found myself, my destiny, and my whole relation to the world. With it, I could conquer everything.

I wrote it all down in a small, brown notebook, which I labeled *Sacrum Arcanum I* (even then I anticipated that there would be many more notebooks; this is *XIX*). I think I ate dinner at some point, or at least some leftovers, but when I went to bed, I dreamt strange dreams, and woke with a fever. I had been coming down with something for a long time and it finally got me then. I kept the notebook under my pillow, and frequently clutched it in my hand. My thoughts, I will admit it, were confused, and my ideas had that fixed and hypnotic power they sometimes hold in dreams and fevers. I had constant shivers and weakness and Sarah set up a TV for me in my room, including, eventually, a DVD Player. ("Mom said 'No' on bringing in the Blu Ray," she said.) I occasionally watched some old movies, but I found it hard to concentrate, and I could barely watch a minute or two of the ballet DVDs. Frequently, the illness was so severe I almost wanted to die. But, in my mind, this was but the first test of the idea, its first weathering. Illnesses often possess this strange suggestive power to those who suffer them, as if they stood for something much higher than themselves. When it was over, I laughed at my thoughts. But at the same time, I felt perhaps those thoughts were right. The weakness of illness is nothing when you have purpose, and I had the Arcanum.

⟨⟩

I went to the kitchen, taking the back way to avoid the living room. No one else was there with me. I idly examined the chaos of magnetic poetry covering the refrigerator door. "I play gift trap." "I want the sun pumpkin." "Despite all my—." Looking for "rage," no doubt. I smiled, and moved the tile for "ø" over. Pete or Dash would appreciate it when he found it. That was when I noticed it, right in the middle of the door: "No lies." An entirely innocent coincidence, but it shocked me. No one could have known how many times I had written just that, the highest principle of the Arcanum. The highest principle since that day, anyway—replacing *Truth above all* and *Manifest the ideal in every act and pursuit.* I could tell that the front door was open. The noises from without were much louder than before.

Oh, Sarah, I was thinking. I would do anything to bring back that girl in one boot and one sock, shorts and a sweater. Pete had set out the liquor from the liquor cabinet on a table between the kitchen and living area, along with a mismatched set of tumblers and shot glasses. I took the Johnnie Walker Blue—I knew what it cost, but I didn't care—and poured it into some ugly German tumbler shaped like a goat. I intended to take only a single shot but my hands were unsteady and I must have poured out twice that. *What the hell*, I thought, *I might as well.* I downed it all at once. Drinking it felt like a cigarette up the nose, and it tasted like a hundred dollars' worth of shit. But it was just what I wanted.

Everyone else had retaken their seats and they were discussing something. Coming back to my own seat, I found that Simon was arguing with Rufus. I was strongly affected by the drink and at first I did not catch what was passing between them, but gradually the argument was becoming clear. Their discussion went something like this:

"So is your idea that the human condition constitutes an 'hour of crisis' (in your sense) and that what we need is someone who can rescue us from this crisis?" asked Simon.

"Yes, that's it," said Rufus.

"And the only person with the power to do so is God?" said Simon.

"Exactly so," said Rufus.

"But God has no antecedent obligation to do so—quite the reverse," said Simon, "because the human condition as we've defined it involves sin and sinfulness, which puts man in the wrong before God as judge. So we cannot call upon God to help him on the basis of a general moral obligation. Sin also violates the primordial harmony between God and man, upsetting any relational obligations man might invoke as a basis for calling upon God's assistance."

"That's right," said Rufus.

"Yet if your hypothesis obtains," said Simon, "then God has offered a new way out of the impasse: he has offered a covenantal relationship through which he freely imposes relational obligations upon himself, in virtue of which man does have the option of calling upon God's assistance in the hour of crisis and feeling assured of God's positive response."

"That's my story, and I'm sticking to it," said Rufus.

"Even granting that God exists, to which you assign the probability of .62—"

"You needn't mock," said Rufus. "I know you have your 'private reason' for belief that you won't share, but I have to stick with my probabilities."

"Even so," Simon went on, "there is a terrible practical objection to this idea. You say that God by granting the covenant would cancel the crisis of conscience—but I say that this covenant would only worsen the problem.

"For what is human sinfulness but an enduring tendency to sin? And what is this tendency to sin except the tendency to value wrongly—to degrade what is good and uphold what is evil, to violate the right and embrace the wrong? This tendency might be explained one of two ways: either we just happen to value things wrongly (and what is needed is better education and better laws), or there is something deeper in us that drives us to sin. But you admitted the problem is of the latter type. Education refines the human being and you can educate a child to beauty, but education has never been able to create virtue. Or, to put the matter in my own way: everyone is guilty.

"So suppose that God *has* offered to covenant with us. Through this covenant we will receive the right to call upon God to show us *hesed*. And suppose that when I ask God to show me *hesed* it is because my conscience has come alive and now I am aware that I am a sinner, under just wrath and doomed by my own inward tendency to strive against constraints, including the will and law of God? How will the covenantal relationship aid me?

"For although God might forgive the sin and say, 'I do not condemn you, go, and sin no more,' what happens? Why, we go and sin again *in just the same way.* That is what we do, for it is who we are. Now we are worse off than before, having not only committed the original sins that called for a covenant to restore our relationship with God, but now also having committed the additional sin of despising God's mercy toward us."

"But is that so bad, really?" Pete asked.

"You have not come into contact with as much sin as I have," said Simon. "I have seen the worst, but that's not what is distinctive about my experience; rather, it is the repetitiveness of what I see that appalls me. Nothing is more repetitive and monotonous than evil. Consider the Hellman case, which I prosecuted back in Greenville. Laura Hellman was the loving wife of one Jack Hellman. He was greedy and selfish, but cunning too, so he frequently succeeded in his endeavors, in his way and after a fashion, and he provided a respectable income. He wasn't much of a husband, of course, as he spent most of his time out drinking with his friends and doing other, less respectable, things. He was a serial adulterer. He was sometimes violent and beat Laura as well—not all the time, she would say, but I think he did it as often as he wanted to. Periodically, as if coming to his senses, he would lay his head on his wife's shoulder, crying tears of sorrow, saying he was sorry and asking her forgiveness. In these instances she regarded it as her duty as a wife (because of the marriage covenant, you see), to forgive him. So Laura stands by his side always, always, while he is growing more and more vicious. She always forgave him and every time she believed he was really sorry and wished to mend his ways. For a brief time, of course, he would, just enough to give her hope; but then the old man would come back, the same monster as before. So they lived, year after year. The police could not do anything because she would not testify against him. I even got into the habit of calling on her during the day, and I pushed her as much as I could, but got nowhere. She refused every time. It all ended suddenly, when Jack murdered her; and by then of course we could put him in prison, but could do nothing for her. Would it not have been better had they never been married, without any covenantal relationship holding them together? For then at least Laura might have simply let the brute go his way, to the benefit of each: for she would not have suffered so much, and although Jack Hellman would have continued to be a wicked man, his wickedness would not have grown so great."

"Sounds awful!" I said. "Well, Dr. Rufus, what say you? Defend yourself!" I knew I was a bit tipsy now, but did not care.

"Your analogy seems flawed," said Rufus. "You've upset the

power balance between God and humanity, since it is surely not the case that we could beat or tyrannize God in the way that the husband in your story does."

"Reimagine the case as you will, it will always come out the same. The man who continually bails out his business partner (to whom he thinks he owes an obligation of aid, because of some youthful agreement they made), and thereby brings the business to bankruptcy, often only after attempting to save things by unsavory means and hiding his incompetence—out of shame before the other; or the mother who continually 'rescues' her son from all his misadventures and misbehavior, with tears and embraces and sincere yet unfulfilled promises of better behavior, until he finally commits some crime; I have been called into far too many of these cases, always too late, always after the offending party made things go irreversibly wrong. Relationships that function this way are no help to those bound by them, either to the one who shows *hesed* or the one who betrays the other's trust. Far from answering the question of what would solve the human condition, covenant between man and God only increases humanity's misery and God's wrath."

Such, or something like this, was what Simon said. I think that the general mood was rather sour at this point, but I was rocking back and forth in my seat, overtaken by a feeling of exhilaration and contradictory emotions. Sarah! You cannot come to me any longer, but I can go to you. Yet the world is so beautiful, and these people are so lovely. Such were my thoughts going into the final conversation we had together that night.

THE BALLAD OF
THE MATIN SEA

"Simon," said Pete, "I'll grant you that the picture you draw is dark, and perhaps we shouldn't want forgiveness if it's going to be like that. But I don't think it goes to the heart of the matter." Pete had gone to school with me at UNCW, and as I mentioned earlier, he double majored in Philosophy and Art. Throughout school, he had lived with a variety of roommates, but it was always he and Dash who provided the center of the group of friends who revolved through those apartments and rental houses. Every summer the two of them disappeared for a month to hike through the Smokey Mountains or the Blue Ridge. He loved to paint in oils or watercolors and specialized in landscape paintings, after the European tradition, that were not quite what they seemed, in which a hint of the fabulous always hovered close to the surface. Occasionally he worked in clay, with indifferent results. His interests in philosophy were eclectic, but he gravitated toward thinkers with bold and imaginative ideas, those who were exciting rather than careful, and especially those whose ideas had a haunting power to change your perception of the world.

"The trouble you've brought up with Rufus's view is that the solution is too external," he said. "It doesn't allow redemption to change who we are, or explain why God would bind himself to

THE HURRICANE NOTEBOOK 163

us so that we can again make claims on him. He leaves this out in order to be clear and establish the framework for his *hesed*-based view. But I have never been able to stop thinking about Maximus' statement that 'the Word of God and God wills always and in all things to accomplish the mystery of his embodiment.'[53] This saying is charged with power. Can the evil that mars the human condition in each of its dimensions be changed? I don't know exactly how to answer that question all at once, so I am instead going to begin with something easier—I will begin with simpler question: *if* the human condition can be changed, how could it be changed? How could we be saved? After addressing that question, I'll deal with the second part, the part that Simon says we're always neglecting—whether we have reason to believe that the antecedent of the conditional is fulfilled."

"That's reasonable," I said. "Now tell us your theory."

Pete was silent a moment while he finished his drink. He stood looking outside, looking past the beachgoers and partiers just down the walkway whose raucous noises still bothered me, out at the ocean beyond. I walked over and closed the door in vexation. The barest hint of the sun shone like a bare glow upon the waters. This Pete contemplated for several minutes before he turned back toward us, and spoke.

"Have you heard of the Matin Sea?" he said.

"No, of course not," I said. "You just made it up."

"Oh, hush, now. You asked for my answer. In any case, it is not really a sea, but a lake, located somewhere in the Baltics or the Caucasus, tucked between two mountains. It is inhabited by a species of spiny creature that is responsible for the ink that pollutes it. When the sun rises, its rays never illuminate more than a few inches of its depths because of the ink produced by the creatures."

---

53 Ed.: Pete quotes Maximus the Confessor, *On the Cosmic Mystery of Jesus Christ*, trans. and ed. by Paul M. Blowers and Robert Louis Wilken (Crestwood, NY: St. Vladimir's Seminary Press, 2003), p. 60.

"Sounds disgusting," I said.

"Worse than that," said Pete, "the ink is also a contagion that infects everyone who comes into contact with it."

"And where did this ink-sickness come from?" I asked.

"No one knows for sure," said Pete. "But there is a story, a ballad almost, told among the shepherds who used to pass through the valley. It is said that at one time the condition of the sea was quite different. The water shone with the light of the sun, and was crystal clear at that time. The creatures themselves were very different as well. They were known as the tevzebi then. Although they are currently covered over with dark, reddish scales, and curving, yellowish spines, in those days they had such delicate skins that they were translucent, like jellyfish, so that their interiors were even more visible than their exteriors. Moreover, the sunlight affected them in an unusual way. When it shone upon them (and they loved floating near the surface of the water in those days), some of the light shone through them but some of the light was absorbed by them. The absorbed light produced a kind of glow, so that for a time afterwards the creatures glowed with a borrowed glory. And thus the sea was bright at all times, even its depths. The tevzebi, these translucent, glowing creatures, lived in a kind of bliss in those days of mountain peaks, halcyon skies, and glowing seas. The shepherds who pass on this story say that when this was still true they used to sit around the lake during summer evenings, when the tevzebi were fat with the light of the sun, as they often came up toward the surface en masse and sang a kind of song—except, it was more like music than like a song, because as aquatic creatures they obviously did not use their mouths to make the music. It seems to have been a kind of resonance created by the mutual influence of one glowing tevzebi upon another, which grew in complexity and volume as more and more tevzebi came together. This happened whenever glowing tevzebi came together, but there were different types of tevzebi, and the music was particularly pronounced when these different types came together in just the right way. For some were particularly beautiful when side by side with each other, and others produced their most beautiful music when one swam below the other, or in some other arrangement, and sometimes the greatest music was made when these were all arrayed in magnificent, undulating geometric patterns, in spirals, pyramids, and fractals formed from the swimming fish. Anyway, according to the shepherds this music was quite lovely and enchanting, as the resonance was naturally harmonious, but it also had a remarkable effect upon moods, and could disorient and disturb someone who listened to it too long."

"But you were going to explain where the ink-sickness came from," I said.

"Yes, a sickness they call the marigold's bloom. They say it got this name from a young girl who lived in the mountain valley, who particularly loved the tevzebi. 'You make no sense, girl,' they said, 'maybe the marigold was blooming last year, when they glowed like the yellow sun, but this is ugly,' for, indeed, the sickness was very unsightly. She was crying out of sadness for the fish, and she just shook her head, saying, 'It's the marigold's bloom,' and refused to explain why. 'They'll sing again,' she said, but everyone else thought saving the lake already a lost cause; the sickness spread impossibly fast. For some reason, perhaps for the sake of a young girl's tears, or perhaps from the dark sense of irony marking those living in those parts, everyone ended up following the girl and called the ink sickness the marigold's bloom.

"As for the spread of the sickness itself, according to one version of the story it struck a single tevzi first late during one summer. It was found by the other fish in a disoriented state, anxious and making unpredictable, sudden movements. It was sort of muttering to itself, moving its mouth and bubbling, and not clearly conscious of the others' presence. Very quickly three changes occurred in the infected tevzi: it lost its translucency, growing dark, reddish scales; it ceased to glow with the sun's light, but instead began to produce ink, from the aforementioned spiny protrusions; and it became, as they say, strange."

"What do you mean, strange?" I said.

"To begin with, it hated the sun, and tried to avoid it. Obviously, since it no longer glowed, it could not participate in the song of the tevzebi either. So it began to behave strangely around any tevzi who remained translucent and glowing. It was suspicious of these and often hid among the rocks so that it couldn't be seen. Of course, the ink it produced (although it didn't produce so much in the beginning) was a dead giveaway. So it needed to hide near the bottom in caves and crevices where the others couldn't see the ink constantly emanating from its spines. At other times, however, it behaved aggressively and erratically, charging at them and sometimes piercing them with its spines. But soon everything changed."

Pete sighed, and for a moment said nothing.

"What's wrong?" I asked.

Pete said, "It's always hard in a story to tell the part where the tragedy comes."

This made me want to hit him. "You're very melodramatic," I said.

"What happened is this," he said. "The marigold's bloom soon spread to the tevzebi the infected creature came into contact with. When the ink entered them (whether because they ingested the ink, or because they took it in through their gills, or because they they were pierced by the spines—no one quite knows), a darkness could be seen growing inside of them, and they would become disoriented and begin muttering, just as the first one infected had. As the darkness grew it produced the reddish scales and cruel spines, and began filling the water with dark ink. Within days the lake had a very different appearance from before. No longer did it shine with the light of the tevzebi, nor did the valley resound with their song. When the shepherds passed through the valley again it was

inky black, and all the creatures were suspicious, sometimes aggressive, and the shepherds soon stopped traveling through the valley,
and the girl's family moved south, into the cities—Tblisi first, then
Poti or somewhere in those districts, by the ocean, that is, the sea.
And the fish remain in their self-induced darkness, unseeing themselves and unseen by anyone."

"That's good," I said, "you've painted a dark picture."

"It is not all gloom, however," said Pete. "The shepherds also
report a prophecy concerning the creatures."

"What is it?" I asked.

He said, "The legend states that when Heaven grows weary of
the darkness and wants the Matin Sea to again reflect its brilliance,
it will plant the Sun within the heart of the Sea itself, so that glory
will reflect glory, and all things be restored."

"A fetching prophecy; what does it mean?" I said.

"It means that one day the Sun will send a savior into the Sea,
who will bring the Sun to them," said Pete.

"Very mysterious," I said. "How could the sun enter the sea?"

"You've asked the right question. Obviously, this will be something of a miracle, so I won't discuss how it could happen, and since
it hasn't happened yet, it can't be adequately explained. But now
that the sea has been sick for awhile, the only person who comes to
the valley is an old woman, whom they say is that girl who named
the disease at the beginning, who wept for the fish when they fell
into darkness. She returns to that lonely place between the mountains to the house she dwelt in as a child. Everyone else, including
her family, avoids the valley from fear of the sickness. She returns
every year in the summer, though it makes her sick to be there,
because she loves the sea. She spends her days keeping trash and
stuff away from the shore, and helping to save plants and creatures
in danger of sickness or death. Every day she weeps for her memory of it. It is this one, it is said, who will one day be granted to save
them. Years ago, the Sun, noticing her efforts, asked her why she

dedicated so much of her life to such a gross and lifeless sea. She explained that the sea is only gross and lifeless right now, but she knows its true essence, what it was before, and she loves it for that. The Sun said that there is a way to heal the sea back to its former beauty, but only with an ultimate sacrifice. She responded that no sacrifice would be too large—she would do anything to save the sea. Then the Sun spoke as follows:

> When Heaven grows weary of its darkness and wants the Matin Sea to again reflect its brilliance, it will plant the Sun within the heart of the Sea itself, so that glory will reflect glory, and all things be restored. To save the Sea, you must swallow my light, which you cannot do. I must prepare the light before it will be possible for you to do so. I promise you, you will not perish until this is accomplished, though it may take many generations before I can grant the light to you. You may continue to carry on your life, for you have tasks yet to accomplish, and continue to return to the valley every year. There will come a summer when I will beckon you into the meadows, into the most lonely place at the back of the valley. You will know it is the moment, because marigolds will fill the valley, and in this most lonely spot, there will be one, just one, marigold with no flower at all. You will find it with its long seeds pointing out, black and sharp. These seeds will contain my light, which I will have prepared over all these generations for you, a particle of my fire sealed within a hard, black shell, to make it possible for you to consume my light. I will call you to this place because you loved the fish, you loved the sea. You must swallow the seeds, and their sharp points will tear your throat, and then you must swim into the sea, and allow yourself to be attacked by the tevzebi until you are torn apart. When the seeds mix with your blood and tears, they will quicken, my fire will enter the sea, and that will be

beginning of the sea's salvation. And I guarantee you that as long as my fire endures, you will never be forgotten.

"That's what the Sun said to her. The shepherds used to say that she received this prophecy not only because of her love for the sea, but because her family was a branch of the famous Zets'idan family, which has a mysterious origin, being themselves descendants of the Sun. That is probably nonsense, but they say that is why she can bear the seeds of hidden fire. When she comes—though she will be old indeed then—she will find the seeds and will know what they mean."

"Of course," I said, feeling sentimental and wistful, yet somehow also very despondent, and excited, too. "She must throw herself into the sea, that is the only way to consummate her love."

"So, on that day, when the creatures attack her with their spines, and poison her with their ink, she will surely die, but her blood and the seeds containing the light of the Sun will be released into the water. The fish cannot resist eating marigold seeds, but these are very sharp ones, and when they consume them, their sharp points will scratch the fish, too, and then the quickened seed will break open."

"What will happen when they break open?" I said.

"The fire, the light of the Sun, will enter the fish who is scratched by the seed and enter its blood. This flame will grow within the pierced creature, for the light of the sun cannot be doused. This causes the creature, dimly, to remember itself, for all its organs retain their old sensitivity to sunlight, but not wholly. So the music begins again in a feeble, broken way. When other fish attack it with their spines, the sparks of the flame will sometimes pass back through the channels of the spines—the channels where the ink flows out—and back into the other creatures. The fire will therefore spread in this way from creature to creature."

"You tell a marvelous story, my friend," I said.

"To us, of course, it seems that way," he said. "To the creatures themselves, it will not even be obvious that anything has changed. The ink is of course thickest around each creature and blocks its sight almost completely, not because it lacks the power of sight by nature, but because it constantly blinds itself by polluting the water around it with its ink. So even tevzebi with the fire alive in them will see very little at first, and only a bit later on, as the fire progressively changes them into light bearers, rather than ink spreaders."

"Why does it take them so long to change?"

"Well, the fire will be the light of the Sun itself, and could easily consume them entirely. But that wouldn't do. What they need is for that fire to slowly consume the ink producing glands in them and make it possible for them to return them to their original condition. So you see, when they pierce a fish with the light of the Sun inside, the fish will pass on the fire to them, but receiving the fire is painful."

"What a beautiful story," I said.

"So he will pass along just a little spark, and some of them try to resist even this. Only those who willingly accept the fire will receive fire within themselves. That spark, though, contains all the power to transform them into what they were meant to be, if they will allow it to work. But the prophecy states that the fire will be hard to bear; each moment, they must accept its continued, painful work, until every part of them infected by the sickness is burned away."

"I see," I said, "so it is a process of transformation, which they must cooperate with to be changed by."

"You've got it. And the next part of the prophecy states that when as the fire spreads among them, the Matin Sea will be restored to its original brilliance. The fish will once again begin following the pattern inscribed in their nature with grace and beauty—and the song will be renewed, as they begin to glow again, and come into harmonious resonance with one another."

"So the prophecy says that the original brilliance will be restored only if the woman who loves the sea is pierced, and then those who pierced her and consume the seeds are themselves pierced?"

"That's right," said Pete.

"And the result of this is that the Matin Sea will be restored to its original glory?" I said.

"Or an even greater glory," Said Pete. "For the tevzebi will have the Sun's fire inside themselves, and glow not only with the light of the Sun but with their internal light and in response to the light inside each other, and the song will never end."

"Is there a reason the fish need a savior," I said, "rather than saving themselves by their own efforts?"

"Suppose that someone came to them and said, turn upward, turn your gaze upward, and see the Sun!" he said. "Would that make a difference?"

"Turning their gaze from the depths to the Sun might be a little different," I said. "But they would hardly be able to see it, because of all the ink. I suppose that some fish could take to floating as close to the surface as possible."

"Wouldn't their ink still block their gaze?" he asked.

"Yes," I said, "but they could float all the way up to the surface itself, to look above the skin of the water, so to speak."

"Wouldn't that be ridiculous?" said Pete. "A bunch of fish trying to stick their faces up above the water?"

"It would be ludicrous, because while trying to get better, they'd hardly be able to breathe, and unable to do anything naturally— keeping their face above water would always been a very unnatural act, and one that they couldn't keep up for long." I paused for a moment. "And, I think that it might not give them what they wanted, anyway."

"Oh?" said Pete.

"According to the myth what they need is for the light of the sun to set them aglow, so they can swim and make the music again. Simply *seeing* it wouldn't change their constitution, if all their effort were devoted just to keeping their heads above water; as soon as they returned to the water, where they swim and make the music, they would again be blocked from the sun and unable to receive its light."

"True," he said. "When they sought purity above the surface, they'd be as much dead as alive, while they would be diseased and unhealthy when they swam in the depths, and in neither condition could they make the music of the tevzebi as they used to, like a symphony of angels."

"So when they were up at the surface, staring at the sun, they can't live like fish; and when they are down below in the water, they can't see the sun. In either case, they can't join together with each other," I said. "Now, what is the meaning of your allegory?"

"It is no allegory," said Pete. "Allegories are marked by forced, arbitrary associations. It is, rather, an analogy. I have described a vision with its own rules and principles, which serves only to highlight our own condition by making its features more vivid to see. The main idea is that you said that there is something wrong with the human condition; not just that evil happens, or that it happens to us, but that it happens in us and through us; and to make a suitable analogy for that idea, I needed a picture in which those features were made apparent."

"I haven't thought much about the difference between allegory and analogy," I said, "but I'll go with what you say for now."

"The difference is important," said Pete. "Extremely important. The reason the Allegory of the Cave is so powerful is that it is not an allegory at all, it's an analogy, and the reader feels the likeness himself, which gives it all its authority.[54] The Sun is like the Good, that is, that upon which we rely to realize whatever pattern it is which will allow us to become ourselves, if we will but receive it into ourselves; but which we do not know, and do not like, so long as we are in the wrong condition."

---

54 Ed.: See Plato, *Republic*, 514a-520d.

"That makes sense," I said.

"So what that means is that there is a pattern we could be and should be," he said, "but we don't live up to that pattern; instead we follow some other way that is inferior to the right one and contrary to it."

"I follow you."

"So if that is the character of the problem," said Pete, "then the solution must be to somehow 'renew' the old pattern and erase the new one."

"That the Problem—with a capital P," I said.

Pete's idea might be represented as follows: There is an old or true or right pattern or principle, a form, of a living thing, what Plato or Aristotle would call an εἶδος, although we might also call this the λόγος of a thing, an account of what it is or is to be.[55] This account specifies how something should live. It corresponds with a way that we are, a set of powers and potentials ready at hand and necessary for our way of life (W): and those powers and potentials for living well when developed are virtue (C). However, we do not manifest W or C. They present themselves as a task to be realized. Yet, the Problem is not this; that is no different from what might be said of an innocent child. The problem is that, instead of having the dispositions uW and uC (potential W and C), we manifest $\mathscr{E}W$, a way of life contrary to W, and $\mathscr{E}C$, a state of character directly opposed to W and to developing C. Trivially, if one brings this into the Arcanum, ($\mathscr{E}W$ & $\mathscr{E}C$) constitutes

---

55   Ed.: Elizabeth here, as frequently, utilizes Greek straight and without transliteration. Εἶδος (eidos) means a *form* or *shape* in everyday Greek or, in philosophical Greek, something like a *natural kind* (such as a genus or species). The idea of form (as opposed to matter) is an essential element of Platonic philosophy, an idea that Aristotle reworks but retains as an essential distinction within his philosophy. Λόγος (logos) has too many meanings to list, but which grows from a base meaning of a *word* but then coming to take on additional significance as a *speech* or *discourse* and then coming to mean a *reason* or a *ground* for something, or an *account* of something, in the sense of an explanation. In the Stoics especially, but not exclusively, it is given the meaning of a kind of *ultimate reason* for everything that is, and it is in this sense that the Gospel of John refers to Jesus as the eternal Son of God.

interference—($\mathcal{E}W$ & $\mathcal{E}C$) $\subseteq \triangledown$(uW & uC)—so that to possess them is to be in a condition of being unable to develop W and C.[56]

"Then how do we overcome the Problem?" I said. "It's our own evil that makes it hard to recognize the good or respond to it when we can make it out. How we live is a function of our character and nature. What we do reflects who we are."

"Doesn't how we live also affect who we are?" he asked.

"Of course, but I wanted to highlight a particular aspect of the Problem—if you asked a group of adults to start living differently, well, you'll fail, because their character is already set. We'd be stepping on our own feet. They won't want to do the things you want them to do, because they are unattractive to them, and they'd do them clumsily, without sensitivity to the nuances and differences among things; and all the time they are doing them, they are starving other aspects of themselves that will storm out at an opportune, wolfish moment to look for sustenance."

"Right," said Pete. "Whatever the creatures do to return to the sun, they are blocked by their own ink. But what if we decided that we wanted our children to follow the right way?"

"But aren't those with bad character the worst at judging good character?" I asked.

"Yes," he said.

"Just like your tevzebi, the ink they are infected with also prevents them from seeing the sun. They don't know what good character would be, and their own character makes them reject it when they see it. It may be attractive in some respect or another, but inevitably, it must diverge from their own character, and that means that it, not their character, but good character, actually good character, must seem to fall short," I said.

"Right," he said. "So somehow we need to know the right way

---

56 Ed.: Elizabeth provides no further explanation for the private notational language she deploys here elsewhere in the notebook. It appears to have been developed in one of her previous (unknown) notebooks.

to live, but we aren't in a position to know it; and, if we did know it, we'd reject it all the same, because it would seem wrong to us."

"In that case it sounds like our situation is impossible to correct," I said. (In the back of my mind, I was importing a principle from *S.A. XVIII*, for 'impossibility' is too strong a conclusion merely from the premises supplied by Pete; but he didn't notice this, nor was it yet explicit in my mind. I will return to this later if I can.)[57]

"Don't forget the prophecy," he said. "When the Sun grows weary of the darkness, it will renew things itself."

"How are we to understand that?" I said.

"It means that every great artist will want to correct his work if it gets ruined," he said. "I'm asserting that, it's a given, from the experience of the artist; but here's the analogy, as it exists in things: if there's a God, then he's the Creator, our Creator, and we're his creation and his work. The relationship of an artist to his work is a three-part relation: an artist has a vision, of something excellence or beautiful or wonderful, and he attempts to embody his vision in the material; when the vision is embodied in it, then it is called his creation, although he didn't create the material in which he embodied the work. For God the matter is naturally different. He doesn't face any preexistent material, but makes the materials himself; so his creations are even more his creations than those of a human artist. But that just means he is more jealous of them and loves them more, and, I should think, is even more grieved to see his work ruined."

"I understand," I said. "When God created humanity, we were created to embody this excellence of his, which he had in mind, refracted or condensed or abridged in our own particular way (that is, our intended way of life and being are a form of finitized or

---

57 Ed.: As the present notebook is labeled "S.A. XIX," this appears to be a reference to the immediately preceding (unknown) notebook.

delimited excellence). But now the work is ruined, since we manifest this other, defective pattern instead, different from the original vision."

"And, in fact, as we said, we are actually hostile to this intended pattern, which we refuse to embody. This is the key point, for otherwise, we would have to say that the failure of the artwork was its creator's fault."

"What do you mean?" I asked.

"Ordinarily, if an artist's work is ruined, it's either his own fault, or it's the fault of someone else, something else, coming along and spoiling it or breaking it. But in this case," he said, "the fault lay with the work itself: somehow, it messed itself up."

"That's paradoxical," I said. "Wouldn't it be the creator's fault for making something capable of messing itself up?"

"I grant you it seems that way," he said, "but it's impossible to create something that is free that cannot mess itself up. I'll explain as we go. Here, I just want to focus on the fact that the creator has a free and living creation that has gone wrong, and he wants to correct it. He could simply destroy it and create another, but an artist wants to correct what he's made, and so does God. Yet the fact that his creation is alive makes this particularly hard. A piece of clay is hard to correct once it is set because it loses its malleability when you fire it. A living and rebellious creation presents another kind of problem. One, you don't want to kill it while you fix it, and two, you need to find a way to overcome its rebellion, to get it corrected even while it is fighting your attempt to heal it."

"Right," I said. "In our case, it's our bad natures that are fixed, and trying to alter them violently could destroy us, but anything short of that, we'll fight against and do all we can to prevent. Plus, there seems to be no good reason to wipe out the old and broken creation, if it's only going to go the same way again—it's better to just fix the whole thing and set it to rights."

"That will be particularly true if you can fix it and reinforce it somehow so that the same thing doesn't happen again," he said. "Otherwise, you'd have a Sisyphean task before yourself, to keep fixing the same thing again and again."

"If Simon is right, it's worse than Sisyphean," I said, "since Sisyphus doesn't wrong the rock; but before we get to that, we need to work out a couple of points."

"As you wish," he said.

"First, I want you to make your analogy clearer—the analogy between God and the artist. It has surface plausibility, but you need to pin it down before you put it to work."

"That's the first thing we'll discuss."

"Next, you need to clarify what you mean by saying that we're a self-vitiating creation."

"Okay, then we'll discuss that," he said.

"Finally, you need to explain what you just said—that God, as an artist, would not simply correct his creation directly, but would instead need to use an indirect method."

"That's the easiest of all," he said. "Let go back to my analogy of God as artist. We say that God is a creator, the creator *par excellence*, because he created our universe."

"Yes, that's what people say," I said.

"Let me introduce another analogy ... although, in this case, it is a more certain analogy than in the first case," said Pete. "We imagine a great artist, a multitalented artist who employs all the arts, a virtuoso unlike any we've known."

"Do you mean *all* the arts," I said, "or just the productive ones like painting and sculpture?"

"Oh, yes…. I forgot you were a dancer," he said, awkwardly. "Let's say it is all of them," said Pete, "but I am going to start by focusing on the creative and productive arts where the artist makes something outside of himself—those where the outcome of the work resides in an existent besides the artist himself, and this other existent is the proper possessor of the excellence or defects of the work, rather than in performance arts where the artist seems to merge with the work of art."

"Very well," I said, "let's start there, but don't think I will let you avoid the other arts if I see the need for an account of their role in this picture of yours."

"That's fair," said Pete.

"Then tell us about the artist," I said.

"God is a creator, isn't he?" said Pete.

"Yes," I said.

"In doing this," he said, "he was aiming to do just what an artist does: to embody some kind of excellence, beauty, and goodness in an independent existent."

"What do you mean by that?" I asked.

"Well," he said, "it's crucial to understand the relationship between an artist and the artistic creation. When a painter produces a painting, for example, there are three main factors—the artist, the idea, and the painting."

"Okay, I understand," I said. "The artist has some kind of conception that he is working with when he paints—something he is aiming at creating."

"Yes," he said, "that's the proper beginning of the work—the idea, the inspiration. There are two ways about this. They seem to contradict each other, but they are both pointing back to the same thing, because their divergence is rooted in this analogy between God and the artist, and the difficulty of any merely earthly artist living fully up to the standard set by the divine artist.

"The *classical* artist looks to the ideal, and his idea comes from outside himself; he finds himself to be dark and obscure, whereas the ideal is something sharp and bright, and in his art he submits himself to this ideal and in his work he strives to live up to the ideal as he knows it, something greater, more eternal, and more sublime than he himself is. He does not aim at realism, but at perfection. He does not paint the average, but the exceptional, and he favors whatever subjects show humanity at its most exceptional and if he could, he would even paint the soul or the divine itself. He prunes everything in himself and in his work wherever it falls short of the ideal, he prunes it sharply and even severely when it lacks harmony and order, and if this involves suffering, he thinks it worth it, even if he suffers every day for it, until finally, through the long, demanding process of assimilating himself and his work to this great ideal, he embodies the ideal in his mind, as his work embodies it within itself."

"I understand that," I said.

"The other approach is the way of the *Romantic* artist. This artist begins with what is inside himself. The world around him is a thick curtain of conventions and falsities, but he gropes in the murkiness within him, and he finds a feeling, or passion, or inkling that must be expressed. This inkling, he believes, is a glimpse of truth, and on this glimpse he stakes everything. He sees the whole world as false if it cannot contain this glimpse, and in his work he strives to draw this glimmer of truth and feeling out of darkness and into the light of day where it can finally be embodied and receive its due recognition in the world of life and light. He works in solitude, strives with the unknown and unnamed, to bring light to the most twisted and hidden corners of the human heart, to whatever is obscure or full of dread in human experience. He strives this way, day after day, until his suffering finally brings that inkling to the light; that inking he did not find anywhere in the world, but only inside himself."

"Which do you think is right?" I said.

"That is not for me to say," said Pete. "Perhaps their contradictions are rooted in the apparently immutable conflicts of human nature. In any case, each of them captures something true about how *God* creates."

"What do you mean?" I said.

"For God himself embodies all excellence to the highest possible degree," said Pete. "He is the most sublime, most eternal, most perfect, and most excellent of all. When he creates, he aims at the ideal, but the ideal is just what he finds in himself. His creation therefore fulfills everything the classical artist aims at while also fulfilling everything the romantic artist aims at. He strives to embody his excellence in whatever he creates—that is what people mean by *the glory of God*—but he also is aiming at nothing more than manifesting what would otherwise be obscure, that is, his own inward insight, and in light of our own predicament, the evil of the human condition is always most obscure to us, and this glory appears most unexpectedly when it shines forth."

"It seems as if no human artist could possibly be like that," I said. "No human being contains the ideal inside herself." That was, of course, a long-standing principle of the Arcanum, one that recent events had only strengthened.

"Perhaps so," said Pete, "but there is no reason its seeds could not be planted there, to be harvested at the appropriate moment ... as in the analogy, perhaps."

"I see," I said. "Well, perhaps one can become pregnant with the ideal and give birth to it in a work of art, once the final elements are in place. I can't see why not. But what do you make of the role of inspiration and influence?"

"Let's come back to this question," he said, "I'd like to avoid that topic for now, so we can develop the main line of thought."

"The 'seed' of the idea is already in your letter from Niakani," said Simon. "Let him go on ... I want to see where this goes."

"Sure," I said. "Go on."

"When the artist has the vision, wherever it comes from, then he sets to realizing it in the material. He takes the paint and applies it to the canvas with his brushes. Through the artist's skill, the material is transformed, so that it embodies that vision or idea. When the artist creates, he creates something that bears the same particular beauty that the idea had. At least, that is what ideally happens; the possibility of success is there if he has the skill and the appropriate materials. If he *lacks* the talent and ability, or if the materials aren't suitable, then he will almost certainly botch the job, and the result will be something that doesn't embody the artist's idea, though he may not realize this. The sensuous intuition of beauty existing in the artist's imagination now exists in the world of things. Whereas in the imagination the idea was private, unstable, and threatened by forgetfulness, the created artwork is shared, with a fixed form and an enduring existence in the world. Art is, in fact, among the most enduring things we know. It now embodies the imaginative intuition, the idea."

"And you think that God is just like this: he too had an idea (although maybe not an imaginative intuition), an Idea of some kind of excellence and beauty he judged to be good," I said, "and he too wished to create so that he could embody this Idea of the καλόν, the noble, the ideal, the beautiful in some external, independent form, in something shared and enduring: a new being?"

"Right," Pete said. "There is a difference here. The artist utilizes skill, which is a kind of manipulation and transformation of what already exists, whereas God creates via his own power. He has omnipotence, which is to say, he has the power to bestow being upon his ideas without having to manipulate or transform them, although he has that ability too—we'll come back to this."

"Yet I wonder if you haven't left something important out here," I said.

"What is that?" said Pete.

"Well, something that may help you with my second question, about the self-vitiating creation," I said.

"That was the next topic," he said. "So tell me what you're thinking."

"Does what you say apply to performance arts?" I said.

"Sure," he said. "Don't you think it captures the essence of what makes classical ballet, well, *classical*?"

"Perhaps so," I said. "That was surely the intention of ballet's inventors, and in the case of the Italian neo-Platonists, at least, it has some plausibility.[58] But that's not quite where I'm going with this. Let's say that for now I am content with your analysis of the cause of the romantic/classical distinction in the inability of the created artist to fully participate in the nature of the Creator. There is, however, a larger disanalogy I am worried over in your account."

"What is that?" said Pete.

"You have focused upon a creation in which the created object is a product of the artist's idea and the passive material in which it is embodied," I said. "Yet, does this not leave out the most important thing?"

"What's that?"

"It only makes sense if we are paintings or sculptures or cleverly contrived robots," I said, "and it will make it entirely impossible to solve your problem of self-vitiation, since the flaw will need to come either from the artist's idea, or the material, and in the case of God, either would serve as an indictment of his choosing to create us."

"Why is that?" he said. "Oh, you mean because he creates the material, too, so both the idea and the material are his."

"Right," I said. "Besides, the analogy of painting or sculpture or poetry doesn't speak to how we experience ourselves with relation to the ideal, or to a Creator who wishes us to embody some ideal. We are not static and passive recipients of an ideal imprinted upon ourselves."

"Now you are going to point to dance," he said.

"Yes," I said, "we need to freely embody the ideal pattern in our own lives, as the dancer embodies the pattern of the music and the choreography in her dancing. The distinction between the true music (the ideal) and the false music (the music of the age, which is the music heard in life) would be essential to this. However, that seems like another long speech, and perhaps someday I could give

---

58   Ed.: See Jennifer Homans, *Apollo's Angels: A History of Ballet* (New York: Random House, 2009), pp. 3-9.

such a speech, but right now I am going to assume we've worked out the disanalogy and go on to another important point.

"Now, here is where your art analogy helps," I said. "Despite our wickedness, we can divine the reason why God would still hold out for redeeming his work—to realize the Idea! Yet, how can he correct it—correct us? How could he change us without breaking us?"

"I see," said Pete. "When you are painting, it's easy to correct a mistake: painting is all surface, so if you can paint over something, you can correct it. So sometimes you can even see a painting with another painting beneath it. If people were like that, if the surface were the only thing that needed changing, then I think God would change us directly—you know, if it was only our way of life that needed changing, only what we did, or our most shallow fears and desires, but—I think we said that there was something more fundamental to us that needed changing, a hardening of character that lies behind our failure to dance the Idea, as you put it. That bars the way to such a simple form of redemption."

"Right, our beginning idea was that our character isn't some accidental feature of our identities," I said, "but is so important to us, that if it were simply wiped out and replaced with something else, this would be equivalent to destroying us and creating something altogether new in our place—as would be the case if someone 'fixed' a pot by simply pulverizing it and making a new one from fresh clay. Do you agree?"

"Right," he said. "We have a self, there is a state or condition of our will that gives us an identity and that stands behind our particular actions or feelings."

"And you think that this self would be broken (like a pot would be broken) by the direct approach?" I asked.

"Well, something like the pot," he said. "Perhaps it would be more like a story where halfway through the author suddenly began writing a character with an entirely different personality. I'm not sure that really would be the same character."

"That does seem pretty violent," I said.

"So I think we couldn't be redeemed like that," he said. "It would be as if the creator wiped us out, just starting anew with a brand new set of creatures."

"I quite agree with you!" I said.

"You do?" he said.

"Yes, I have a whole theory about this—only, I can't seem to remember how it goes right now," I said. "I can provide you with the argument later, if you like. Anyway, the only way to understand this idea of changing us without breaking us seems to be that a person must change via what we'll call a 'coherent narrative path.' Such a path is a series of changes in which each step is intelligible in terms of a person's beliefs, goals, values, and changing circumstances. Their change would not be equivalent to an author changing a character mid-story from A to some completely different character, B.

"Second, the really important thing here is the unity of the passions, since that is what we're most concerned with here—the person's sensitivity to and appreciation for the good, and their internal responsiveness to it, whether they *love* it or not. A coherent narrative cannot simply replace a person's old loves and values with new loves and values; but it can involve a person being exposed to new goods, new values that they might love, and coming to new beliefs that modify those loves and values. The mind, will, and character of a person cannot simply shift from one condition to another but can be guided along its own path, and this is the path that governs any story ballet, where the ultimate truth is the human possibility of the passions it depicts and the story it tells of them.

"We already accepted that the Creator wants to realize the Idea by embodying it. This is the ground both of creating us and for redeeming us," I said. "Therefore, a person can move from one condition to a new condition by means of becoming gradually aware of or sensitive to new values, new information, and so on. That is the pattern of transformation we agree would not 'break' a person but would constitute a genuine redemption from *our* self-vitiated character to the proper character that would allow us to dance the way of life God has made for us, and so allow the Creator to realize his Idea by gradually bringing about its embodiment in us dancers."

I noticed a film crew outside, trying to capture the first early moments of darkness outside, the ambiguous time when the sky is blue but darkening and the beach still feels alive. I smiled for no reason, and I was wishing they would capture something beautiful, but who knows if that is what they wanted? Perhaps what they wished for was some brutal and ugly scene, and maybe that's what they deserved to have.

I went on, saying, "This will allow us to make use of what you just said. I take it that for someone to follow such a narrative path, two things would be necessary: first, the person would need to encounter these new goods and values in order to love them or otherwise be passionately related to them, and second, the person would need to acquire the capacity to recognize them for what they are. Therefore, if God, our Composer, gave us some kind of example of the dance we could see, where we saw the dance performed, then that would supply the first condition. That would allow us to encounter the Idea embodied in a form we could become passionately entangled with.

"Then, if somehow we could have an active principle implanted in us that was striving to help us appreciate the true dance, to make us sensitive and aware of how lovely and lovable it is, then we could become passionately entangled with it in a way allowing us to embody the Idea by making us more sensitive to it when we see it and wanting to become such, then we would gradually be growing closer to being it. That would allow us to overcome our self-vitiation. So, if the Composer, God, could somehow be actively at work within us, dwelling in us somehow, pushing and prodding us so as to do just this, then this would provide just the active principle called for. That would supply the second condition. That is just what your legend presents, as an analogy—the analogy of the fire of the Sun. So, together, we have a picture of how an artist God, a creator God, could and perhaps would redeem his lost creation."

Pete was silent a moment, taking in what I had said. "Then we now understand the overall structure of redemption, the Great Task that God takes on and shares with his creatures, by analogy to the artist's wish to redeem the work; this is expressed in the Legend as a covenant, which supplies the normative framework that would otherwise be missing," I said. "Converting the analogy to our own case, God doesn't have an obligation to vicious creatures, but if he makes a covenant to redeem his creatures, this would let them know he is concerned and working on their behalf, and allow them nonetheless to call upon his help. It is contingent, since the Creator voluntarily takes on its normative obligations, but it's not arbitrary, since he has the artist's reason for making the covenant. The covenant becomes a middle term that creates the mediating language between creatures and Creator."

"Right," he said. "In this case, the covenant isn't hopeless, because it is linked to God's transformative enterprise, the 'Great Task' as you put it."

"For our part," I said, "accepting the covenant would mean joining that Great Task, that is, we must love the Idea and want it restored, we must want to dance it and to have everyone dancing it, for at the bottom of everyone is a dancer."

"That's great," said Pete, "and I hope someday you can explain what that means. But you're right, when redeemed creatures join in the Great Task themselves, they become one with the Sun as much as possible by doing so, just as much as they become themselves as much as possible. This is the most beautiful part of the Idea, the idea of union in love. For the essence of the task is love, love for the idea and for the Creator and for the other bearers of the Idea. This is working out the mystery of the incarnation: that the Idea returns to the world in power to bring everything back to itself."

"You're running together a lot of things in that statement," I said, "but I take your meaning." Yet, what he said about love had me thinking, as became clear later.

"I turn now to the second part of my promise," Pete said. "We just explained the hypothetical part—a combination of what redemption *must* look like, if there is a redemption from the human condition, and when there was no way it must be, but several, we allowed that this is what it *could* look like. Now we still need to provide the other premise, so the *modus ponens* can terminate in a conclusion."

"That's right," I said. "We've got a pretty picture now of what a redemption should look like. But how do we know such a thing exists, and how can we take advantage of it?"

"Are you familiar with Pascal's Wager?" Pete asked.

"Of course. I hope that you are not going to rest everything on that," I said. "I will be severely disappointed if so."

"You've probably only heard a bad version of the argument," Rufus said.

"Well, no, professor," I said. "I learned the argument from you ... I remember everything about the argument from dominance, the argument from expectation, and the argument from dominant expectation, and so on. I know the math is perfect, and the business about Diderot's counterargument being based on a mistake—not grasping how Pascal aimed to secure the partitioning of possibilities, and so on."[59]

"You do seem to remember it well," said Rufus.

"Okay, okay," said Pete, a little impatiently. "Let's grant all this. Let's grant that the probabilities are perfect, and so on. I don't accept the Wager because it seems to rest on a mistake of a kind."

"If the math is perfect, then you must reject one of the earlier premises," I said.

"Yes," he said, "I meant one in particular—the idea that the

---

59 Ed.: Elizabeth here made a note of her own: "See Hacking," apparently Ian Hacking, *The Emergence of Probability*, 2nd Edition (Cambridge: Cambridge University Press, 2006).

will desires nothing but happiness, and then staking everything on what's more likely to produce that."

"Good point," I said. "Why, these days, I desire practically anything more than I desire my own happiness."

"It makes the argument appear a bit sordid, putting it all in the dress of a gambler who is trying to figure out what number to bet on to maximize his yield. It's foreign even to Pascal's own religious life, and surely no way to approach God," he said.

"No, I can't imagine approaching him like that," I said. Perhaps Pascal let his discovery of probability theory run away with him, but he is such a careful observer of the heart I must believe he had more in mind and had intended the Wager to function as a kind of diagnostic tool for the wandering heart, not a proof for the curious.

"Instead, I will make my case in another way," he said. "Do we know if God exists?"

"Simon may have his 'private reason,' but I don't know that myself," I said.

"What if Rufus is right and the probability of God's existence is .62?" he asked.

"If you only know that the odds of something's being true, you don't know it."

"But is the redemption we described beautiful and wonderful?" Pete said.

"Yes, it is," I said. "It would be like a great dance more beautiful than any thus far imagined."

"Well put," he said. "And do you know *that*?"

"Yes, perhaps I do know that," I said.

"So it would be beautiful and wonderful if God offered grace and redemption in this way, to make our glory reflect his," he said.

"Yes, it would," I agreed.

"And it would be beautiful for us to accept his offer of redemption and to participate in his plan to redeem all things?" he asked.

"Yes, that's right," I said.

"More beautiful than refusing to participate in this plan?" he said.

"Yes, that seems right," I said. "We wouldn't want the ink to continue polluting the Matin Sea."

"No, indeed!" he said. "That would be terrible. So we are faced with two possibilities: either there is a God who offers a salvation like we described, or there isn't."

"That's logical," I laughed, but I also felt my mind was slowly growing clearer as the intoxication of my drink receded.

"Moreover, we pretty much know where to find this, if it does exist; we've described the gospel of Jesus the suffering savior, who comes to the world to redeem it and fill it with glory," he said.

"That's so," I said.

"In that case, we've provided some reason for thinking that the gospel of Jesus Christ could be the solution we need, if indeed it's true; and it's beautiful in the way that the Wager is not," he said.

"Correct," I said.

"But we don't know if the gospel *is* true," he said.

"That's also true," I said.

"Here's the wager I'll describe. It begins with this premise: We shouldn't just pursue happiness, but we should respect the taste for the divine, for what is eternal, infinite, and free, that we have in us, and strive to live in ways that are noble and beautiful," he said.

"Certainly so," I said.

"We are perplexed by our own participation in evil, and we are uncertain whether there is a redemption like this from that evil, but we know it would be beautiful if there were," he said. "The third premise would be that the dance of love is certainly beautiful, just as you said."

"I did say that," I said, but I was now very much thinking about what he had said earlier about love as the essence of the Great Task. It was not so certain to me now that matters stood just as we'd agreed.

"Now, the next premise is that, if there is no redemption, then we are justly condemned beings. And if we are justly condemned, it's inappropriate for us to reject that; we ought to accept it and live with it."

"I agree with that," I said. "It's no good lying to oneself about it."

"Very good," he said. "However, even if we are condemned, we should still seek what is best and most beautiful, even if it won't be for us. That follows from our first premise," he said.

"I'm following," I said.

"Now, there's either an offer of redemption or there isn't. If there is, it's certainly best to accept it, and to seek to make the world as glorious and beautiful and possible."

"A good premise," I said.

"But if there *isn't*," he said, "the dance of love is still beautiful, and we should help it along, even if we aren't going to be redeemed. We should try to love as much as possible and live as if there is such a dance, because this is the best way, and accept that we might not be saved, but that this will still be for the best. There is something noble in accepting one's condition but still hoping to make the best of the world for everyone else."

"Ah, now that's an interesting premise," I said. Pete did not catch the element of foreboding in what I said, although Simon's face twisted into something between a smile and a grimace. He had been listening very attentively throughout, but did not share a hint of what he was thinking.

"So, on the basis of this argument, we ought to wager that God exists, and participate in the dance. We should live as if there is a God, and there is a redemption, even though we do not know if we will be rescued or not. We should do this because it would be the best and most beautiful way to spend our lives."

Pete was flushed and smiling when the door was pushed open by Dash, and the crowd of revelers outside began coming into the house as well, filling it with laughter and music. "It's all right!" Dash said. "I'm here now. You can start the party." He had his guitar and was crooning for a couple of girls who had come in with him, the kind of silly beach goers I avoided not on principle but out of instinct. I was relieved that I did not know either of them. The group had been drinking and conversation quickly devolved into bits and nonsense. It wasn't long until Pete had his harmonica, accompanying Dash on the guitar. I don't know how long I stood there, saying nothing; I must have been the only observer present, uninvolved in anything going on.

When I finally became myself again, I didn't see Simon any longer, and Rufus was in the kitchen talking with an older lady who had come in with the others. They were making tea. Walking over to Pete, I whispered to him. "I've remembered what I forgot before, about our identities."

He looked at me quizzically, not knowing what to say.

"I can't accept the Wager," I said. "I have to go." The music and sounds of the partiers was swelling, pounding in my ears. I stepped out of the house and quickly descended the wooden stairs to the beach.

It was night. Leaving the warm glow behind, my eyes slowly adjusted to the cool light outdoors. I walked down the shore and did not look back.

CODA

What I found in her apartment:

There were two meadow voles, a little one and a big one,
who in their mischief had many adventures and found out
many secrets together. Returning from an adventure one
day, a new whim seized the little one, and she climbed a
beech tree. The other vole said, "Come down from there.
Are we tree dwellers?" The little vole said, "I want to live on
cheese and beer, like the squirrels," and the bigger vole was
disgusted. She turned, saying, "Stay, then, I never knew
you," and she left for another land. It was summer when
she left, the too-fat summer, but fall came, and leanness,
and finally winter. And so the grain ran out and the beer
no longer ran, and when the cheese spoiled the birds flew
south, and no one could find the squirrels. The little vole
was all alone. She sat in the beech tree and watched the sun
rise and she watched the sun set and the clouds flew across
the sky. The night was long and the bigger vole did not
come. When the sun rose again a new seed was planted in
the ground, but no one sat in the beech tree.

Man is neither angel nor beast,
and the unfortunate thing is
that he who would act the angel
acts the beast.

Pascal, *Pensées* 329

THE BLACK SWAN

"Joshua," (I envision myself responding) "I know I haven't been dancing, but when I play chess, I can do what I couldn't do on the floor—I can embody the music in my game, and draw the other player into the music too, the silent music only my opponent and I hear, which emanates from somewhere in my soul."

I know he wouldn't approve, though. In chess, making the other player hear the music is a kind of seduction, to trap him. Joshua's too much of a romantic. He'd be tempted to use the music the way a dancer does, to make the other player win. It was hard to start thinking about Joshua again, but now I find I can't stop thinking of him. About him, and about dance, but mostly about him. Not that I've let him out of that little shrine in my mind. I feel I daren't touch him at all.

Nonetheless, I hope I can see him again someday, and explain myself to him. What do I hope from this? That he will absolve me for my life? I know neither he, nor anyone else, can do so. Sarah is gone, lost through her own despair, but also because I did not extend my hand on her behalf, and she took any forgiveness she could offer with her when she took her own life. Still, I feel I must find one person on earth who understands me. With or without forgiveness, that is necessary.

How would this go? I remember Joshua once shuddering at *Swan Lake*. I teased him and made fun of his squeamishness over the ballet's dark ending. "It's all just spectacle," I said, "beautiful, wonderful spectacle." Yet it may be that he was in the right; perhaps *Swan Lake* is very dark, as dark as human life itself. Then, given the chance, perhaps I would tell him about myself through something like the following. Though he and Sarah were no more than acquaintances, I think he would understand. He would grieve for me, because grief is elemental, it isn't restricted by desert. He would grieve for me even when I despaired of grieving any longer for myself.

℘

You shuddered when you saw Odile enter during Act III, my friend, but why was that? What did you sense that you could not name? I shuddered too, but it was a shudder of delight: when her entrance is handled correctly, there is no scene anywhere as magnificent as that single moment. The whole ballet has led up this moment, everything in it points to it, but only as a yet to be revealed mystery; and this moment when she enters not only unifies every earlier thread, it also contains in itself the whole conclusion of the ballet. She is already beaming and triumphant; she stands as if on an entirely different plane from any of the prospective brides entreating Siegfried for his hand. When she enters, the audience feels an overwhelming sensation of life.

I do not retract my reaction, not at all, I am sure it is entirely correct, but I suspect now that there was more to your shudder than I granted. I laughed at you, saying "She is going to wrap Siegfried around her finger because she is so magnificent, so much greater than anyone else in the room!" But you were right too, and that is what I want to talk about.

Let's start with the obvious: *Swan Lake* is a tragedy of unhappy lovers, and Siegfried and Odette are like Romeo and Juliet in that their love ends in their joint suicide. Now, I'm sure you'd grant me that the spectacle and grandeur of the ballet overwhelm the senses of the audience in a way no play could, and that the unearthly beauty of its dances is unmatched, and the music—oh, God, the music, there is nothing like it to grasp the wonder and sorrow of life. Yet the comparison with *Romeo and Juliet* reveals a possible weakness, or an ambiguity, in *Swan Lake*, something I was always ashamed of. For it was the point of Shakespeare's play to show that it was not the magical power of the stars over human destinies so much as the "eternal contradictions" of human nature—the divergent characters of love (as the free and spontaneous gift of oneself) and of human society (as the binding of naturally warring individuals into groups of mutual protection)—that doomed their love; in *Swan Lake*, however, the theme appears to be just the reverse: it is not the human condition, but Von Rothbart's sorcery, that prevents the lovers' union.

This has the regrettable effect of nearly making the ballet a farce upon love, which is why many might laugh, as I did, at taking the story too seriously, whereas others are reduced to justifying it with limp, empty platitudes. The audience is made to think, If only Odette and Siegfried had been left alone by Von Rothbart, all would have been well! But is this not a very naive view of love, my friend, to imagine that only the intervention of a superhuman power could spoil a vow of eternal love? There is a childlike quality to the ballet that one becomes ashamed of when it is compared with a more mature work of art. *A Midsummer Night's Dream* likewise gives to magic an ample role in deciding the fates of the various lovers, and yet does not suffer in this same way. This is because there magic represents in visible form what is already latent in human nature itself. Magic becomes the imagination's way of making the invisible visible for the audience.

This was what I thought. However, when you shuddered, my friend, was it not because you sensed that the magic was much more than a daydream? Odette is transformed from woman into swan, and Odile is transformed from Odile into Odette. If the magic is not simply a poet's nothing, then the transformation must be something rooted in the nature of Odette, as the children's innocence and immaturity corresponds to the piper's power to enrapture them. Odette contains within herself the potential to become the swan, but this potential is not activated without its condition, which is provided by Von Rothbart. Since the swan state is represented as what is new, and her original form is that of a young woman just coming to maturity, the swan state must correspond to a potential existence she might take on as she completes the transition from girl to woman. Odette is the swan by day, and the woman by night. Since "day" represents what is manifest and obvious to all, it is the swan form that is visible, whereas the form of a young woman is merely her inner nature and her inner potential to become something other than the swan, for "night" represents what is hidden and uncertain. The young woman might become many things, yet under the influence of Von Rothbart, she is drawn to become the swan. It must be her own obscure longing into which Von Rothbart has sunk his hooks and that is responsible for such a transformation, for no other type of transformation would be worth attending to. He activates the longing within Odette that draws her among the other swans and traps her with them to live upon the lake.

The memory of innocence draws her back each night to an original form that might yet become something else, something other than the swan. Odette's transformation into the swan is therefore a manifestation of her own inner potential for transformation, and the form of the swan is something found in her, and not simply imposed upon her from without, by Von Rothbart. What then is this role played by Von Rothbart, the "sorcerer"? Critics complain when a production makes him into too much of a show, into a cackling sorcerer with flame colored robes. The best productions show his power primarily through his gestures, movements, and interactions

with the other dancers—above all, through how they pair his dancing with Odette's. He provides the condition for Odette's transformation, a condition that corresponds to her own inner potential
for the form of the swan. The most masterful productions show
this through careful choreography, such as making Odette's arching back mirror Rothbart's arching arm when Tchaikovsky's "fate"
motive plays, so that when we see the sorcerer raise his arm, hand
outstretched, we see Odette twisting back toward him, drawn by
his power over her. Though the audience is sometimes confused
whether Odette is in her swan form or a young woman again, they
always understand that this linked motion signals her loss of freedom and transformation into the swan.

Still, there would be no point in shuddering, my friend, if there
weren't more than this. The best productions show that Von Rothbart's power is over not just Odette, but over any young woman;
thus Marcelo Gomes's Von Rothbart dances with all the prospective brides at the ball, and he entrances even the Queen herself.
The sorcery is something that might happen to anyone, and suddenly, we understand that the two different realms of the ballet,
the court and the lake, collapse together: we realize that just as the
swans were all once women themselves, any of the women of the
court might themselves become swans and be entrapped at the
lake. That is, Odette's fate is a *universal* fate: it hangs over each of
us as a possibility, a sword of Damocles that might fall in a careless
moment upon us.

This lake forms an important part of the overall image. Whereas
the image of the sea or ocean suggests surpassing power, infinitude,
and divinity, and a river suggests temporality, flux, and possibility,
a lake has a peace to it that invites a different interpretation. The
lake, we are told, has been formed by the tears of Odette's mother,
weeping for her transformation into swan—a very suggestive fact.
For what is the lake then but a symbol of the mother's grief at
her daughter's transformation from immaturity to maturity? The

mother grieves that her daughter is leaving the young womanhood of potential to become the swan, to become that which was within her but which could not be activated without the condition provided by Von Rothbart. Now the mother hardly recognizes the child; she grieves for what she herself has borne when it enters maturity, when the young woman's freedom becomes lost in her transformation. The lake contains all the grief at the transformation of the child's infinite potential into something fixed, finite, and particular, the swan, something the mother does not recognize as her daughter at all. With your shudder, I am sure that you saw this, and it was not mere superstition that made you turn your head.

This grief suggests something else as well about the transition, something embodied within the form of dance. Do you remember, during intermission of *The Nutcracker* that one year, those old ladies talking outside? One of them complained that her seats were too far back, but her friend said it was better to be back from the stage, because if you see the dancers sweat it ruins the illusion. She is right, but why is this, my friend? It is essential to the dance that the dancer makes her movements appear effortless. The dance is the embodiment of the music in motion, and it is the task of the dancer to effect this embodiment at every moment. The music, let us say, is beautiful, and every movement of the dancer should embody this beauty, through the harmonization of the physical and the ideal. Motion is the force of this embodiment. Effort indicates a lack of harmony—it displays the fact that these are not immediately united with one another, but are united only through the straining of the dancer. Barre exercises and training make the dance possible, but they do not change the fundamental fact, which is that the ballet always exists at the limit of the dancer's powers. The existence of the straining is itself the dancer's lack of harmony in herself, something that can be overcome only with a complete concentration of self into the dance.

What the audience wants to see is a ballerina who exists in a state of immediate self-transcendence, in which she has always overcome the distance between the physical and the ideal. Since the ballerina's body is not a tool (as the artist's hands are) by which the work is achieved, but is the work itself, it must disappear wholly into the work, into beautiful movement. Her potentiality must be completely and utterly transformed into the ideality of beauty. For the ideal to be achieved, such self-transcendence must be immediate, not achieved by work, or the power of the dance is lost, for it is no longer merely beautiful movement, but movement and effort, and it might fail.

Sweat is a sign of the dancer's effort, art's failure to hide itself. Perhaps you'll secretly think I say this because of my own case, but I envy the ease, the *sprezzatura*, with which the artist hides his effort; the effort is hidden in the artist's studio, and what is seen is only the work itself. The dancer also works in the studio, but her efforts are directed not toward the dance itself, but toward acquiring suppleness, instinct, ability—the potential for the dance. She brings her body into the condition where it might, just possibly, embody the beauty of the dance. Yet even after so much effort in the studio, the dancer sweats, because the body still resists. It is this resistance, so unharmonious, that must be hidden as much as possible. For there is a necessary imperfection in the transition from potentiality to ideality; she cannot completely transform herself into beautiful movement and in every moment her physical being resists the transformation and its resistance must itself be canceled and conquered. Thus the transition is always potentially imperfect.

In the same way, to return to *Swan Lake*, the transition from the potentiality of childhood and young womanhood to the actuality of adulthood is not just a process of finitization and limitation where the indefinite freedom of childhood is transformed into the defined sturdiness of adulthood. For there is always that in us which resists and must be canceled and conquered in the process of transition. We cut off and lop off those parts of ourselves which cannot make the journey, and so we lose some of ourselves in the movement. But likewise, the very effort of cutting and lopping represents a loss for the movement itself, as our efforts are divided. The transition therefore is always missing something. But whereas the dancer can hide her sweat, reality is not so kind, and the girl becoming a woman has, compared with the dancer, many fewer chances to practice her steps. Do you understand, my friend? In all this effort, even if she hides her sweat, does she make the transition flawlessly? Does she not step wrong at some point? It is jarring to see a dancer for a moment walking rather than dancing upon the stage, or in seeing an Odette so focused upon her dance that she forgets that she dances not just for herself, but with Siegfried, with Von Rothbart.

But there is a disanalogy between dance and life concerning this matter of the false step, and *Swan Lake* is focused on this making this matter clear. Whereas the dance exists as ephemerality, as pure movement that is always canceled from one moment to the next, the young woman's transition is not so, for in history some steps are cumulative and the wrong step then persists in the next step. Once fate enters, it is inerasable. This is why the ballet struggles so much to represent the mother's grief. It represents the danger by portraying it as the threat of Odette becoming something else that is beautiful (for everything in a ballet must be beautiful), a swan. But even a beautiful swan is not a woman. This is how the ballet must represent her false step. The young woman has an ever shortening period of days in which she may correct her steps and find the right way through her transition, but her time for correction is not long, and eventually, her error will become her identity forever, never to be escaped. The errors she makes in the transition become part of the form she takes on. To be a swan is to be beautiful, and to be queen of the swans is to be both beautiful and great, yet to be a swan is to be finitized and unfree, inhuman. The child is the most human of us all because the child holds unlimited potential, whereas the adult has hardened, and is growing more and more into a statue of fixed qualities and instincts whose free origins lie in an ever-receding past. And so although to be the swan is to be beautiful it is a curse to lose the more beautiful freedom of the young woman whose twinkling eyes still suggested her identity as an eternal being.

The difficulty is this: can the young woman avoid error, if the conditions for actualization are not ideal? Von Rothbart is not only the condition, but he is represented as wicked, as an evil man. So too every young woman comes into herself under unfavorable conditions. There is a wickedness in the world that she cannot avoid because it speaks to her and to her own possibilities. When she feels herself drawn into becoming who she will become, the longing itself is beset by the power of this evil. This is why it is so helpful for a production to show Von Rothbart's influence upon the prospective brides and upon the otherwise forgettable figure of the Queen. The audience must understand the full range of Von Rothbart's power to understand the terror. To make the transition, then, the young woman will have to make effort, she will have to transcend herself and conquer the wickedness that is embodied in the conditions of her actualization. But where will this power of self-transcendence come from? From her mother, that is, from her freedom? Thus the ethicists always insist, but the ballet disagrees. She is born of both freedom and necessity—she is born from freedom into a set of conditions she cannot control, and her transition is always a union of these two. Since it is a union neither may be disregarded; the condition is always present in the act, shaping and determining its nuances and direction, shown in the carefully linked choreography of Von Rothbart and Odette. Asking her to make the transition without a false step is like asking a dancer to perform to the wrong music, when to dance is precisely to embody the music in oneself. Does the dancer remember the music? She thinks she heard it once or twice, when she was a child, perhaps another time when she fell in love, and in a rare moment when the sun shone sublimely over a field and she dreamed of dancing over the heads of the wildflowers and escaping into the sky with wind-like feet; but how shall she recall it now when is asked to dance, and the music is wrong and she hides secret griefs in herself?

If she were the self-transcending being the audience demands, she could do it; she would *be* the music she had to embody. But Odette has no power to cancel Von Rothbart's sorcery, and the young woman can never complete the transition without going wrong. For the wickedness of the world is also her wickedness, through the condition, and she incorporates it into herself and makes it part of her identity. So she goes wrong. Her mother grieves each time as necessity, history, and society conquer her daughter, and prevent her from making herself according to freedom. The motion of her life lacks the harmony of beauty, is marked by a discordance that isn't canceled in the ephemerality of motion, but which persists and shapes each subsequent step.

This is the curse upon Odette, the fullness of her mother's grief, and the great problem of the ballet, the problem that makes the ballet strain at the limit of what is possible within the medium of dance.

Now, the lake is also the center of the action. What does this mean, that grief holds the center? Why should grief dominate all in this way? Let us turn to Siegfried. Melancholy Siegfried, who is bored even while celebrating his birthday festivities, comes to the lake by chance and finds Odette. Odette can be saved (returned to her state of innocence and freedom) only by a vow of eternal love, and Siegfried is ready to offer such a vow. Consider, however, that he sees her as a swan before he sees her as a woman. Her avian beauty is no less than her human beauty, and this beauty arrests his intent to hunt and kill, but it is only after this that Odette the woman appears and he professes his love for her. This detail is telling. The inner potential that she retains in a hidden, closeted fashion appears only at night, and it is this form of Odette that the lover falls in love with. The swan is beautiful and entrancing, but it is the young woman that Siegfried loves. Let us not forget that.

Siegfried promises a return to Odette's form as a young woman; he promises to liberate her from the curse that transforms her into a swan and freedom from the sorcerer Von Rothbart. What does this amount to? He returns her to the form of a woman because love infinitizes the beloved. It views the beloved with visionary eyes, where all of her limitations are transcended and she becomes not who she is or who she might be, but a kind of supernatural being, a glorified being who performs the impossible and attains actualization without sacrificing her potential. For the lover, the beloved most fully *is*. Love promises to break the curse because it represents this constant possession of potential in actualization not only for the lover's eyes, but in reality as well: love opens the heart to love and the beloved to the lover's vision of the beloved's true self. Love would allow Odette the power of self-transcendence. Love therefore breaks the hold of Von Rothbart because it destroys the power of the condition to limit her and force her along the path of development she has begun. It allows her to return to the past and to the time before the fatal meeting with the condition that activated the particular direction her soul has embarked upon. This is what Siegfried's love means for Odette.

The ballroom provides the axis upon which the ballet turns. Picture this scene again, my friend, though it was here that you shuddered. The potential brides invited by the queen mother draw boredom from Siegfried, for she does not realize that he has fallen in love, and has eyes for only one woman. Now Von Rothbart intervenes; rather than lose his precious swan queen to Siegfried's love, he prevents Siegfried from making a vow of eternal love to Odette by sending his daughter Odile to seduce the young prince. This move would be as foolish as the queen mother's except for one thing: he possesses the magic of transformation, and he makes Odile to appear as if Odette. Siegfried has eyes only for one, but according to his eyes, Odile and Odette are one and the same woman. Odile's dancing is not identical to Odette's, yet it is made up of the same distinctive components. Those who are embarrassed by the magic sometimes explain this as Siegfried's immaturity. They say that he has too much passion and has not yet learned to love. Yet Siegfried's variation, his most significant dance in the whole ballet, which is prompted by Odile's appearance, is not a dance of desire or dark passion; the dance, in its leaps and kicks, resonates with a joy every lover can recognize from his own heart. Oh, my friend, it was not passion or lust that did him in, but love itself, and was this not what made you turn your head? When you watched the *pas de deux*, you felt fatality tap upon your shoulder, a premonition of the shortening of days we cannot escape. Not just infatuated desire, but love itself, all forms of love, are brought under the ballet's wings at this moment. And what does it have to say?

Note that Odette and Odile are so much alike that the prima ballerina plays both roles—another very suggestive fact. Who is this Odile, so much like Odette? She bears the same appearance as Odette. She displays the infinitized form of pure potential, she is Odette as seen through the eyes of love. She has overwhelming power over Siegfried; her 32 fouettés, far from being a simple display of the ballerina's technical skill, are the signature upon her seduction, her mastery. She is Odette as she would be through the transforming power of love. But she is also the daughter of Von Rothbart, the daughter of the condition that transformed Odette into the swan. She appears the same as Odette, but her connection to Von Rothbart is permanent and incontestable: she is his daughter, she is his creation and his pride, just as Odette is her mother's creation, her mother's grief. She elicits the vow from Siegfried that dooms Odette to be a swan forever, for in vowing to marry her, he breaks the vow of eternal love that would have saved Odette.

What is the meaning of this moment, the decisive turning point of the whole ballet? If the magic is nothing but the poet's vain imagination, a spectacle to dazzle and amuse the audience, then it is meaningless; for what can it mean that love will triumph, if only an evil sorcerer does not intervene with his curses? What can it mean if the only way a vow of eternal love can be shaken is through bewitchments and invincible illusions? Unless, that is, human existence truly is marked by curses, and human love really is beset by illusions. For then the ballet would be a work of great and dark genius, teaching a dark truth hidden beneath a vibrant spectacle.

This, my friend, is what I think you struggled to name when I laughed at your fears: Who is Odile but *Odette herself*? This statement would perplex most balletomanes, and the critics would regard this statement as absurd. But let us consider. Von Rothbart is the condition for Odette's transformation and adult identity. She owes her potentiality to her mother, but her actuality to her father. They each symbolize the universal condition of the human individual, for each individual contains a balance between freedom and possibility on the one hand and necessity and history on the other hand, which in childhood weighs toward freedom and in old age toward necessity. When a girl becomes a young woman she stands in between these two. Her freedom is not yet lost, it reappears under the shroud of night, a hidden possibility. In the light of day we see only the specific, finite, and manifest identity that she is bound to through the intervening of history, society, and, above all, the condition that activates what was within her and draws her into its orbit through her own inner tendency. No matter how she might deny her parentage, she is as much a child of necessity as of freedom.

In Act 2, Odette appears to Siegfried in her infinitized form, without limits, glorified with the glow of a self-transcendence that can actualize itself without losing its potentiality. The eyes of love see a vision no one else can see; but is this vision true? Acts 1 and 3 do not take place in any magic lake, but in the everyday world of the court. The overarching mood here is—boredom. Siegfried is melancholy, bored by all he sees in this realm. It lacks the element of the ideal. The image of a lake is used to create a world set apart from both history and eternity, a miniature, self-contained world where the ideal can appear in time. When Odile appears, Siegfried briefly believes that this ideal, the transcendent Odette he met at the Lake, can be brought from this miniature world into history. But can the young woman as seen through the eyes of love actually accomplish the transition?

Von Rothbart hovers ominously over the ballroom scene, symbolizing the way that the condition hovers over the young woman. Nureyev and Fonteyn show how to portray this in their performance of the *pas de deux*; whereas many male dancers disappear beside the ballet's prima ballerina, Nureyev brings Siegfried alive in this scene, matching Fonteyn with a dance that mirrors her Odile in a visibly impressive way. There are other dancers who attempt this, but the effort always seems to go to waste; not with Nureyev. Such sensational mirroring makes her hold over him palpable to the audience. The weakness in their performance is that Von Rothbart becomes too small; in a perfect production, we would see both Von Rothbart's powerful sway over Odette and Odile, something made extremely vivid by Gomes and Gillian Murphy for example, and also Odile's sway over Siegfried. For then the audience could more fully understand the tragic nature of Siegfried's vow. He vows eternal love, but is undone the moment he attempts to actualize this eternal love in time by proposing marriage. It is Von Rothbart's presence that seals their doom, for he is the condition.

Some might protest, "How can his vow be tragic, if Odette is Odile? How can his vow seal her doom as the swan, her perpetual servitude to the sorcerer, if Odette is Odile? How can making such a vow lead Siegfried to his death, and not his death only, but Odette's as well, if Odette is Odile? Should not the vow free her? Should not eternal love transfigure her? Should the lovers not be happy, now they have one another? How can Odette be Odile?"

But Odette is Odile. Love if it could would live out the eternal in the day to day. The whole time the lover has beheld the beloved, time and eternity have been reaching out toward each other, and in this decisive moment when he would seize eternity by binding himself and the beloved together forever, their outstretched fingers touch. However, Odette contains duplicity within herself, as we know, for she is both swan and woman. Siegfried is deceived by love; he is tricked into thinking she can retain her innocence and infinite capacity for self-transcendence, that love can rescue her from her destiny, from becoming the individual history, society, and the condition have prepared for her. No, the infinitized maiden seen by the eyes of love is an illusion, a perpetually unrealized possibility—the "true self" one never becomes.

In one very dark Swedish production of the ballet, they communicate this through showing Siegfried drinking from an enormous drinking cup at the end of Act I immediately before encountering Odette at the beginning of Act II. It is no mistake that Odette is so passive, whereas Odile is active. In Odile the finitizing force of the condition upon action is in evidence, whereas in Odette it is love's power to transfigure the beloved that is evident, and her passivity is a warning that Siegfried's love is painting her with powers she does not possess, just as Von Rothbart's magic covers his daughter with a form she does not possess. The tragedy of the vow is the tragedy of love, that it sees something that cannot be, the deified form of the beloved, which is stolen away in the process of becoming as the freedom of the maiden is transformed into the inhuman beauty and straitjacketed nature of the swan. Von Rothbart is her father, and what he provides is essential to her and so inescapable. The vow of love is undone by the inherent duplicity of human existence.

We imagine that humanity stands above the animal kingdom by our freedom. But our freedom belongs to our youth; once the condition appears, once age intervenes, necessity appears along with them, and the individual becomes something solid and unchanging, the swan. Love presents an intimation, a glimpse, of a self beyond ourselves. We can see this self in the eyes of someone who loves us. This is its power. But yet this vision of the self that could be, the self-transcending self, is not a self we can actualize in history. It is not pure illusion, for this glorious self is rooted in our potentiality. But this self history erodes and finally, after many skirmishes and slow sieges, utterly destroys. So the vow of eternal love is tragic in itself; it commits itself to a form of the beloved that will vanish all too quickly, a form that will disappear utterly in the end, to the consternation of lover and beloved both.

Love is the power by which one person puts hooks into another. I don't mean any of those passing intoxications or partial attachments we see everywhere in the world. Love is being torn open to the reality of another person and affixed to that person; it's a passion that makes of two persons Siamese twins. You wonder what I mean? I mean, love makes you open to another person, aware of that person, delighting in that person, ardently attached to the person, sure that your own being can only be completed in the presence of that person, and it fixes you to this person with hooks you cannot remove. It fixes us, most particularly, to a vision of the other's true self, their best self—this never to be realized potentiality. Put otherwise, it is our way of trapping each other, luring them to us, and then binding them to our fate by hooks and chains deadly to remove. True love is in itself an eternal vow. Now we begin the dance toward finitization, toward Swanhood! And yes, what you loved will pass away and be forgotten, the person will at best dimly recall what you loved in them, while you will never be able to escape, and the power you found in your beloved that was so essential to achieving your own self-hood—this power will recede into the past, as a recollection, but no more a hope. Love kills from the inside out through the ongoing power of betrayal and memory. Yes, that is it, my friend, that is what love is, and that is why I am confessing to you. I do not ask your forgiveness, do not worry yourself, I only need one person on earth to understand me.

The conclusion of the ballet is almost too dark to speak of. If love is loyalty to the infinite and free self that time destroys, then love must pursue death. The joint suicide of Odette and Siegfried, far from being inferior to that of Romeo and Juliet in its power to speak of our condition, actually represents a darker truth than Shakespeare attained to. It represents love as failing not due to a conflict between love and the conditions of social existence, but failing of itself. The vision of the lovers ascending together to heaven represents love's last hope: that, love's impossibility notwithstanding, there is hope that in death we shall transcend ourselves. But what is this hope? Is it not despair to speak of love so, that only the intervention of a God and an afterlife could resolve its difficulties? Are we back to Socrates' "philosophy is preparation for death"?[60] Since ballet is beauty and harmony it is entitled to hope for this ultimate harmony, but it is suspicious; it is like the moment when the dancer hides her sweat and allows the audience to believe the world can be harmonized in beauty.

It is well known that the Soviets, in keeping with their illusions about the possibilities of human transformation in the here and now, gave the ballet a happy ending. We owe particular blame to Konstantin Sergeyev, so-called "People's Artist of the USSR." This was their characteristic folly, to imagine that the conditions of human transformation can be corrected within time and that history can set itself to rights. They imagine that some moment, the moment of "the Revolution," a burst of violence will overthrow the condition and cancel Von Rothbart's power. In the future, the dancer will no longer sweat. However, to imagine that the ballet could end happily cancels its whole meaning and relegates it to the realm of pure fantasy. When Korsuntsev plays Siegfried with Sergeyev's revised choreography, which includes a violent struggle between Siegfried and Von Rothbart, he grins in disbelief at his triumph, looking upon Von Rothbart's torn wing with amazement. His incredulity is fitting, for the moment is as disconnected from the rest of the ballet as an episode in an airplane would be.

Sergeyev got what he deserved when he received those four

---

60 Ed.: See Plato, *Phaedo* 67e.

Stalin prizes. When I asked you, you shrugged, because you would rather speak of anything else. But I hope that you understand what I mean. I fear that if you do not understand how wicked it is to place a happy ending on this ballet, you will not understand me either. It should be obvious that if the ballet gets at something true, there can be no resolution to its tragedy in this life. It must end as it does, first with the deaths of Odette and Siegfried, then with the deaths of Odile and Von Rothbart. In some accounts of the legend, it is explicit that Odile dies, though of course, every performance of the ballet depicts only three figures: Odette, Siegfried, and Von Rothbart—another nice detail. All perish, for Odile is Odette, the young woman is the seducer and the Black Swan is the Queen of the Swans; all perish, for Von Rothbart, the wickedness whose words call her into being, is only the condition that actualized her; there is nothing of him left to endure once she passes away.

So, my friend, tell me, was this what you shuddered at, when I was ecstatic at Odile's entrance? At this thought that behind the spectacle of *Swan Lake* lies a great, and dark, message? In it is embodied the whole problem of life: that we, who have freedom for our mother, nevertheless come to adulthood under the conditions of history and necessity, and lose ourselves in the transition from potentiality to being. The lover finds the potential hidden beneath the manifest surface of our lives, but, lacking the power to activate that potential again, this discovery destroys the lover, who perishes, bound and dragged into the darkness of the human heart. On this point, Nureyev's drowning scene is the most poignant and effective of those I've witnessed, for although he is such a powerful dancer, he is completely overwhelmed by the superior power of the waves. His production also includes a disturbing detail: the audience cannot tell if Odette and Von Rothbart die or not, for the whole focus is on the death of Siegfried, dragged to death by his love. If Odette does survive, of course, then we must imagine that she becomes a Von Rothbart herself. Nureyev's genius, completely contrary to Sergeyev, is found in that even when he changes the ballet, everything still points to the same idea.

Was this what you shuddered at? Then you'll have the sense to shudder at me. Everyone about me keeps talking of sin, sin, sin, and so I will join in; *Swan Lake* is my definition, my doctrine, of sin, this account of freedom and its loss. So I'll grant your point: it's a bad thing to play chess the way I do, to enchant and draw the other player into the music only to destroy him. It's thoroughly wicked, but that is who I am, my friend, and it is better for you that you left to follow your dream of dance. You would not have found your destiny in Greenville, but had you stayed, perhaps I would have destroyed you, too, as I destroyed Sarah. My friend, this is what I am saying: love is death, being loved is to kill.

Have I gone too far? Would this not mean that love is sin, and sin is love? Perhaps I have gone astray; indeed, I know that I have. In any case, I do not know whether the message of the ballet is true of all, whether it is true of you; perhaps some dance to life the way that you danced in the studio; perhaps someone who held the music in his soul would not be ensnared by the sorcery, would still dance true when the condition was false, but I know myself—that I am the black swan, and that I betrayed the one who loved me most, who needed my love the most, who saw something in me I lost sight of in myself. When I repudiated her, she lost herself and she perished. Having understood me, will you grieve on my behalf, my friend?

JOUSKA

For you beautiful ones my thought
is not changeable
Sappho[61]

---

61   Sappho, *If Not, Winter,* trans. Anne Carson (New York: Vintage, 2003), fr. 41, p. 83.

September 7

When I stand upon the beach, I am entranced by the unbounded horizon and the limitless expanse of the ocean's waves. Strain your eyes to see as far into the distance as you may, and yet still they go on, and on, further than you see. The sea laughs at our attempts to limit it. No matter how safe you feel when the surf warms your toes, you know that the ocean is only playing at being gentle. It treats our boundaries as an adult might treat capture in a childhood game, tearing apart our bonds at will, a flimsy artifice of paper. It is holding its force in reserve, for reasons of its own. On a moment's notice, it sheds the mask and opens its maw to reveal overwhelming chaos and power, a frightening vision of wrath pursuing to consume us.

In a painting, we can render its image charming, but in truth, its beauty is too big for us. The ocean waters resist attempts to make it beautiful, demanding to be treated in terms of what outstrips the human. Outside of our lies, it is a vision of eternity, a vast, intolerable, infinite blue.

Perhaps it was only here that I truly knew you, Sarah. As you said, one can never predict which memories our hearts will hold onto. You left out, however, that neither can we predict which they will forget, even when these are the most essential particulars.

℃

Just after dawn, near the end of the strip of beach, far beyond the realms popular with beachgoers and up a narrow, grassy bluff that rose like a finger over the waves, I came upon a beautiful garden abutting the beach, attached to an unusually richly constructed home. This was at the end of one of my forays into the city, which I had begun at 3 AM. What had begun as a quest for observation became a desire to be alone with the waves, and I left my car behind to journey off heaven knows where. The house was large and quite old, perhaps from the late 18th century, done in brick after the colonial style. It had been kept up and added to throughout the years. The first story had been modified at some point, the porticos replaced with a flagstone exterior. It was surrounded by a stone wall with an iron gate that, remarkably, showed no signs of corrosion. It looked a recent replacement. The gate was ajar, propped open with a large, dark stone.

Within, the garden betrayed an Italian influence. There were several statues and fountains of marble and, at the garden's center, a small table. Upon the table was a chess board with pieces all set in their rows. The place seemed familiar, but I couldn't place it.

Curious, I entered, for the garden seemed to beckon any visitor who had made the rough trek to come within, particularly, so I supposed, another member of the universal chess community. For otherwise, why place the board out this way with the gate a propped open? I walked in slowly. From somewhere I caught the scent of roses.

The chess set, when I approached, looked weathered, but still in good condition. I picked up the white king and held it in my hand. I liked the weight of the piece. It was heavy, carved from some sort of stone. I could just see into the house in the morning light. Whereas the exterior conveyed history and durability, the interior appeared very modern, functional and streamlined, in an elegant Eastern European style.

I sat in one of the garden chairs and picked up the white queen from the board, putting down the king. The waves were crashing on the shore and I could not escape thinking about what Sarah in her letter to Aunt Helena had said about the record. I'd received this letter at the funeral. Our aunt, who was ten years younger than mom and just twelve years older than me, had always seemed a kind of compatriot to us—a secret ally we had among the grownups. Sarah had written to her in Bali two years ago, but by the time the letter arrived, Helena had already left. The letter was received by some of her friends who had stayed on, and they forwarded it to Sydney, where they expected her to be soon. But she had not gone to Sydney, as they had predicted; instead she had gone to Cancun, and then to yet other places, before finally arriving in Sydney six months later. Her friends there told her that they had received a letter for her, which they had forwarded on to Cancun. The friends in Cancun, however, had decided to hold onto the letter and wait until her next visit to give it to her. It sat in a drawer there until May, when Helena retrieved it. In August, far too late, it had come to me. Why had that damned LP meant so much to her? What had I misunderstood?

Sunk in contemplation, I pondered such impossible questions for what seemed an interminable stretch of time. Suddenly, I looked up. There was someone moving within the house. The door from the house entering into the garden opened. It was Simon.

"Now I *am* going to accuse you of breaking and entering," I said, standing up, queen still in hand. I was not as surprised as I pretended.

"And do you have any reason to be here?" said Simon.

"The gate was open," I said. "Besides, I've been here before." It had been two years ago, but I had not recognized the place until now because in the past I had entered, as people usually do, from the front. I had not seen the garden except through the window.

"Yes," he said. "It's the home of your one-time classmate Sal."

"But what are you doing here?" I asked.

"I'm here for Sal, of course," he said. "But he has made scarce."

"What do you mean?" I said.

"I did come to help Rufus, but I had another reason for coming to Wilmington," he said. "Your friend Sal, you see, is a very interesting character."

"What has he done?" I asked.

"It is not so easy to explain just what it is he has done."

"Something to draw the attention of the Feds?"

"Indeed," he said.

With this, he fell silent, and become thoughtful. His expression was pensive. He was holding the black king, examining it intently.

He seemed to want silence. The crashing of the waves below the bluff was the only sound.

I understood the desire for silence, and sat down in one of the two wrought iron chairs set by the table. I placed the white queen back in her place and played d4. Simon stood a moment, staring at the board, before sitting in the chair opposite, replacing the black king and playing d5. I played c4, the Queen's Gambit. He accepted and we played the game without speaking.

☙

I met Sal in a freshman seminar on *Moby-Dick*. We disagreed frequently. The professor once asked us whether, when Starbuck challenges Ahab over the reasonableness of seeking vengeance upon the white whale, Captain Ahab's response suffices to meet the challenge:

"Vengeance on a dumb brute!" cried Starbuck, "that simply smote thee from blindest instinct! Madness! To be enraged with a dumb thing, Captain Ahab, seems blasphemous."

"Hark ye yet again,—the little lower layer. All visible objects, man, are but as pasteboard masks. But in each event—in the living act, the undoubted deed—there, some unknown but still reasoning thing puts forth the mouldings of its features from behind the unreasoning mask. If man will strike, strike through the mask! How can the prisoner reach outside except by thrusting through the wall? To me, the white whale is that wall, shoved near to me. Sometimes I think there's naught beyond. But 'tis enough. He tasks me; he heaps me; I see in him outrageous strength, with an inscrutable malice sinewing it. That inscrutable thing is chiefly what I hate; and be the white whale agent, or be the white whale principal, I will wreak that hate upon him. Talk not to me of blasphemy, man; I'd strike the sun if it insulted me. For could the sun do that, then could I do the other; since there is ever a sort of fair play herein, jealousy presiding over all creations. But not my master, man, is even that fair play. Who's over me? Truth hath no confines."[62]

Professor Andrulis then asked us: "This is an important passage, but what is at stake? Starbuck is upset with Ahab's commissioning the ship to pursue Moby Dick—but why is he upset? Ahab makes an argument that he is in the right, but is his response convincing?" She waited a moment, and then reframed her question: "So is Starbuck right—is Ahab's mission blasphemous?"

"I think it's sad he wants to kill a whale," said one student.

"The whole book is about killing whales," said another.

"But what did the whale ever do to him?"

"Besides eat his leg?"

"I mean, I know, but, before, I mean, didn't Ahab try to kill him first?"

"Isn't the point the bit about pasteboard masks?" I said. "You know, and the wall?"

"'That wall, shoved near to me,'" said Professor Andrulis.

"I think the wall and the prison represent necessity," I said. "Starbuck can't understand offense at something governed by necessity, rather than freedom. He calls it blasphemy, because rejecting the laws of nature is rejecting God, who set those laws. Ahab doesn't quite up and say it, but when he says there is an inscrutable reason behind such necessities, and he strikes back at that reason, he's suggesting rebellion as a way of life. That's why he's wrong," I said. "This whole picture of necessity ... it's wrong."

"What do you mean?" the professor asked.

---

62 Ed.: Herman Melville, *Moby-Dick: Or, the Whale* (Berkeley, CA: University of California Press, 1981), p. 167.

"Because the laws of nature are beautiful and elegant, and conforming to them is not like running into a wall," I said. "Besides, those laws are part of what we are."

"Nature is bloody in tooth and claw," someone said.

"Nature is mathematics," I said, "and mathematics is beautiful."

"Ahab is right," Sal suddenly interjected. His face was furrowed with an intensity that, however, seemed to be directed toward something absent.

"What do you mean?" I said.

"Ahab has grasped the same thing that Father Mapple said in that sermon earlier. Sure, to some degree, we embody necessity, the laws of nature, history, biology, psychology, whatever. Nature is necessity, but we are nature mixed with *will*. What the will wants, mainly, is to assert itself and to distinguish itself from other forces by asserting itself. So we have a choice between obeying ourselves and disobeying ourselves. For Mapple, since God is the source of all truth and all necessity, obeying oneself is disobeying God; and disobeying oneself is obeying God. For Ahab, disobeying himself means submitting to the reason of things, but obeying himself means asserting his will and striking back against the world that would confine and constrain him."

"That's a bad idea," I said.

Sal was thinking about something. "I'm not so sure," he said.

What had he meant the other day by saying, "One must imagine Ahab happy"? And now, Simon being here!

☙

I played quickly, instinctively. I hadn't played against Simon in years, and was confused by how his maneuvers worked together. A chess player's style is like the signature of his thought and mind. If you understand how he thinks, then you can predict his strategy and tactics, predict how he will take a given feint or sally and how, in the end, to draw him too deep into his own expectations and hopes for him to realize you are just one step further than him, and his hope your lure, your victory. This requires, of course, that he cannot do the same and read your thoughts and intentions.

Simon had taught me to play this way, and I was young when I last played him, and much his inferior in understanding the principles of the game; but even then I had grasped his thought and been able to know, sometimes, how to intuit his intentions and turn them against him. As my teacher, I knew him, and that should have served me. Yet somehow I could not penetrate his mind. He teased and toyed with the idea of attack, made moves whose purpose was suggestive but opaque, and his errors all contained further traps. It was nothing at all like playing my old teacher, and although I thought I had surpassed him in the intervening years—I was sure I had—I struggled to make any gains against him and gradually his traps drove me into an impossible situation. I tipped over my king.

"You're not the same player," I said.

"I've been studying, recently," he said.

"Do you have time for that?" I asked.

"It was part of the job," he said, shrugging. "You are not the same, either."

It was my turn to shrug. "I've become a better player and a worse person."

He toyed with his bishop, holding it between thumb and finger, turning it back and forth. "A melancholy sentiment."

"Lying to yourself makes it worse."

"True," said Simon. "But—well, nevermind that. Isn't such resignation to be left for old men at the end, who've played their hand and seen it come up short? Your early twenties are the springtime."

"Spring?" I said, and laughed. It was a bitter laugh.

⁊

Does not even summer contain the winter within itself? Is the eternal recurrence of the seasons, so that there is no springtime that does not fade and wither, a symbol and sign for us, that each generation that is born is born with a false strength that will fail it in the crucial moment? It is not that its strength is too small, for that would be nothing. To fall short, with one's will one's own, is still victory, spiritually understood.

It is not that we are born with too little strength. It is its falseness that I wonder at.

☙

The grandfather clock was ticking in the dining room. It was six years ago, October. I was at home. I had declined to enter university at 16, on the good advice that it's hard to be so much younger than everyone else. But I had finished high school, had finished long before May in fact. Joshua had left town, gone to the Joffrey in New York. Sarah was at school, mom and dad were at work. I was alone. The chess board sat open upon the table before me, but I wasn't playing. One of Polgár's books lay beside the board, but I wasn't reading it either.

What was I doing? I remember sitting there, but I can't recall why this memory is so important. I was staring ahead, and the grandfather clock ticked, ticked, ticked.

☙

That memory creaks with weakness, though I don't grasp why its recollection makes me feel so impotent. Yet such is the law of polarities that the same autumn included my moment of greatest strength, the day I discovered the Arcanum.

It was a sunny afternoon when the light was glowing, suffusing the room with brightness. The Sacrum Arcanum spread out before me, written on the mirror. I can still see the awe on my face as I took in what I had constructed and expressed on the two walls. Everything followed from but two assumptions, that the ideal is articulable and that the individual is sufficient for her relation to the ideal. What infinite strength I felt at that moment! What invincibility against all enemies! Truly unconquerable is the one who possesses herself within herself.

Compare with that with a third moment, that moment when I

was standing alone in the dusty light, filtered through the carelessly strewn curtains, and found the record in her apartment. I knew that, however far back the string of events leading to this discovery stretched back, it ultimately terminated with myself. It was I who had set this in motion and made it possible.

Why can't I find the missing thread of my self?

SARAH

"Do you think that a person can avoid going wrong?" I asked.

"What do you think, after all I said the other day?" said Simon.

"You did imply a dark view," I said. "You said that everyone is guilty. But that's not quite the same, and many would say that if you must go wrong, you can't be guilty, and, contrariwise, if you are guilty, then you could have avoided going wrong."

"So they would," said Simon. "I take it that you think differently?"

"I don't truly know," I said, "but I think it is very hard, the hardest thing of all, to go right, and much harder than we usually admit."

"Oh?" said Simon. "Did you murder anyone on their way over?"

"No," I said.

"Or steal from someone?"

"Not that either," I said.

"Then did you lie?" asked Simon.

"I've tried not to," I said.

"I see," said he.

"That's not really getting at it," I said. "It has to do with who we are, what kind of beings we are, and how we go about this process of becoming."

"That sounds very abstract," he said.

☙

I was 12 when I met Joshua, the first day I began studying dance at the Greenville Civic Ballet. He was two years older than I. He did well enough in school, but was indifferent to academics, having made up his mind before I met him that dance was the only thing he would do with his life.

In the studio, everything he did was perfect. I was not so, though not for want of practicing; in those days I was completely devoted to dance. My efforts did lead to some success, and I got the better parts as often as not—becoming blindingly jealous when I did not—and I remember a recital when we performed some *pas de deux* from the standard catalog, and seeing Sarah in the audience. I think it was "The Sleeping Beauty," and Joshua as Prince Désiré had just brought me back to life. When I finished the dance, Sarah was watching, so, so intently.

"What were you thinking when you were watching?" I asked her afterwards. "You were staring at me so hard!"

She shrugged. "I dunno," she said. "You looked beautiful."

I knew you wanted to say more, but you hugged me instead with one of those wild embraces you used to give that made me feel like you might hurt me or break my neck. You may not have known how much strength I got in those days from those silent embraces, for I never told you that I never felt more loved than when you did that. If I forgot how your wild embraces felt,—but, you know, I think I am forgetting.

☙

"Set the board back up," I said to Simon. "Let's play again."

"As you wish," he said, and he did. This time he played as white and I as black.

"What is melancholy, do you think?" I said.

"As a state of soul?" said Simon. "To see the beauty of the world and to know that every beauty that is grasped is lost, but remains beautiful."

"Is it the world that is doomed, then?" I asked. "Or oneself?"
He smiled, slightly. "Are you still thinking of that letter from yesterday? Put it as you like. Perhaps it is to see the beauty of the world and to know that it is oneself who is doomed, for despite all this beauty, one can't own it, one must let it go, at the risk of destroying it oneself, or being destroyed in it."

I let out a sigh. "What is beautiful about Myshkin in *The Idiot* is also the reason for its melancholy mood. Melancholy is marked by longing for an absent possibility, by the sweetness of contemplating a glimpsed goodness that will not come to be, but is present as possibility nonetheless. I cry when I read the novel because I taste how close their happiness is, and yet everything is lost in despair, and one hardly sees how to prevent it. Sometimes, the beauty of this possibility is enough to provide a contemplative joy, but it is a sad joy."

"Ha!" said Simon. "What a sentiment. But, I do agree. An experience of true joy, when it cannot be repeated and perhaps was absurd from the first—such a joy may leave you melancholy the remaining years of your life, yet recollecting this lost joy may become your sweetest occupation. Hmm," he said, tapping the board and contemplating the position, "I wonder that your view is already so dark. Fifty or sixty years will be a long time to live with so much in your heart."

Ignoring him, I said, "You know, keeping with Dostoevesky, in *The Adolescent*, Arkady expresses joy on hearing Vasin declare that idea-passion cannot be canceled without being connected to something else.[63] For, he reasons, that means that if his idea is challenged or even disproven in his own mind, he will still be passionately committed to it, and that was what counted, it would give his life meaning. He didn't need to worry that someone who was better at arguing than he would take it away from him."

---

63 Ed.: See Dostoevsky, *The Adolescent*, p. 54; Pevear and Volokhonsky render the term "idea-feeling" while Garnett translates the same as "idea transmuted into feeling."

"A striking thought," Simon said, "meaning, the bit about being excited that Vasin also understands idea-passion, something Arkady knows is rare, and probably not understood by anyone in the room but him and Vasin and Kraft, and not the others, whose thought—and life experience—lacks the category. About the other, I mean giving his life meaning—he's a bit naive about that."

"Perhaps," I said. "I actually brought this up because my problem is just the opposite," I said.

Simon took a bottle of cognac from Sal's kitchen and poured it in a tumbler.

"Isn't it a little early for that?" I said.

"You're stealing my line," said Simon, joking awkwardly. He held out a second tumbler, and when I declined, he replaced it and drank from his. "What do you mean about your problem?" He asked at last.

"I mean, I can't escape the idea, I get no relief from it; it is grown to such proportions that I am consumed by this new wrinkle, the suspicion of being fated to go wrong, not because anyone else makes it happen, but fated to go wrong because I will choose to go wrong, because I cannot do what is right and remain myself, nor go right by choosing to become someone else," I said.

"Your idea remains obscure," he said. He played e4, and I responded c5. The Sicilian Defense. "Perhaps you'd better explain it to me."

෴

How is it that I can't tell any story of myself without pain? But I won't flinch. We used to spend hours in that big playroom with its polished oak hardwood floor in the big brick house our family had in Greenville. It was always full of light, its large windows facing south and east. All our toys were contained in the low pine shelving that lined walls on three sides—dolls and dress up on one side, Lego bricks and building blocks of all kinds on another side, and a miscellaneous assortment of books, toys, and playsets on the third wall. The last wall had the door and the closet, with a couple of big posters framed and mounted on the wall.

In one corner was a table with an old record player. We would drag the player out into the middle of that dark circular rug in the middle of the room and pull out our parents' old records, which were piled up in a basket underneath the table, to play whatever happened to catch our fancy, dancing in circles around the room as children do. We listened to a lot of music that we didn't understand. There was a lot of old blues and jazz, alongside the typical favorites from the '70s, like Neil Young, Jimmy Buffett, Diana Ross, The Beach Boys, Leonard Cohen, and Fleetwood Mac. That will make the collection seem more unified than it was, however; it contained, besides what I now recognize as a core of typical music from our parents' youth, a lot of purely miscellaneous material that didn't betray any single taste or style. Our favorite one summer was the International Marching Band's collection of John Philip Sousa's marches. The girl on the cover, looking as innocent and American as mom and apple pie but her leg raised scandalously high for someone wearing so short a skirt, seemed a bit silly to me. Sarah thought she was cute and would sometimes dress up and pull the cat around in a wagon as if leading him on a march. I am still amazed he allowed it.

Toward the end of that summer I found a record with a woman all in white standing in what at first appeared an impossible position, bent backwards with her head upside down and visible to the viewer. I was struck by the juxtaposition of the sharp and piercing beauty of her face and shoulders with the dreamlike appearance of her body. Her face was sharply outlined by something like a white crown while her arms extended purposefully, yet almost languidly, to either side like the wings of bird in downstroke. Although her hips aligned with her shoulders, her left leg was turned a full ninety degrees, so that one saw not the back of her foot, but the side, and indeed, she did not even seem to be standing; she appeared to be floating in cloud-like mist, her body rising from ghostly insubstantiality to diamond-like brilliance.

Sarah was not at home that afternoon, and I stared for some minutes at the cover, entranced. Finally, I put the record on the player, unprepared for the playful mastery of the opening of Leonard Bernstein and the New York Philharmonic's *Swan Lake Suite*. Listening to the record made me feel uncertain and excited all at once. I tried to share it with Sarah when she got back, but somehow things seemed wrong when we tried to dance it together, so I danced to it alone. It was only later that I saw *Swan Lake* first on DVD (forty or fifty times), and later still, live in performance. I kept the record in my bedroom as a kind of private possession. I hid it in a drawer and imagined becoming like the woman on the cover. It was a source of shame and secret pleasure, for reasons I didn't entirely understand.

I remember the first time Sarah saw me attempting to dance to it, it was an accident and I was embarrassed. She was staring at me, curiously. What was she thinking? I didn't ask. But she always watched me dance, and she never said a word about it, except that it was beautiful. I think I could have fell flat on my face and she would have said, "It was beautiful, M." This always struck me as wrong, because I did not feel beautiful, though I loved beauty more than anything. And she always said, "It was beautiful, because you're beautiful." But she couldn't say anything more about it, and I didn't believe her. "You're the beautiful one, Sarah, not me," I said, but she shook her head.

It turned out I was right. There is a beauty out there that I longed for, more than anything, and I wanted to give myself to it, be possessed by it. I was a bit gangly for a ballerina, even for one of Balanchine's dancers, but I practiced religiously and developed a technical mastery that impressed my teachers. Despite my efforts, I lacked a ballerina's peculiar grace, that magical fusion of music and movement. I could not convert the pathos and passion of the music into expression and motion, and so I gave up dancing when I went to college at 17.

∾

I had almost forgotten Sarah's fondness for poetry. She herself almost seemed to have forgotten it; I can't recall a recent example except a single poem I found in her apartment. But our childhood was full of her nonsense poems and limericks. I can't remember the nonsense, but I do remember some of her limericks. I wish I could remember more of them.

They typically came out like this: I would be sitting in my room, doing something or another, probably reading a book, and Sarah would enter dramatically, tossing her arm across her forehead, suddenly reciting:

> There once was a marvelous schooner,
> Whose captain, a wily harpooner,
> Accepted her fate
> When she shot her first-mate
> And her whole crew did justly maroon her.

"Are you she?" I said.

"I am," she said.

"If you are justly marooned, then wouldn't it be wrong to help you?"

"Then I will die," she said. "I cast myself upon your mercy, lonely hermit."

"Hermit!" I said.

"Yes, you're clearly a hermit," she said, "holed up all alone in this room."

I playfully hit her with my notebook.

"Where'd you get that limerick from?" I asked.

She shrugged. "Made it up."

"Did you write it down?"

"No," she said.

"You should."

"I want to go out and play," she said. "Will you come?"

Who would she be, without the poems to round out who she was? But she almost never wrote them down, and now no one remembers them but me, and I don't remember more than a handful.

☙

I was fourteen and it was summer. We were in the Outer Banks, Sarah and I, running down the beach. We had been running for a long time.

"Wait up for me!" you shouted.

"I can't stop!" I said. "I'm under the magician's spell! You have to save me."

"*Expellere aoctes!*" you shouted.

"What!" I said. "You just killed all the others…" I kept running.

"*Incipit arcanum!*"

"The mystery begins? What are you even saying?" I kept running.

"*Capio sororem!*" You leaped and tackled me from behind, just grasping my ankle, so we both fell on beach.

There was sand in my mouth, but I was trying to laugh as we wrestled. "Yes," I said, "you captured your sister … after all."

Finally, you got off of me, and we sat up. The sun was high overhead, its heat not oppressive, but its light filling the air with life. We were alone, and had found a part of the beach we hadn't seen before. There were little tufts of beach grass and scattered flowering sneezeweed and duney aster, along with some larger yaupon bushes. These formed a sort of tangled grove upon the rise. Some of them had reached the size of small, twisted trees, which stood sentry before a deeper grove of oak, loblolly, and beech. There was a bird pecking at the fruit of one of yaupon shrubs, which, having retrieved the berry, flew away.

"Yaupon," you said. "Let's make tea."

"Have you had yaupon tea before?" I asked.

"No," you said, and you bit your lip. "Does it really make you vomit?"

"That is just a myth," I said, laughing. "It's just tea. Like black tea. Or green tea. Just tea." I had stood up, and was fingering the leaves of one of the shrubs. "Let's take some of the leaves back. We can grind them at home and steep it in the coffee carafe at the house."

You agreed, but finding a place to put the leaves was a difficulty. Finally, you knelt down, opened your small leather pouch—your "creature bag"—and let out the little seven-legged crab you had been carrying in there, and which you had carefully cast to one side as you tackled me to avoid crushing the creature. "There you go, little buddy," you said. "You go home. You won't get a chance to meet the others, but I'll let them know about you…" The crab scuttled off on its seven legs, and in an idle thought I wondered whether it even had the sense to be bewildered by its double change in circumstances. We stuffed as many leaves as we could into the creature bag.

However, the grove was dense and unexplored. Its mysterious prospect and unknown quality made the lure of going further into the grove irresistible. Who knew what interdunal ponds, interesting creatures, and other treasures it contained? Something about it, some sinister quality, inspired foreboding. You reached out for my hand as we went into the grove. The sound of the waves was muffled by the vegetation. "Sarah," I said, "We have found the grove of Apion," I said. "It's inhabited by a powerful sorcerer … the sorcerer of Apion."

"Oh, gosh," you said. "Crap. How'd we get here?"

"His spells brought us. But he can't defeat us, so long as we keep our arcanum. So, let us go boldly into his grove, defraud him of his secrets, and defang him."

"Yeah," you said, "let's kick him in the nuts."

☙

The waves were surging up on the shore, strongly but not violently, and we were running into the water and rushing back. A few yards up the shore stood a sandcastle we were building, and we were bringing back shells from the water to decorate and buttress its walls.

"Look, look, look," Sarah was saying. "Look at this one!" She was holding out a whole and unbroken sand dollar.

"That's great," I was saying, "Sarah, did you know an unbroken sand dollar is very rare? I've never found one." I could be a pedant. "Why don't we put it in the middle of the castle, like in the courtyard."

"No, no, no," she was saying, "why don't we, let's put it right here!" She placed it on the wall over the gate, the hole gaping.

I whispered to her, saying "Put it in the courtyard, where it's hard to find ... like it's a secret."

"*Arcanum aracanandum,*" she breathed, excitedly placing the sand dollar right in the middle of the courtyard. "That's so perfect, M! You're always right. Let's go find some more shells!" And she ran back into the water before shrieking, "A *jellyfish*!"

"Wait for me!" I was shouting above the roar of the waves, which were growing louder.

⌘

Joshua stood to one side, watching the younger dancers begin practice at the barre. I felt nervous and uncertain, and ashamed at these feelings, a miserable spring of energy. "Joshua, what are you looking at those younglings for?" I said. "Look how stiff they are." I don't know why I said something so pointless and untrue.

Joshua turned his face to me. "They're the past, you know ... the future."

"What do you mean?" I said. "Don't talk nonsense." There I was again, trying too hard.

"I mean, that was me, I was like that dancer there, I mean, you and I were ... and that's the past. But when I leave—"

"You can't leave," I said, "and you were never like that dancer." True. You were so perfect.

Joshua was silent a moment, staring at the dancers again. "I'm flying to New York tomorrow," he said, "to try out at the Joffrey."

My stomach was tight and twisted, my nerves aflame. I didn't say anything.

"Please don't be like that," he said. "Let's dance the thing from yesterday, the—"

I shook my head. "I don't want to dance." I didn't say anything else, finally sitting down against the wall and staring at my ballet slippers. He sat next to me and tried to put his hand on me, but I remained cold, though I was burning inside. Finally, he walked away. I didn't see him leave the studio, staring at my slippers until the bustle at the end of the so-called younglings' class, when I got up and left the studio myself.

I couldn't have said what I felt. When I went home, I argued with my parents at dinner over something stupid and shut myself in my room. I was lying on my back in bed, reading some magazine or other, when Sarah came half an hour later looking to cheer me up with one of her limericks. She came in shouting, "BumpatabumpabumpataBUMMMMMMMMMM" and then recited:

> A battle of brute was occurring,
> 'Twixt I and the god-sea enduring,
> Till she lapped at my bow
> In a playful kowtow
> And did blush when she saw me demurring.

Then she stood there smiling, not suspecting how savage I was to be disturbed at that moment.

"What does that even mean?" I said.

"Well, the sea is fighting with the captain, you see ... and then she kind of flirts with him."

"Why would the sea flirt with him?" I said.

"She stoops to conquer," Sarah said.

"Is she blushing because he rejects her, or because she's embarrassed she didn't trick him?" I asked.

"Well, I don't know, maybe it's both."

It was just nonsense, I thought. "She should just crush the captain and feed him to the sharks." I sighed, and rolled over to face the wall, my back to Sarah. "Just leave me alone, Sarah. I don't want to talk."

She left, and I heard her put on music somewhere. I dwelt alone with my thoughts.

℘

In one of Melville's letters to Nathaniel Hawthorne, he wonders whether the ultimate secret of existence, the "Problem of the Universe," might not be unlike "the Freemason's mighty secret, so terrible to all children. It turns out, at last, to consist in a triangle, a mallet, and an apron,—nothing more!"[64] Yes, what if the secret of existence were like that? Something opaque in which one could not find any trace of an analogy to oneself? But this seems to be just what my dream of formalism was driving to, for what if the secret of existence is a mathematical, a geometrical formula of some kind, like

$$C(n,k) = \frac{n!}{(k!(n-k)!)}$$

or

$$P(R_n) = P(R_n \mid W)P(W) + P(R_n \mid \overline{W})P(\overline{W})$$

or

$$\sum_{(k=0)}^{(s-1)} \left(\frac{(r+s-1)}{k}\right) \text{ to } \sum_{(k=s)}^{r+s-1} \left(\frac{(r+s-1)}{k}\right) ?$$

Would that be a comfort to know—if one couldn't find oneself in the formula properly, I mean, if the formula doesn't include oneself and one's freedom as an ultimate and complete variable? Would

---

64 Ed.: Herman Melville, Letter to Nathaniel Hawthorne, April 16 [?] 1851.

one even know what to make of oneself in that case? I can see Joshua laughing. "I don't know how to dance that." Well, would you prefer to have found the mallet, which at least can be used for hitting things, to knowing oneself that way?

It was a cold September, the last time we danced to the record player. I remember that, though I remember so little between us afterwards. Then came all the years of adulthood, of my intellectual passions and pursuits; my investigations of the darkness in human action; and what did all this end in? In the discovery of a record, a letter, and a poem, each of which confounds me, and in that confounding, confirm that together they somehow constitute the answer to the knotted, undanceable problem of my life.

I am sure that I gave up using the record player before Sarah did, but I certainly didn't think she was still using it even after two years in college, whereas I had almost forgotten its existence years ago, and would possibly never have thought of it again, except for what happened. That is not so remarkable; we forget most of our childhood toys, for we have no cause to think of them. Thus I had not thought of such things since the moment I stood before the mirrors contemplating the Sacrum Arcanum for the first time, with its two assumptions—that the ideal is articulable and that the individual is sufficient for her relation to the ideal—and its injunction of truth over all. I stood before those two mirrors upon which I had written my system of thought, and in the evening glow reflected therefrom everything, myself included, seemed to contain an added luminosity and deeper existence. Everything, that is, except what that mirror perforce excluded, which is what was non-ideal, childish, or trivial, and for these things, my sight grew dim.

What is remarkable is that I even forgot about the LP, the one I had been so enchanted by, with its ethereal ballerina surrounded by mist. For surely my whole prior life contained no more significant encounter with beauty and ideality than that early confrontation with *Swan Lake* and Tchaikovsky's sublime music. How did that happen? How did I forget something so essential?

It was I who went to her apartment, after. Dad was tied up and couldn't come until later in the week, mom couldn't make a plan and stick to it; she was trying to do this, and do that, and did none of it. So it fell to me, and I was calm, right up to the moment.

When I entered her apartment, I was overcome by disgust. She hadn't cleaned recently or, I thought to myself uncharitably, perhaps ever. Empty wine and beer bottles were stacked in one corner next to a garbage can that was overflowing with discarded bags from Taco Bell and Chick-fil-A. There were more on a heavy round table that might have served as a good kitchen table for a family of four. The walls were decorated with surfing posters and a couple of band posters, featuring boy musicians that I imagined she thought attractive. I ended up throwing all of the posters away, and since I knew so little about current popular music, I can't say now who it was she had put up there. In the corner of the room opposite the front door she had mounted a number of record albums on the wall. The light was poor and it was difficult to immediately make out the albums she had hung up on the wall above the player, nine of them, hung three by three. In the left hand corner I saw the Beatles' *Abbey Road*, but most of these were unfamiliar to me. One showed the portrait of a woman with a confident, worldwise look and long, reddish hair, standing with palm trees behind her. It felt of weary despair, so that I appreciated the irony of its title, *Paradise*. Another, with a black frame, I recognized as a sepia-toned portrait of Leonard Cohen. I briefly ran my finger along the edge of his face. This had been a favorite, one we shared. Beneath this collection she had a small table upon which she had set an old record player, which I recognized as that same one we had used as girls. It is hard to describe how disconcerting I found this.

I went into her bedroom. The bedding was a mess, and there seemed to be something tucked into it, something like a book or cardboard display. There was a pile of clothing in a corner by the closet—dirty or clean, I didn't bother to try to find out. Managing her laundry was clearly low on her list of priorities. Well, I said to myself, would you have bothered, under the circumstances?

God, how bitterly I regret that thought. I felt I was violating her in some way by standing in her room and was about to return to the main room, but something about the piece of cardboard sticking out from her bedding tugged at me. I pulled the bedding back and unwrapped it from the sheets, and found the *Swan Lake* record. I didn't understand how Sarah had come to possess it, and the poem I found there further confounded me. But that was how I came to remember, and found that she had treasured to the end, what I had forgotten.

e/o

We'd grown apart in those intervening years, ever since the year between high school and college. I had redoubled my devotion to chess, to formal systems of understanding, and incorporated whatever I found meaningful in them, I mean, meaningful for understanding human nature and its principles of action; and when I discovered how dark the human heart could often be, I clung to my own virtue the more tightly. In every outward respect I presented myself as the perfect daughter, and so I took myself to be.

Yet how unwelcome it was to learn that Sarah, too, was coming to Wilmington, and coming to UNCW. I did not see how she and the life I had now could possibly be combined. She had called me breathless with excitement when she knew she had gotten in, and my first words reflected this unease on my part; they were not congratulatory, but almost scolding, and although this quieted her it hardly changed her certainty that she must come to Wilmington, must come to UNCW.

"It wouldn't just be surfing and partying, Sarah," I said. "You'll have to be more serious if you want to succeed."

"I'm not coming just because of the surfing team, M." she said. "I know you're a thousand times smarter than I am and you do all these amazing things. But it's got a lot of things that will be good for me too, and you'll be there."

"I'm not that smart," I said.

"You're the smartest person I know," she said.

"Well, you'll meet others," I said.

Unfortunately, she was better at drinking and partying than at studying, and her avowals could only combat this for so long; by the end of her freshman year I was avoiding her on principle.

℘

The mystery I pondered over was how it was that Sarah ended up with the *Swan Lake* album—which I certainly recognize as mine; the creases and imperfections on the cover were, that is, *are*, distinct—and, in fact, I didn't remember losing it, though I hadn't possessed it for years. Then this mystery was compounded when I saw Aunt Helena at the funeral, and she gave me the letter that Sarah had sent to her; for the letter told how Sarah had received the record, but added to this the new mystery that she had received it from Aunt Helena; and I think I certainly would have remembered if I had given it to her. Moreover, I would never have chosen to give it to her, as such a gift would have made no sense, and in fact, though Sarah continued to adore her, Helena and I had almost had a falling out in recent years.

When I pondered this in my mind, the mystery of the record grew so that gradually it seemed to be wrapped up in a thousand ways with Sarah's despair and death, and my whole understanding of her from the past five years—above all, my role in her life going wrong, which, I am convinced, goes beyond a simple failure of sisterly concern, although I certainly failed in that. Yet what did I do? How did I go so wrong?

I can't seem to find the answers.

℘

Remember that day two years ago, when you came in from the water, laughing, your blue and black wetsuit hugging your limbs, gleaming in the light of the glittering, too bright sun? You'd just wiped out surfing. The others were there, the people you were hanging out with that year, you were talking and laughing. I loathed them and I despised you for liking them. I was sitting on my beach towel, full of my own self-disgust. I'd tried practicing the Lilac Fairy's steps but I found the sand too slippery and kept losing my footing. I was sure if I were a better dancer I could manage it. Eager to insulate myself from my own sense of failure, I was now reading *The Rebel* instead. You came running over to me.

"Sis!"

"What?"

"You've gotta come to Kill Devil Hills tonight, M." You were wringing the water from your hair with your hands. Your hair was beautiful and it shone in the sun.

"Why?"

"Party. Fred's place tonight. We'll all be there. We might have a bonfire."

Your brown eyes were looking into mine, searchingly. I met them for a moment, squinting because the sun stood behind your head. You wanted to find yourself somewhere in my eyes, I know. You prayed for my acceptance and the answers you believed that only I could provide for your life. You felt life coming upon you as a raging chaos and sought a foothold and would make me that foothold, that sure guide for your life. I resented that you would do this to me, when there was nothing I had that I could share with you. "Bonfires are illegal in Kill Devil Hills, Sarah."

స

Six months ago in March, what seems only yesterday, we argued by the Kenan Memorial Fountain. I wish every word I spoke that day back into my mouth. If I had said nothing, I couldn't have done worse by you than I did.

"I won't get to go to Greece," you said.

"Oh." I genuinely had no idea what you were talking about.

"Do you even know what I'm talking about?"

"No...Um. Did you apply to go?" This was a standard stupid

followup question when someone tells you something you had no idea they were considering.

"I told everyone over Christmas break! You were there with mom and dad and everyone." I had spent break reading and working on my own problems, my own ideas. I certainly didn't waste an ounce of concentration on anything anyone was saying, idiotic as it all seemed to me at the time. I wonder how many chances to save someone's life slip through one's fingers this way?

"Why did you want to go to Greece, anyway?" The "anyway" was probably the worst single word of that day.

"God! Why do you hate me so much?" What if I had decided to listen to you at that moment? What if I had embraced you or said something else, taken you tenderly in my hands and apologized for my indifference? Said *something* that showed you that I loved you still despite the distance between us? That I wanted to bridge that gap? Could I have done so, and saved you, even showing my concern so late?

"I don't hate you. We just don't—" I didn't hate you. But I found nothing in your life attractive or worth thinking of, and you must have known this.

As you turned away from me, the slanting rays of the setting sun shone in the sparkling spray of the fountain's bitter cold water. That moment is now frozen in my mind, twisting and turning, and it is always that cold March day, the sun is always sparkling in that water, and you are always turning away while I stare at your back, not knowing what to say. I still don't know what the right words would have been. I would have to have been a different person to have said something different, to have said the right thing. Perhaps the person I was seven years ago, eight years ago, would have said those things. I don't know what I could have said, Sarah. I don't know how I could have rebuilt what was missing to make it possible to save you.

᳁

The letter you wrote to Aunt Helena:

Dear Aunt Helena,

Hi! I thought you might enjoy some good old-fashioned snail mail while you're soaking up the Bali sun. Sooo jealous! How are the waves there? Please crush a pipeline for me and let me live vicariously through you.

I was really glad to see you at Dad's birthday last month. The record was greatly appreciated—I had no idea you'd kept that! It has yet to leave my turntable. I'm not sure what it is about Swan Lake music that makes me so happy. Just nostalgia, I guess. All those days spent watching M dance the same dance over and over again, and being too young to get bored of it. It's nice how the music takes me back. We can never predict what memories our hearts will hold on to.

Hey, guess what I found last week when we were cleaning out the basement for Dad's party?

Quid credis Tu? Opto dicere aoxi

    quidcumque

Dicamus aoxi arcanum

    arcanum arcanandum
      Incredo

Quippepippe aox ior pulchra agit. Lingua arcana non SOLUM arcanandum arcanum nobis solis

nonnumquam agentes pulchra need nova verba habere vitae

QUIDCUMQUE

People who do beautiful things sometimes need new words for their life! Twig Latina aoxi placit. Credo.

Numquam

Tu impossibilis es

The arcanum nobis
No aoxes

AOCTES

Fhhh, whatevs M
Arcanum arcanandum

Do you remember this? It's that secret language that M and I made up when we were little kids. I still remember all of the phrases we used the most, I think. It was actually pretty complex—M made it, obviously. I guess it's mostly Latin, but we didn't follow all the rules, and there were other rules, and I'm not sure where they all came from. Anyway, I thought you'd like this part because we were actually talking about you here. "Aox" meant someone other than us, although not just anyone, mostly just someone nearby. It was during our family reunion trip to the gulf, when we were watching you surf from the shore because the waves were too big and we were too small. We had been writing back and forth to one another, and she wrote "opto dicere

aoxi" which meant "we should tell her." She meant that
we should tell you about twig latin. I was confused at first,
because she had been very adamant about it staying a perfect secret just between us (that's "arcanum arcanandum,"
we said that a lot). So I wrote Quidcumque? which meant
"why on earth would you want to do that?" although it
also meant a lot of other things. And then she said "secret
languages aren't *just* for keeping secret. Sometimes people
who do things that are very beautiful need some new words
in their life. I think she would like twig latin." I was hard
to convince! Apparently I was quite the secret-keeper. But
I couldn't deny how beautiful your surfing was. Of course,
we didn't end up showing you then because we were so shy.
But I'm glad you know now; she wanted you to know.

Anyway, hope this letter finds you tan and sandy! Take
lots of pictures and avoid jellyfish pleeeeeease, because you
need to surf these crazy El Niño babies with me. Love you!

-Sarah[65]

Discovering your letter, which followed the strange mystery of
finding the LP itself in your apartment, put me in a state of panic.
I could not understand the panic, which itself made me feel even
more disturbed, uncomfortable with myself.

My first instinct was to throw the thing into one of the boxes

---

65 Ed.: Sarah explains most of what the "twig Latin" means in the letter, and some of the
words ("quidcumque," "quippepippe") have no clear and definite meaning, so I will not
provide a translation here. However, it is interesting to see that in the letter, Elizabeth—
whom Sarah consistently calls M., suggesting this may be a middle name—corrects Sarah
on the nominative plural form of "aox," insisting it is "aoctes" not "aoxes," which suggests
a 3rd declension noun. But earlier for the dative singular she uses "aoxi" not the expected
"aocti," suggesting that either the word was irregularly formed or she was being unrea-
sonably hard on Sarah for making, essentially, the same mistake that she had just made.

destined for storage and to let if fall into oblivion like everything else. But I distrusted this instinct. *No lies*, I said. This was the moment when that phrase began its ascent up my hierarchy of imperatives to its current place of ultimacy. *No lies*, I said to myself. *Why does this disturb you?*

It required incredible effort to focus upon its words. I repeatedly found myself suddenly having jumped down several lines from the last thing I genuinely read, having somehow skimmed without comprehending what I was reading. This vexing failure put my nerves into a state of intense agitation, alongside my general disquiet. I found myself gritting my teeth, and my head swirling, all, however, without knowing why. I wondered if I was getting ill, and spent several minutes contemplating the possibility, before returning to myself with those simple words, *No lies*.

I read it again. "We can never predict what memories our hearts will hold onto." "Arcanum arcanandum." You never stopped surfing. Or did you, that last year? I have no idea. I used to surf. When was the last time I did it? It must have been with you. We used to do so many things together, during those summers especially—not just the surfing, but the games, the exploration, and the dancing; and always, always, my brain was occupied with this endless imaginative construction of possibilities and transformations of the everyday into something else. The Grove of Apion—what a marvelous place that became that summer, the heart of our quest to imaginatively transfigure all things into beauty. But the surfing. What was I unable to remember?

ও

The *Swan Lake* record: how had it fallen into Aunt Helena's hands? This thought, more than any other, made me very uneasy. When I contemplated this, I did remember something, didn't I? And then forgot it again... A dusky dawn, the sun not yet up, and the clouds hanging in the air to choke off its still thin light. A porch. The early morning hint of winter in mid-autumn. The sighing of the trees. Disgust. Agony. Disenchantment.

The memory fluttered into my mind, dimly grasped, and I lost it several times before I pinned it to myself, so to speak, so I could never forget it, by writing it on my bathroom mirror, alongside the phrase, "No Lies."

You had the record. You'd practically died holding it. What the hell. What the hell. What was it you'd said, so long ago? God, it was ages ago.

Somehow, connected to this, was the memory of us lying on our towels on the beach. The sun was setting. It was one of those late summer sunsets when your legs ache from living so much. Yes, I had been surfing too, and it had felt so good, and now we were lying side by side on the beach, staring up at the sky above.

We were staring up at the sky as the stars came out. You said, "When I'm surfing, God, M, when I'm riding one of those big waves, I feel like I can handle anything else life has for me. You know?"

I smiled.

But something was not quite right. I am forgetting something.

"It's like when you dance," you said. "It's the only time I feel beautiful."

Now, why had you said that?

I laughed. I remember that. I couldn't understand your self-doubts on this front. "Do you know why?" I said, instead of arguing with you.

"Why?"

"Beauty is the dance of finitude upon the edge of infinity."

☙

There is something wrong with this memory. I am still missing something. Why did Helena have the LP? How could she have had it? Again, that dusky, dimly lit morning; the clouds are all overhead, I am standing on a porch somewhere. The birds are all awake, they cheer the morning, and I hate them for it. The sun will soon rise, and I dread it. The power lines run overhead, among the tree branches, whose leaves have not yet fallen. I want to crawl away.

I must pierce this memory and tear it open.

⁂

The new game was developing as strangely as the first. I was devising a dozen different strategies around that c5 bishop, but I was sure the thing was an apple proffered by a serpent, and not at all what it seemed. Yet I was very uncomfortable making a defensive move here. What was the meaning of his strategy?

I made the aggressive move Ne4.

ON THE FRIEND

Kierkegaard's Constantin Constantius says, "People are always shouting that a melancholiac should fall in love, and then his melancholy would all vanish."[66] What is this that the people recommend, and is it so? Considering the idea will explain much.

The melancholiac is someone who has made two discoveries: he has tasted of the beauty and sweetness of life and he has realized that, given the conditions of existence, such beauty and sweetness are not to be his. This is the melancholiac in the strict sense. The first explains why the melancholiac feels himself to stand above his fellows. He perceives that they have not downed the same draught and looks askance at their merriment as out of keeping with inward maturity. In Keats's words, he is the one whose "strenuous tongue / Can burst Joy's grape against his palate fine," and naturally not everyone has either the "strenuous tongue" or the "palate fine."[67] The second condition explains why, despite this view of things, he may also view himself as inferior to every one of them, possibly as

---

66 Ed.: Søren Kierkegaard, *Fear and Trembling/Repetition* (Princeton, NJ: Princeton University Press, 1983), p. 133.
67 Ed.: See John Keats, "Ode to Melancholy."

not even deserving to live at all. Keats speaks less well of this, for he says that melancholy "dwells with Beauty—Beauty that must die," placing the emphasis upon the ephemerality of *things*, which might be how the non-melancholiac experiences melancholy, but is not true of the strict melancholiac, who senses there is something in *himself* that prevents him from joining beauty.

This must be said in particular with regard to the melancholiac who has tasted the ideal, that is, whose mirror-part has grasped some fearful and glorious word and grasped what it would be to become in beauty, becoming the ideal self who is marked by harmony, unity, and completeness, fully open to, and reflecting this fearful glory. He knows it and he longs for it. However, not only has he so far failed to reflect the ideal in himself, he has come to suspect, is perhaps even certain, that he cannot embody it within himself. The word speaks his doom, as the sum total of his being can never be integrated with that glory; no available course of action would bring him that harmony, completeness, or blissful submission of soul to the ideal.[68]

Now, when it is said that the melancholiac just needs to fall in love, we should guard against a possible confusion; the speaker might mean that the melancholiac needs to know the beauty and wonder of being in love, a redundant suggestion, since it is a requirement for melancholy that one have already become awake to the wonder of existence. Falling in love would only intensify the first condition without canceling the other. However, the speaker

<hr>

68   Ed.: This is he first time in S.A. XIX that Elizabeth has approached a problem in the type detached tone seen here, in what one might term "the essay form." Perhaps—as seems plausible—this is her ordinary tone in earlier notebooks. In any case, this paragraph seems to invoke concepts—"the ideal," "mirror-part," "fearful and glorious word," "ideal self," "harmony, unity, and completeness"—developed prior to S.A. XIX. The idea seems to have been that individuals become their ideal selves by grasping some idea, which they have the purity and strength to reflect in themselves and concretize the self on its basis. The melancholiac then is one who grasps the "word" but cannot concretize it.

might have something deeper in mind. He might be recommending not the awakening of wonder associated with being in love, but the partnership and purpose embodied in a love-relationship. This suggests a wider scope than the initial formulation; it suggests that what the melancholiac needs is an especially significant loving relationship with someone who will help him struggle against the great tasks of life, and whose existence will itself give him purpose and hope in life.

Without prejudging the exact relationship type, I will call this person the friend. What is friendship? Aristotle said that it is a combination of εὐνοία and συζῆν, good will and shared life or action, and that true friendship was only possible between two virtuous or at least decent persons, and that its most authentic beginning is goodwill developed through time into a deep intimacy in which the proper object of love, the other person's *nous*, is properly known and loved. Noῦς is usually rendered understanding or intelligence or intellect, though none of these are really a very good translation of the word; *nous* is something like a person's intellectual and moral core, that power by which someone grasps theoretical and practical first principles. *Nous* is the power by which we grasp and yearn after what is *kalon*, another word with no good translations; I'll refer to it as goodness and beauty or the ideal. What we love most in a friend is their grasp of goodness and beauty and their yearning to live a life marked by these. Since virtue is a stable state, an excellent person's *nous* is unlikely to change, and Aristotelian friendships are very stable.

However, consider the Nietzschean friend. Nietzsche describes the friend as a "mirror" in which we can see ourselves as we are and, more crucially, as "an arrow and yearning" that points us toward, and motivates us to pursue, a better version of ourselves. Nietzschean friends are each on a path of individual becoming, and Nietzschean friendship is directed toward self-development. The friend stands between the "I" and the "Me" and helps us to write the self we yearn for upon ourselves.[69] Since Nietzschean "better selves" are highly individual, such friendships are not notably stable; each individual's path may go a different way, and one should love even the enemy in the friend.

I have never had an Aristotelian friend, for I have never been a virtuous person. My strongest claim to virtue is that I made it my deliberate and constant aim to embody the ideal in myself, and become virtuous. But if I was aiming at it, then I hadn't achieved it yet. And who among my acquaintances could count? Perhaps Sal was a Nietzschean friend, for it would be too much to say that we shared our feelings or our lives with each other, or were united in mutual good will; yet I suppose we did push each other on, we were, at times, "an arrow and a yearning" for each other, "in one's friend one should have one's best enemy," and, yes, perhaps we each regarded our "yearning for a friend" as "a betrayer," as Nietzsche said, and what we loved in each other, if love it was, was "the unbroken eye and the glance of eternity"—but one shouldn't overstate things. It's not as though either of us was for the other "an arrow and a yearning *for the Overhuman*"[70]—both of us, for different reasons, would have laughed at that. But beyond all of this, were we even friends? I do not think I would say so. Nietzsche thought that women were not capable of friendship. Well, I can judge as harshly as Nietzsche can, and I know that in love one's judgment can quickly and easily become occluded, even dominated, by a few vivid impressions from life—and isn't this talk about "woman" really all about one woman—Lou Andreas-Salomé? And not even about her, but about Nietzsche's disappointments with her?

---

69 Ed.: See Friedrich Nietzsche, *Thus Spoke Zarathustra*, trans. Graham Parkes (Oxford, UK: Oxford University Press, 2005), p. 49.
70 Ed.: For these quotations, see Thus Spoke Zarathustra, pp. 49–50.

Well, let us bid *adieu* to dear Friedrich, unlucky both in love and in friendship. In my own life, a different form of friendship has been most crucial—what Plato describes in the *Alcibiades*, a kind of relationship that falls between these two types of friendship. It is *nous*-centered, like Aristotle's, but focused on becoming, like Nietzsche's. This, I think, gets at the core of friendship as I've known it—with Joshua, with Sarah, perhaps the only two friends I've possessed—and even if there are oddities and errors in Plato's account, he does get the main idea right: our friendships are not partnerships of complete and virtuous agents, shining, self-sufficient Apollos, but ragged, friendly alliances of human beings in the process of becoming, who walk in a twilight of dimly perceived possibilities. Aristotle's mistake is in forgetting that friends are most essential to us when we are in the process of becoming and yearning for the ideal that is not yet embodied in us. In the *Alcibiades*, however, *the friend is that one with whom we may become our ideal self.*

The background condition for Platonic friendship is our specific developmental nature. We aren't generated all at once; we follow a gradual process of development, like other organisms, except that for human beings there is an added complication: our development occurs partly through instinct interacting with our environment and our material conditions—the way it does for other organisms—but also partly through choice or freedom, however we may understand this. Our final development is self-directed. Such development, however, depends crucially upon the role of others in our lives. Self-directed development is not usually, and cannot always, be engaged in alone. We require friends with whom to take on this task.

The friend is that one with whom we may become our true or best self. For Plato and Aristotle, our truest self is *nous*, that intellectual and moral core that grasps the first principles of being and goodness. I am going to develop the account with this idea of our

core in mind—that *nous* is our grasp and yearning toward goodness and beauty—but generally follow Tal Brewer's formulation
in terming this a person's "evaluative outlook."[71] The goal of the
developing agent is to perfect their *nous* and for Plato this meant
an assimilation to God and a cleansing of the soul so that *nous* may
grasp and reflect as in a mirror the Forms, the ultimate standards
of existence. But that kind of unearthly mirroring first required an
earthly mirror in which we can see ourselves accurately as we are
now. In *Alcibiades*, Plato therefore applies this image of the mirror
to the figure of the friend, whose "eye" must be our mirror:

> Socrates: If the inscription [know thyself] took our eyes
> to be men and advised them, "See thyself," how would we
> understand such advice? Shouldn't the eye be looking at
> something in which it could see itself?
> Alcibiades: Obviously.
> Socrates: Then let's think of something that allows us to see
> both it and ourselves when we look at it.
> Alcibiades: Obviously, Socrates, you mean mirrors and that
> sort of thing.
> Socrates: Quite right. And isn't there something like that in
> the eye, which we see with?
> Alcibiades: Certainly.
> Socrates: I'm sure you've noticed that when a man looks
> into an eye his face appears in it, like in a mirror.
> ...
> Alcibiades: You're right.
> Socrates: Then an eye will see itself if it observes an eye and

---

71 Ed.: See Talbot Brewer, *The Retrieval of Ethics* (Oxford, UK: Oxford University Press,
2010), p. 24. But this work was also published earlier in "Savoring Time: Desire, Pleasure, and Wholehearted Activity," *Ethical Theory and Moral Practice* 6 (2003):143-160,
esp. 149ff.

looks at the best part of it, the part with which it can see.
Alcibiades: So it seems.

...

Socrates: So if an eye is to see itself, it must look at an eye,
and at that region of it in which the good activity of an eye
actually occurs, and this, I presume, is seeing.
Alcibiades: That's right.
Socrates: Then if the soul, Alcibiades, is to know itself, it
must look at a soul, and especially at that region in which
what makes a soul good, wisdom, occurs.[72]

"If the soul is to know itself, it must look at a soul," but not any
part of the soul, or even the whole soul, but rather, the part of the
soul that can know and exercise wisdom: that is, *nous* must grasp
itself in *nous* and perceive itself in that mirror.

But what kind of mirror is *nous*? If *nous* were merely the intellectual core of a person, then we could assume that the function of
the friend was to provide us with accurate, unbiased information
about ourselves and about the world. Someone who provided this
would indeed be useful and would provide us with good advice.
Yet *nous* is also our evaluative core. The mirroring of *nous* in *nous*
will therefore be something rather different, and deeper.

Perhaps we should begin, as Aristotle did, by turning to the
person's own self-relation: how the agent's *nous* is mirrored in itself
(NE IX.4).[73] We can define someone's *self* as the person's *nous* insofar as this *nous* grasps itself and is made the agent's own project,
subject to the agent's own attitudes and agency. That is, *nous* can
grasp the good, and grasp a vision of what it would mean for itself
to be good, grasp what kind of thing it is and where it is now, and

---

72   Ed.: Plato, *Alcibiades*, in *Plato: Complete Works* (Indianapolis, IN: Hackett Publishing, 1997), 132d–133b.
73   Ed.: The reference is to Aristotle, *Nicomachean Ethics*, IX.4 (1166a5–6).

endeavor to make itself over into that vision. Then the person's *ideal self* is a fully developed evaluative outlook that adequately grasps the good and the beautiful and which has been developed to reflect that outlook.

The starting point of the *Alcibiades* is that this initial grasping of *nous* by itself is not very stable or successful. A person's *nous* may adequately grasp some matters, but is also bombarded by a dangerous array of passions and desires, and above all, by public opinion. We therefore begin with confusion with respect to the good that endangers the development of our ideal self. For a developing agent, *nous* remains in a state of flexibility: it is not yet fully solidified into either a virtuous or vicious self. The friend seems here meant to be a kind of ally in knowing ourselves and properly becoming ourselves. What, however, does this mean spelled out in greater detail? What happens when our *nous* is mirrored back to itself in the friend's *nous*?

This means several things:

1. We grasp something of our friend's evaluative outlook.
2. We can grasp both our *current self* and what would be our *ideal self* in light of our friend's evaluative outlook: we know how we measure up to what we see in his or her eyes and what our *nous* would need to become to more ideally satisfy what we grasp there.
3. Where the evaluative outlook of the friend complements our own, filling it in where ours is weak or solidifying it where it is vague, our *nous* can obtain a much more complete grasp of the good and the beautiful and transform our own grasp of our ideal self.
4. Where the evaluative outlook of the friend overlaps our own, our openness to the friend feeds this yearning for the good back into us: to our own sensitivity is added our sensitivity to the friend's yearning and to the friend's approval of our own yearning.

5. Because the love in such friendship is an openness of our
    nous to the friend's *nous*, our sensitivity to the good as
    grasped by the friend is deep and enduring.

Thus, whereas the Aristotelian friend loves and delights in contemplating his friend's *nous* (NE IX.4, 9), the Platonic friend has a
more complex and deeper relationship with the friend's evaluative
outlook. I cannot pause to cover each aspect in detail, yet it is clear
how these elements make the Platonic friend uniquely useful in
strengthening our resolve against external pressures and in pursuit
of our shared grasp of the good.

We can therefore see why a mentor should ideally be a Platonic
friend, but a Platonic friend need not be a mentor: a mentor's
particular form of guidance can provide the reinforcing role if the
mentor has him- or herself acquired greater solidity of *nous*, greater
resistance to contrary social pressures, and greater balance within
the self. However, a friend who is not a mentor can provide the
role of the Platonic friend if that friend is not more advanced, but
nonetheless balances us in crucial respects—by strengthening our
grasp of and yearning for the good where it is weak, by comple-
menting our grasp of the good with their grasp of the good, and by
giving us a crucial voice contrary to the voice of society on the very
side we are most susceptible to its pressure and most prone to self-
doubt. The Platonic friend is therefore not necessarily a *mentor*, as
Plato depicts it, but is essentially someone who shores up our weak
sides and whose friendship aids us in pursuing the good: the friend
is like Enkidu in the Epic of Gilgamesh, who provides the necessary complement to the boisterous boy king Gilgamesh for him to
become a great king. In fact, it is not hard to find literary models of
such friendships—such as that of the agnostic Charles Ryder and
the Catholic Sebastian Marchmain in *Brideshead Revisited*; that of
the elder Zosima and the young Alyosha Karamazov in *Brothers
Karamazov*; the love of Dante for Beatrice—and in every case,
one or both persons grasps the self they are to become only upon

meeting the other and depends upon the relationship to acquire the resources to make progress toward that self. Dante's progress requires him to meet Beatrice's eyes, then turn toward his goal.[74]

Then there is no reason that two people cannot both be Platonic friends to each other. If the *nous* of each friend grasps the good but each corrects the imbalance in how the other understands it and allows them to move toward the ideal self more surely, then each can be a Platonic friend to the other. This mutuality may, in fact, be a crucial component even in a mentoring friendship, insofar as the younger friend will, at the very least, provide just the contrast of youthful openness and flexibility of *nous* that the more hardened *nous* of the older friend requires to continue pursuing the ideal self, and of course there is no reason that the younger friend may not also be able to provide a complementary evaluative outlook that would benefit even a Socrates—who, indeed, seemed constantly refreshed by youth.

Juxtaposed with Aristotle's conception of friendship as based in joint activity and mutual admiration, then, we have this idea of the friend as one with whom we engage in mutual self-making, and the concomitant idea that such a friend is necessary to make progress toward the ideal. The truly great friendships are those in which the friends did not merely exercise their powers together, but acquired their powers, and themselves, through each other.

The friend provides the grasp of the ideal we require to embody the particular pattern by which we can come to be whole, harmonious, and complete, crucial in particular to grasping and yearning for the pattern by which we would embody the ideal in ourselves.

Such friendships may come in varying degrees, depending upon how deeply someone allows the friend to define her, and

74 Ed.: Dante speaks of looking into Beatrice's eyes at several points in the Commedia; for example, in Canto XVIII, lines 20–21, he says: "Turn and listen: not in my eyes alone is paradise." *Paradiso*, trans. John Ciardi (New York: Mentor, 1970). This list of friends reproduces Niakani's.

how crucial he is to her grasp of the ideal. What Niakani said has to be completed by a second thought. Self-making passion and the pattern can equally belong to both a passion for something other than another person and a passion directed toward another person. Similarly, Platonic friendship is indeed self-making, but it need not be self-making in the sense that Niakani means it: it can be finitely self-making rather than infinitely so. What distinguishes the former I will not say; but regarding the latter, self-making passion allows an intensification of the openness of *nous* to *nous* carried out to a maximal or absolute degree. Similarly, in a self-making relationship of the type Niakani describes, the shared activity of the two individuals is specially related to the activities in which the person's life is most ideal, that is, becomes most coherent, unified, and complete. It is also Niakani's idea, I think, that the relationship speaks the glorious, fearful word into the person's soul, in that through the dynamics of the relationship itself, where *nous* mirrors *nous* and the person inhabits her perfect pattern, the *kalon* appears all of a sudden in the space between the friends and writes itself into the mirror-part of their souls.

However, the idea is not yet clear in Niakani's writing, because he does not clearly see why we need such friends: the fact that, generally speaking, our constitutions are marked by imbalance, and it is this imbalance that prevents us from embodying the ideal. The friend whose *nous* grasps the oblique side of the same ideal, and whose *nous* we allow to become constituted in our own *nous*, provides the strength and vision to overcome this limitation. For, if the ideal is beauty—that is, harmony, wholeness, and completeness—then we presuppose that there is a way of reconciling the different factors of a person harmoniously; and the fact that the possibility of harmony is a question implies, further, that these factors are somehow not balanced as they come from the hand of nature, and our weak grasp will lead us astray.

Embodying the pattern in ourselves is like walking a tight rope whose starting point is the moment of infinitization and whose endpoint is our end—the self we would become should we unify all we are in ourselves. This image of the tightrope implies that the chief danger is falling to one side or another. The ordinary man would regard this as an overdramatic image; he would feel that the idea of becoming could be just as well depicted in the image of someone walking along the ground as walking along a tightrope, for he would regard the ordinary situation of choice as a finite movement in a particular direction; and the addition of a finite quantity in one direction can be subtracted by the addition of a finite quantity in the other direction, and he would regard imbalance as akin to a poor compass that points just a bit to the West. The ordinary man, that is, views becoming as a process marked by a series of small choices that make him a little more of this, a little more of that, and what ought to be feared is not the anxiety of a sudden slip off a rope, but the blockheaded stupidity of one who walks a mile off the path and perhaps finally in his blockheadedness refuses to admit his compass could have led him astray, and so, in a final fit of stubborn idiocy, somehow falls off a cliff, dives off a bridge, or what have you.

Less optimistically, when Augustine traces out his life in the *Confessions*, he cannot find an earliest point when his sins were not part of him. The *libido dominandi*[75] at the heart of sin is present in the newborn infant and seizes the desires for pleasure, for honor, for friendship, and for wisdom as soon as they appear, choking them and reconfiguring them into images of itself. Then, again, and for a different reason, there is no falling off the tightrope, for one fell immediately to ruin.

Against the first, it must be said that *nous* does not operate in spatial categories, but rather in categories of sensitivity and

---

75 Ed.: Latin phrase meaning something like "lust for domination," "desire to control."

passion; and these admit of both quantitative degree (*how* sensitive and *how much* passion), but also historical development, maturity, and injury; and whereas it is natural to take the first as a matter of finite, reversible changes, it is not at all a matter of course that the latter operate this way. Everyone knows the environment of an organism during its development has significant and all but permanent effects on its mature form. Is the human organism exempt from this in her moral development? Historical-developmental categories are particularly apt to apply to those powers whose exercise modifies themselves (for example, it is as if an organism's developmental function takes the organism's environment as one of the variables and the organism's current form as the other) and in this way are distinctly unlike the proffered analogy of locomotion. A power that operates in historical-developmental categories, however, is such that in decisive moments its exercise modifies the power itself, so that later exercises of the power always reflect that moment in themselves.

Now, someone's *nous* is her sensitivity to certain goals, activities, objects, and patterns as *good* and *beautiful*—that is, as eligible and desirable possible objects of action or contemplation or embodiment, in herself or in another object. *Nous* is simultaneously a yearning or draw toward those objects and a hope to find happiness in them. When fully developed, *nous* contains a grasp of what its objects are like and how they all hang together, if they do, that is, if the Ideal is realizable.

What Augustine says about evil being from the beginning is hard, and hard to evaluate. For it implies that somehow the developmental function, as such, is broken, or that the material of the human is, as such, incapable of receiving the right form. That is not the hard part; what is hard is that the decisive blow to development is made without any involvement of the agent's own *nous* or freedom. It implies that moral development is like biological development in taking its decisive variables from the person's environment and the person's current condition, and that function yields sin.

Augustine, however, expresses another idea about moral development in the *Confessions*, one that is clearer and essential to grasping the way that human agency *is* involved in its own overthrow. His depiction of his own life is punctuated by moments when he decides to embrace some good he already senses, but embraces it in such a way as to distort its value; and, most importantly, he shows how, in these moments, his free commitment creates an all but irreversible internal commitment that he cannot back out of later. These decisive commitments occupy just those historical-developmental categories mentioned above: they are asymmetrical exercises of a power, our capacity to love, whose result modifies the power itself and is presupposed in all later moments.

For Augustine, commitment to something—pleasure, honor, friends, wisdom, God—is about love. Everyday English shows the same proclivity: we speak of loving to do this or that, loving to eat such and such, and so on, without much particularity. It might be clearer to distinguish *caring* and *loving* and so to segregate these different activities into different boxes, in particular in order to distinguish love for persons from caring about other types of objects and activities, but here, I want to focus on what they have in common, and will call them all *love*. What we notice about love, unlike simple desires or inflamed passions that so often flare up and then die away, is that love is often *irreversible* and represents a movement from flexibility to inflexibility in the structure of the self. What we love becomes a constituent of the immediate self, like our biological drives, our histories, etc.

Loving, however, is not how we fall off the tightrope, for love is a constituent, and therefore it is imbalance, not yet falling. Falling and imbalance are related as event and explanation. Readers today generally think that Augustine is too hard on himself over his desire for sexual pleasure, which we today generally classify as a drive or instinct rather than as something he needed to take responsibility for, but this fails to notice that what he wanted, specifically, was the pleasure for its own sake, without commitment and without any clear appreciation of the other person. There is something highly selfish in the way that he describes his sexual appetites, which is to say, it was tied up with the *libido dominandi* he finds wrapped around all human desires. Is being "in love with love" compatible with truly loving another person?[76] Moreover, when he views life as utterly unlivable without sexual pleasure, as if it were something simply necessary for human happiness, this must be understood in the following way: what he viewed as necessary for happiness was an enjoyment of another person that was most fundamentally the use and instrumentalization of another person. Augustine seems to have thought the implicit instrumentalization to the end of selfish pleasure and idolization of the other person *qua* object of sensory pleasure could never be removed from the drive.

The reader will find that Augustine does the same with honor, friends, and wisdom—Augustine encounters a prospective draw to these things, enthusiastically welcomes them, he finds them *kalon*, and he comes to love them; and then afterwards, when the love has formed and acquired fixity in his will, he finds he is again in the wrong, and that the prospective good has been transformed into something other, something different in his heart. As a universal story of the human heart, Augustine gives us this for self-examination. Has not the same thing happened in our *own* hearts when we embraced our most beloved objects and persons? Didn't Joshua become a burden to me precisely because I clung so tightly to him? And—no lies!—hasn't even the Arcanum become a burden, made a burden only because I have tied myself to it? But what is it that happens between the time when the prospective

---

76 Ed.: See Augustine, *Confessions*, Book III.1.1.

good appears and the time when the love has grown up in our hearts, what is it in that moment that, like a choking vine, grows up alongside, covers, and distorts that love? It is that hidden event I wish to know and understand.

The ideal self is what we grasp when we grasp ourselves in light of the ideal we grasp by *nous*, including that glorious, fearful word, and envision our harmonization with that ideal. The ideal self is the envisioned harmonization of function through which the constituents of *nous* are related to each other. The ideal self is built from the person's constituents as they stand, and can include, exclude, subordinate, or elevate various elements in its envisioned harmonization. Such an ideal self may be far from ideal. It may leave out something essential, or essentialize something accidental. Imagine if someone regarded wearing a certain style of pants as essential to their identity—and then, having gone out of fashion, these pants were no longer available! That is an absurdism, but this is how I took Sarah's fixation on surfing, as a kind of mistaken concretion of a favorite activity within the self, leading to a whole series of absurd further choices. But that was the ideal self she envisioned and yearned for: to be the surfer, forever the surfer; thus an accidental quality, once charming, now seemed sure to become some fixed, dull eccentricity.

In grasping such an ideal self, *nous* can make itself its own project, and affect its own development, insofar as it may strive for greater or lesser sensitivity in some area, even to the extent of searing some part of itself from itself in order to fit itself to some procrustean bed it makes for itself. This is what I wished Sarah would do—I would not say that I was waiting for her to do it, but that I abandoned her due to her refusal to do it, to sear the eccentricity from herself, to become something better than her childish self. Whether I would have become friends with her again had she done so, I do not know; my way did not allow many friends, only those who walked similarly, and could she have followed there? I suspect not.

Every love has its associated aversions and despite for what is antithetical to the love. When love finds objects of aversion within itself, it creates a problem for harmonization, insofar as these pieces press against each other, and create the necessity of possible dissociation of one element or another of the self; for what cannot be harmonized must be excluded, but yet, what cannot be changed cannot be excluded; and the perplexities of such contradictions and their universal possibility are what together give tragedy its power over the soul, which senses, either dimly or explicitly, its own predicament therein.

Now, infinitization is the possibility of positing an ideal self, of *nous* making *nous* its own project. If such an ideal self is merely a desire, a hope, an imagined fancy, then it is a dream, it is not posited; it has no iron. Insofar, however, as a posited self is itself the object of love and care, or is grounded in the outflow of what we love, it acquires iron: for these passions have a degree of permanence in them. It is the iron in the mirror.[77]

When we make *nous* into an object for itself, we set to work on it and those changes themselves, because they belong to the historical categories of development and injury, have their own iron. This task requires us to bring the materials of the self into a harmonious whole; when the materials prove recalcitrant, there is the possibility of forging the self incorrectly, leaving it unharmonious and unbalanced. When imbalance is hardened into a false pattern, that is the fall. In that moment, *nous* will have maimed itself, and maiming is an irreversible change. Such a change in what one views as good and beautiful will be presupposed in all later acts, and will therefore equally maim those acts.

Thus my image of the tightrope walker traveling across a

---

77 Ed.: Here we get a further development of the concepts that preceded SA XIX; she seems to have used "iron" to refer to the result of concretizing some word or idea (or whatever other object might become trapped in the "mirror-part" of us).

chasm, for to stumble is often irrecoverable, for the fall is decisive: the person has fallen to that side and has failed to reach the destination on the other side of the rope, this pattern in which the self is harmonized. Perhaps even the minor stumblings of childhood may assume decisive significance, in the way we often see when someone has begun walking unsteadily, and now finds it increasingly hard to keep her balance; those initial steps bear so much influence, more than it seems they ought.

Prior to the first such moment, we are rising upon the ladder, but set no foot upon the tightrope. We do not even discern the goal, but merely hear rumors of it. Then, the first awakening of maturity, and infinitization: the opening of the possibility of *nous* making itself its own project, of positing an ideal self. We stand upon the dais atop the ladder, everything swirls before us, spinning in our novice's gaze, and—we take our first step toward the goal. So dizzied are we that we cannot even tell in what direction we are being told to step. Where is the goal, where is the rope? Do we dare try to support ourselves? Upon what can we place our hands? Then, in a moment that will shape us forever after, we simultaneously take a step, and discern the goal, we place our foot delicately or clumsily down and so begins our walk along the tightrope.

We need the friend because of this imbalance. We proceed along an axis of becoming (this is the rope), but are weighted too much to one side; the friend, let us say, holds our hand, ever so gently, and balances us. This is the meaning of that old conundrum over whether 'opposites attract' or 'like attracts like' (another point on which Aristotle is quite disappointing).[78] They are true in different respects. The friend has an axis parallel to ours, it points in the same direction, but the friend has a different balance of

---

78   Ed.: Aristotle addresses this in Book VIII of the *Nicomachean Ethics.*

factors; and it is this different balance of factors that helps us to correct our imbalance, showing us a different perspective on the very same thing. The *nous* of each grasps the same good but they correct the imbalance in how they each understand it, and their mutual encouragement and assistance allows them to move toward the good more surely. Mutual pursuit causes them to increase in yearning for their goal. Love unites us with the friend. It is the hand we reach out while walking the rope. If it is met by the other's hand in turn then we will be each other's ally in the great task of life, like blood brothers.

But if someone extends her hand, and finds none there to take it—well, then she cannot help but fall, for if she had been strong enough to walk alone, she would not have reached out her hand; and just as it is rare to embody the ideal without needing to go through the process of becoming, very rare, so it is quite rare to find someone born so strong, and so well balanced, as not to need a friend to go through the process of becoming, someone who will keep one from falling down the chasm, twisted and stumbling.

This problem of imbalance runs deeper than the tightrope analogy suggests, since it is our *nous* that is imbalanced and this affects not only our balance while walking—that is, pursuing the ideal, or the good—but also our vision; for *nous* is what grasps the good and holds fast to it with yearning. Thus the imbalance will also make the goal appear other and vaguer than it actually stands.

It might seem as if someone could compensate simply by consciously correcting for bias of this kind, like a player with an overstrong attachment to bishops, taking care to calculate carefully when your figurative bishops are involved. However, the more correct analogy would be an affinity for a certain style of play, a certain kind of strategy or opening, something written into a player's bones by secret instinct and thousands of repetitions. When someone has a flawed approach written into her that deeply, and and the flaw doesn't lead her into a straightforward blunder that she could see by pausing for a moment of calculation, but sets her off course from the beginning and at every moment when the outcome is still charged with possibility, she is slowly led to the point where the opponent has the advantage. She could try to play another way, but these ways don't make sense to her properly, she doesn't have the feel for them, and either blunders or plays too slowly when she adopts them. They do not fit her temperament and instincts. Thus the dilemma: if she follows the approach that makes sense to her, she will slowly but inexorably be led into a manifest material or positional state of disadvantage; but if she tries to correct her approach, she will spend too much time calculating, and she cannot calculate fast enough to traverse the field of possibilities that makes up the opening and mid-game during the limited time of life, when what is needed is vision and intuition and practice. The timer is ticking, she moves, and—the right move, the right move, a good move, a clever twist, and then the blunder.

The imbalance in how you perceive the goal is with you at every moment, and meanwhile, time is moving, and you must act; but with each act, you are subject to a bit of draw to one side, an imbalance potentially distorting each motion. But the imbalance is not just an impulse—which is what the metaphor of a literal imbalance suggests, the impulse of gravitational pull—rather, it is something like a pattern of fit you are drawn into following after, and fitting your actions into, even without discerning the import. And so finally you find yourself in the wrong pattern.

Then the problem is that you are walking the tightrope, and it is the friend who gives you balance; but the goal is *the pattern*. Life isn't a walk to the store. It is an attempt to manifest the proper pattern in one's life. That is how we fit our life to the ideal. So the friend, the one who was walking along a parallel axis to you, he holds your hand—but now suppose we consider the goal. The two of you will only walk in parallel if the goal for each seems close to the goal for the other, so that you can walk together.

There are two possibilities here. The first possibility is that you are right: you are both headed in the same direction, your axis of becoming runs parallel to that of the friend. The second possibility is that you are wrong: precisely because of your imbalance, the two of you are mistaken in thinking you share a goal, and your true axes are not parallel.

Since the supposition of this whole discussion that you cannot see the goal correctly, it would be an unexpected stroke of good fortune if a person found a friend whose axis of becoming seemed to run parallel, and whose imbalance seemed to balance hers, and these things were in fact true. It must be chance if neither has an independent way of checking their own flawed scales, except by means of those very scales.

This is the primary problem. Yet consider the other side, too—suppose your axes *do* run parallel to each other's. But isn't it quite possible that at some later moment, when you become disconcerted as the glare of life grows too bright and varied, it will come to seem that the two axes part from each other at last, and that, on closer inspection, the apparently overlapping goals now seem quite far from each other, much too far to hold each other's hand? How fraught our relationship with the friend is! How little support it provides us in this attempt to walk the tightrope—despite being, as I said, quite necessary for us, per-haps the most important thing we could ever find in this life. For although the friend can provide us with balance we desperately need, and we can provide the same to them, there is the ongoing possibility, this probability, this dare I say necessity, that at some point our axes will either come apart or seem to come apart, and in this crucial moment, our imbalance will affect the other's imbalance, upsetting both of us. If what I have done, all along, is to pull you a bit to one side, and now, suddenly, I push you toward the other, toward the side you've always favored—or if, having held you up so long, I now seem too distant to provide any support, well, now, when this happens, you will experience your imbalance all of sudden, and possibly more forcefully than before. You may grasp at me to try to draw me back, or push away from me to try to keep yourself from falling, but at this moment, certainly, there is every danger that we will now fall, either or both of us together.

The image of falling represents the irreversible misstep. What is irreversibility? Something done that can't be undone. That is rather unclear, though, and useless. Irreversibility implies a change in the condition of something from one state to another, and that this condition can't be changed so that the first state again obtains. If you gut a fish, perhaps you can un-gut it, too, but you can't unkill it. It's dead. So it is with words, and memory, for what has been said cannot be unsaid if it leaves a charged and vivid trace in memory. Even if we take back what we said, what we said lingers. Of course, someone can forget, but even then, I'm not sure the heart always forgets. The feelings and attitudes may linger on much longer than the memory.

Suppose someone said something to another person that was very hurtful to her. Can the first person take back what she said? It might make a difference if she showed regret for what she said, repented, and asked forgiveness, but suppose that the reason what she said caused pain was that it revealed her own true attitude toward the second person, and this attitude was incompatible with the relationship the second person thought she shared with her and with the goals she thought they shared. What if the first person's words reveal her own deepest self? Then it would require a very profound repentance to mend things, for what would it mean to take the words back otherwise?

If the first person says she is sorry, but her attitude is still the same, then what is the outcome? Is she merely sorry that the other person found out and was hurt? Could it mean, however, that she has a different stance on the attitude, that she now holds it at arm's length or wishes it were different? Yet suppose that the offending attitude were too deep a part of the first person for her to hold it at arm's length. Some attitudes, some concerns, are so deeply ingrained in us, or their alteration so unthinkable, that we cannot separate ourselves from them. No matter how we change ourselves, these elements remain part of the picture; and even if their precise significance changes, they remain nonetheless, and are not canceled.

This is often apparent in love, although also in hate. We do not, in any simple way, choose what to love or hate, even if we can choose to put ourselves into situations that make it likely to arise. Love for place and home does not arise by choice, but by virtue of a gradual attachment that occurs before we are aware of it—behind us, as it were, while love for a certain work of art may strike us all of a sudden, as soon as we encounter it, and become deeply essential to us, not because we chose to do so, but because our nature and affinities made this possible or inevitable to us.

Nor do we choose to cease loving. Once I love someone, or something, although it's possible to lose the thing along the way, it's damned near impossible, in a positive way, to get rid of it. As Sappho said, love, "that loosener of limbs," is a "bittersweet creature against which nothing can be done."[79] We experience love and loss of love more as patients than as agents: we lack immediate voluntary control over love, though love is our primary form of connectedness to the world.

Let us then distinguish between two kinds of love: those that we could lose, without much else seeming different about us except the loss of an item of inventory, and those we could not lose

---

79   Ed.: See Sappho, frag. 7.

without seeming to radically disrupt the structure of our lives and how we understand ourselves. The former comprise such "loves" as love for fettuccine alfredo and all concerns isolated from our other concerns and relationships, most especially from our fundamental sense of our*selves*. If I love someone, but that relationship doesn't have much to do with how I relate to anything else, or to myself, then this isolation from our web of concerns portends an ease of loss, a concern that might slip away without notice until it is well into the past.

The other type of concerns, however, are those whose loss would disrupt the overall structure of the self, either because this concern is integrated with other concerns, shaping or influencing them in various ways, or giving them their peculiar cast—concerns, in short, that are part of how we understand our self, and that ground the stance we take upon our self. In the process of becoming, when we take up attitudes toward ourselves, there are loves and concerns that take on an important role in the process by shaping our attitudes toward our other concerns, and become, in fact, our deepest source of such valuation. Losing these is especially difficult and disruptive, and perhaps this is what is meant by "conversion": a change in the factors, the loves and concerns and whatever else that plays a vital role in our self-evaluations.

Others, which may not play the same sort of fundamental evaluational role, may still be highly integrated with our other concerns, so that their loss is severely disruptive. Dropping one shakes all the others it is connected with and opens them to new interpretations and roles.

A love that falls into either of these groups is especially hard to change. Parental love, for example, falls at the fundamental level: parents usually describe becoming a parent as a transformative experience, which is to say, it changes their own deepest values and sense of their own identity. Yet love for children arises spontaneously, and even though adoptive parents choose to adopt, they do not choose to love; adopting a child is, rather, one of the things we can do that "put us in the way" of acquiring a love that we naturally are possessed by under certain circumstances. A parent naturally begins to view him- or herself in light of this love, and if they don't, then something seems to have miscarried—not the child, but the parent, for it's as if the parent were supposed to be born along with the child, but this didn't happen.

Now let us return to the irreversible misstep. Imagine that what someone does or says implicates these fundamental evaluative concerns: she doesn't only show her real attitude toward the second person, which she at least might repent of or distance herself from; she shows her real attitude and this attitude is at the core of her own identity, in terms of which she evaluates all other concerns. She cannot repent this.

Yet, it is worse than that. Loves are often bound up with despisings, with hatreds, for in loving something, you become bound to oppose what opposes it. So love for beauty is is bound up with despising ugliness that falls short of it. If you love beauty, you must despise the ugly, the ignoble, the low, the tawdry, the cheaply bought, clumsily realized, all the half-thoughts covered with poor taste's luxuriant praises. Whatever shows the inability to distinguish the beautiful from the maudlin—that is despised. Yes, love for beauty entails hatred of the despicable.

So, what do you suppose happens if that love for beauty you have, your love for the ideal, leads you to despite? And let us suppose this love is fundamental, an evaluative concern that's bedrock. Then you say something and it hurts someone precisely because it emerges from this despite of yours—that is, it shows you for who you really are, in the deepest sense, and it goes against the other person? To the extent that the other person values you and a relationship with you, won't that hurt them? And how could any degree of sorrow over harming them correct things, since you cannot repent the core of yourself?

That would be very hurtful and hard to repent. But there are others, as I said, because it need not be one of these negative attitudes, like hatred or despite. It could involve an incompatibility between your fundamental evaluative concerns and the relationship that the other person wants, so the difference is indirectly reflected upon the person ... that is, your disagreement about something extra is only about the two of you insofar as it shows you have different concerns. And yet these concerns are right at the heart of you. So how can you hold together, or correct your relationship?

This is how the irreversible misstep happens. You have a goal, and that goal is shaped by what you love. The reason it turned out we needed the friend was our internal imbalance, that is, our tendency to fall too far to one side or another in our attempt to complete our development. We needed the friend to help us see the goal correctly. Now, however, you see that in this bonding, there is a danger. Our progress toward the goal includes irreversible steps, and these irreversible steps can themselves create discordance in our relationships ... above all in our relationship with the friend, the one whose hand we hold. A misstep of this kind will introduce evaluative differences—that is, differences in how we see the goal—that we cannot take back, and that themselves may push us too far toward, or too far away from, the friend. So the irreversible step becomes a misstep, and your relationship with the friend becomes poisoned in some way that you cannot take back. Since it was the friend you depended upon for balance, you now cannot pursue your goal properly ... rather, you are subject to imbalance again. Unchangeable factors in yourself and these little missteps in what and how we love make your relationship with the friend impossible, and therefore, also make reaching the goal impossible.

The result is, it is your own life that is out of keeping with the ideal, the ideal that you love, and there is nothing you can do for it once you've fallen from the tightrope, and perhaps taken the friend with you—you, who offered and asked for such tender support, and brought not only yourself, but the friend as well, down to ruin.

Now it will be understood when I say that "This is the only form of friendship I have known" just what I meant by that statement: Joshua, myself, Sarah, we three.

JOSHUA

I was in the studio, practicing with Joshua. It was April or May, the sun was shining outside, just beginning to set, shining in the windows and reflecting off the mirrors. I was trying to explain to him some idea I'd had.

"I think that all human beings are secretly sad," I said. "We're sad because truth is the golden ratio, but we're accidental, so we're not."

Joshua laughed. "So we're sad, are we?" He went over to the sound system and put on "Pathétique," the fourth movement.

Perhaps that was not exactly how I put it; it's hard to remember for certain what I said. I was often excited by new ideas in those days, and I couldn't keep my excitement to myself. I told them to everyone, but I especially told them to Joshua, all of them. He would listen, he absorbed every word I said, serious or smiling as called for, but then he would laugh, and he would get back to dancing, and he would draw me back with him. He chose Tchaikovsky on this occasion because my idea was melancholy, but had it been happy, he would have played Debussy or something lively; or he would do the reverse, if that were his whim, or something completely unexpected, Carly Simon or Taylor Swift.

Whatever he chose was always perfect, which is why I told him everything, even though he laughed.

He began to dance, and I joined him. It was something new, something that reminded me of one of those Petipa *pas de deux* from "Don Quixote," but original, deft, and exacting. Somehow I knew how to dance it with him. It was sad, but it was wonderful, and it was perfect.

℘

Where did this love for dance come from? When, why did I lose it, and if I lost it, why do I still yearn for it?

℘

I was sitting at the dining room table, and the grandfather clock was ticking, ticking, ticking. I was reading Polgár, but grew bored, or rather, irritated—about what, I don't know, and didn't know at the time—and stared out the window, in disgust at I know not what. The world outside seemed strangely dim. The twisting plum and apple trees, which had once intrigued my imagination, felt dull and lifeless to me, like the abortive peach trees nearby, which had never grown to maturity, in dumb resistance to the blandishments of the North Carolina climate.

I looked back at the chessboard, and in a fit of pique flicked my king over, using my middle finger and hitting it harder than I expected, so that it flew off the other end of the table. I sat back, full of this nameless irritation, and wondered whether anything would ever come from it all. Damn it, Joshua, why did you leave?

℘

Sarah, we learned to surf together and you were always better at it. I am so repelled by that crowd now, but then, things were different, we were young and the world was bright. Those summers were so full of days you felt they would never run out.

That's not all of it, though. I thought differently. Else: why did I wrote to you, *nonnumquam agentes pulchra need nova verba habere vitae*? (How is it that I didn't know how to express need!)

Why else, but that I then found the way of life of someone like Helena to be beautiful? She hung flowers and seashells in her hair, she floated through life with a thousand smiles, and knew how to join our games and make them even better. Then what turned this all to disgust instead?

Beauty is the dance finitude plays on the edge of infinity. When I discovered the Sacrum Arcanum, I discovered solitude, and its power; for when I stood with all those propositions and imperatives, that complex web of relations and entailments, the elegant structure of development toward the ideal, the Arcanum formed the hinge between the *I* and the *Me*. It gave me the strength and power to face myself in the light of whatever truth I knew, and to drink that truth back into myself—to make it iron in my will. The highest proposition, before the rise of *No Lies*, was *Truth above all.* I remember Sal saying that was his highest principle as well. How funny that is—the root of the respect we shared for one another, though we could never get along. But it was too optimistic.

The Arcanum was my own mind writ large enough for me to fit myself to it. The task required one be with oneself, and absent anyone else. It made me immensely strong. It was also as sharp as anything—with it, I could cut through circumstances and confusion. I could see the right action when there was no more distance between right and wrong than between two grains of sand. My amusement with providing mathematical reductions for games was rooted in the Arcanum, for which they were a training exercise and an application. It was incomparably higher, of course; it was truth conceived as a razor and a compass to the ideal.

But nowhere in it did it contain the thought: *Beauty is the dance of finitude upon the edge of infinity.* Except, there is another memory intruding here, I feel its ligaments reaching out, but what was it I am failing to remember? *Beauty is the dance of two mites upon the edge of infinity?* Those are not my words.

৩

I was sitting at the dining room table, and the grandfather clock was ticking, ticking, ticking. The fall leaves had not fallen, and filtered the sunlight coming into the room.

I was reading Polgár, but grew bored, or irritated—about what, I don't know, and didn't know at the time—and stared out the window, in disgust at this I know not what. The world outside seemed strangely dim, the twisting trees dull and lifeless. I looked back at the chessboard, and in a fit of pique flicked my king over with my finger.

I didn't know if I hated Joshua or myself. I would never be a dancer, never, never, I knew that. I got up, went to my room, took the whole lot of ballet DVDs and threw them in a bag. I threw my dance outfits into another, for some greater fool than myself. I gathered my Tchaikovsky CDs and threw them into the first bag. Finally, I stood over the LPs, looking at the Leonard Bernstein "Swan Lake Suite," and wondering if I dared. Could I really throw it away? In violence, I tore the act from myself, I did dare, I stuffed it into the first bag with the DVDs and CDs. Then I took the two bags out to the garage and shoved them onto the shelf where we kept outgoing stuff for Goodwill.

I went back inside and deleted the voicemail I had been saving for weeks, the one where Joshua said he was "so excited" and had been to Times Square and all that garbage. He had sent it three days before my birthday, but hadn't said boo to me since. I found his number on my phone, and brought my finger over the delete button. *Go, and be a fool by yourself*, I said to myself. I didn't know I had such fury in myself, or where it had come from, so suddenly overwhelming all my reason and self-control.

But I didn't press the button. Was that fair? Wasn't it I who kept saying the wrong thing? No, I said to myself. Don't back down. A storm of feelings flooded my chest, and in that moment I argued both sides an infinite number of times. Every thought included the conclusion that none of our conversations made sense anymore, anyway.

I deleted the entry. Irritant gone, and feeling a sort of restless peace, I lay down on the couch feeling exhausted. I took a nap. When I woke up, Sarah was coming in the door. Feeling bleary-headed, I snapped at her, though we later made up and binge watched *House of Cards*. (Mom and Dad didn't know.) But I had a terrible headache and went to bed after only our third episode.

The next day, I woke with a sense of awful loathing for life, and I reversed my actions from the day before. I added precious Joshua back to my list of contacts and brought everything back inside. I lingered over the dance outfits, held them in my hands, and touched the fabric to my face. They were divine. But, I could not convince myself that they were for me. Still, perhaps ... there was always a perhaps. I brought them back in. I couldn't imagine myself without them. The LP was one of the things I brought back inside, of course, along with all the CDs. I didn't understand how I could have imagined getting rid of them. Had I been mad?

It was then I decided that I would go to New York.

℘

I convinced my parents that letting a sixteen year old drive to New York alone was entirely reasonable. I could be very persuasive, and they trusted me, perhaps too much. It was only nine hours and change, I said, and hadn't I driven to Washington, DC already?

So off I went to the big city. However, I have never been much moved by spectacles, amusements, or immensity, and I was likewise unmoved by New York. My life has always been animated by its ideals, and at this moment, all of my ideals centered on Joshua, who was, you might say, my hope for the future—a phrase I rolled over in my mind, but to which I could put no definite meaning. Nonetheless, he was my hope for the future, and perhaps, even to this day, this is so, all the more so since the failure of the Sacrum Arcanum. When you are traveling to see your hope for the future, of course, no skyscraper, city lights, or monument can impress you. Your soul is immune to all foreign influences but the influence of that to which it has pledged itself!

The drive was extremely long, more than twice as long as the drive to Washington, and much more taxing than I had imagined. The thought of being even a minute late distressed me. Throughout that drive I continually considered this thought that Joshua was my hope for the future. To dance, you see, is to embody the ideal manifested in the music by enacting it in idealized action, and so only dancers are truly lovable. That is what I thought then, and who knows, perhaps I still think this. Only God, they say, knows the heart; I hardly know even my own, but it has always throbbed with life for dance, a throbbing that grows to world-symphonic proportions the moment Joshua steps into the room. I hadn't seen him in months, and worried that our increasingly fragmented conversations revealed that our relationship was in a trend toward disintegration. Yet one moment in his presence and I felt I would know all and, probably, everything would be whole again, perfect again, feel bliss—or whatever that completeness was that I experienced with him, it may not have a name, but be too rare for any human language to contain its name—again.

In this state of mind, I arrived in the City.

☙

I was with Joshua at a coffee shop near Washington Square Park, three blocks from the Joffrey Ballet School.

"What's it been like living here?" I asked. "The big city, the Big Apple, all that."

"Oh, it's been wonderful," he said, and spoke effusively about Times Square, Central Park, and other things I had no interest in hearing about.

"But isn't it expensive?" I said. I didn't know how to ask the questions I wanted to ask, so I asked others instead.

"Oh, gosh, yes," he said. "All my money goes to rent. Somehow I get groceries. You dance all the time, so you have to eat all the time, too, or you starve yourself. It's weird that no one has a car, but … now the weird thing is that I don't find that weird."

"Yeah," I said. "That's not weird, I mean, it's not weird that it's weird." I was drinking coffee, which I didn't normally do, but it was New York, and it made sense to me that I ought to do so. "What about the art and culture?"

"You know, I thought I'd get to see all kinds of things, but somehow, there's never time," he said. "The city is just so big, and dancing—it just takes everything to do it."

And so it went. We talked about everything but ourselves, though I was carefully reading his face all the time, and I saw nothing inward revealed. There was a knot in my stomach that was growing more uncomfortable every minute, and I was feeling sick from the coffee.

☙

I did, of course, visit the dance studio he trained in. He insisted, though I very much didn't wish to. Still, he may not have realized that it upset me to be asked; I didn't precisely say I didn't want to, and what I did say could easily have been taken to be nerves and false modesty, and so he may have felt this was exactly what I wanted; and yet nothing upset me more than this, that he was trying to make me happy by asking to do what we loved to do together. That may seem to make no sense, but any reader who knows the mood will grasp what I felt; and in any case, Joshua ought to have known I suffered from no nerves and no false modesty.

The studio itself was not really any different from the one in Greenville, except of course the dancers were better; yet one always begins with barre exercises, and those are the same everywhere. The dancers might stretch deeper or with a better line than those at home, but it was precisely in these elements that I was as strong or almost as strong as they.

Visitors were not permitted to participate in classes, but a couple words on his part and all was fine. I was impressed, almost intimidated by the atmosphere of intensity I encountered. I had no definite attitude toward the women I observed there training with Joshua; they were wonderful dancers, I was sure, but my youth introduced a distance and ambiguity between us. I did, however, watch them all with a sharp and squinting eye. I examined each dancer one by one. When my gaze fell upon one, I traced her line and judged her form, and when I judged her unworthy of being Joshua's partner, I went on to the next. Besides this, I kept careful watch in particular of every interaction that involved Joshua. I would follow these dancers after their interactions with him, too; when one of them walked away I would spy her in whatever corner of the room she occupied.

The attention I paid to those interactions! He spent more time with me than with anyone else, but I weighed the significance of the movement of a single finger, the slight turning of a head, the fraction of a second it took a dancer to go *en pointe*. No artistic director could have had a sharper eye than I did that day, but it was all for nothing, as my indefinite attitude could never be resolved into a firm judgment. And what was I looking for? Not for errors, though I certainly noted every weakness, but I honestly didn't know what I wanted to find. Perhaps I wanted an enemy with a face and body and hands against whom I could direct all my twisting, contorting passions. Perhaps I just wanted to *know* something to satiate my burning uncertainty regarding whether my friendship with Joshua still existed. Though he had insisted I come here, I felt it was I who was forcing him to bring me. So were these women clues to finding that answer? Perhaps I wanted this, though I also knew that having found such an enemy, I could not resolve anything. So much of this passion hinged upon my own agony, my inability to complete the circuit of the self, to return to myself again as the person I wished to be with the destiny I wished to possess, and what could any other dancer have to contribute to answering those uncertainties?[80]

---

80   Ed.: What is "the circuit of the self"? Elizabeth has either envisioned the self in electrical terms (as an electrical circuit, which, when broken, causes something else—an appliance, for example—not to run, or to cease running; or as a race of some kind, perhaps, in which what happens is that a runner goes out, complete the race circuit, and then returns to the starting point. In the first case, a person's self is required to empower their personality with energy, etc., or the like; or, in the second case, the self is the result of a journey from which one returns with a firm sense of one's identity.

Was I longing for evidence supporting the *negative* answer? I'm sure I did want that, but I must have also wanted an affirmation, a set of angel wings to fly away upon, and yet, past a certain point, only the negative answer will really do; once a certain *punctum crucis* is crossed, any affirmative answer lacks the firmness to resist being dissolved by the assembled forces of anxiety set up in the soul. What a funny thing despair is.

My eye was of course also on Joshua constantly, weighing every movement of his finger as well, but above all, on his face and eyes, and I could not judge what I saw there. An instructor walked by, observing dancers intently with a long finger held by her mouth. She adjusted dancers' poses ever so slightly as she walked by, doling out praise and censure. She was severe with Joshua's positioning during stretching, but when practicing the steps for *Giselle*, she exclaimed, "Joshua! You are excellent. You *live* it. Continue!" This all made me feel more ashamed, for the truth was, my own performance was quite lackluster, much worse than I could have done; and for a time after she said this, I performed at the utmost of my abilities, almost against my will. I felt so many conflicting feelings I simply could not embody the music of the dance, and so my performance quickly became flat again. I couldn't live with his perfection, since I couldn't have it. Was I jealous? But there was no one to be jealous *of.* Perhaps that was what I wanted: a dancer whom I could stare at with green eyes of jealousy, so that I could understand myself: *the jealous girl, the one he left back at home.* Without this other girl, the one I could be jealous of, what was I? I didn't know what to say.

The worst was Joshua's encouragement. He would praise me in the very moments when I knew I was performing below my own standard. He was upbeat, kind, too kind, anodyne. "You're doing fine, Betsy, just fine," he said. Didn't he see I wasn't fine? Why would he say such things unless he had given up on me? I'd rather he frown at me then give me his artificial smile, the one that piles up ambiguity. I don't want your *kindness*, Joshua. I want *you*. Your kindness can't hide that when I reached out my hand, there was only a void to grasp; you took yourself away to somewhere I can never follow.

But who can argue with necessity? It was necessity that took Joshua where he went, and necessity that barred my following after. For him to do other than he did would have marred him, and it was unthinkable to wish that for him. But it was my own necessity to go another way, to ascend a diverging stairway; I could not go the way that he had gone. Such consolations were much to me.

ↈ

Joshua shared his apartment with two roommates, Sybil and Marie. Sybil had dyed her hair black and dressed carelessly. She did everything else meticulously and took some kind of pills twice a day. She had a job as a bartender at a popular nightclub, and when I asked her what her dreams were, she said, "I want to die." She said this with a smirk, as if she were sure I didn't get the joke and were enjoying some facile sense of intellectual superiority. I pretended I didn't understand her reference to *The Waste Land* out of sheer spite.[81] It offended me that such a twit had a deeper and more complete sense of Joshua's life than I now did. Marie had hair whose color seemed trapped between red and blonde, like a rosy flame of some kind. Her face was beautiful but dreamy, and she sang enchantingly. She worked at Madison Square Garden doing something I couldn't understand.

For some reason I was sure Marie and Joshua were dating. It made me unbearably uncomfortable to see the two of them

---

81 Ed.: The poet T. S. Eliot's most famous poem, *The Waste Land*, begins with a quotation from the Latin poet Petronius, as follows: *Nam Sibyllam quidem Cumis ego ipse oculis meis vidi in ampulla pendere, et cum illi pueri dicerent:* Σίβυλλα τί θέλεις; *respondebat illa:* ἀποθανεῖν θέλω. In English, *For with my own eyes I saw the Cumaean Sibyl hanging in a jar, and when the boys said: Sibyl, what do you want? She responded: I want to die.* The Cumaean Sibyl had been granted immortality by Apollo but without eternal youth.

together. There was a coolness to their interactions that seemed to mask something else behind the surface, and she sometimes smiled at him in a way that made me feel sure I'd missed something. He was extremely kind to her and sensitive to her needs, but I felt there was something concealed or unexpressed in his words as well. However, when Joshua and I were alone, he said he didn't know what was going on with Marie, and that she kept acting like they had a secret that he didn't know. She was volatile and difficult to live with, hard to please and full of expectations she didn't communicate and was upset to find unfulfilled. He was considering moving out to get away from her. "Everyone's mad here," he said, "but it's the only place I want to live, so here I am." I didn't know if I believed him. I wanted to, so I didn't.

I fell asleep on the couch easily, but awoke in the middle of the night and tossed and turned restlessly, obsessed with the way he had handed her the saltshaker at dinner. For a whole hour I was sure he was lying to me about Marie, until suddenly it all seemed so absurd that my suspicions vanished in a puff of air. But something else was gnawing at me that I couldn't articulate and I slept with troubled dreams.

❧

On my second day in New York, I insisted that we go to Washington Square Park, famous for its many outdoor chess games and blitz matches with chess hustlers, paying a few dollars per game to the winner. It bordered The Village Chess Shop, one of those iconic New York locations more people visit to see than to buy something; naturally, a few years later, the store closed with the owner mentioning that, after forty years in business, it had "become more of a curiosity or portrait" than a viable business. I was disconcerted to realize this and to know that even if I returned to Washington Square I wouldn't find the landmark there any longer. This is all preface to mentioning that despite browsing through everything, I only bought a little knight. I got green gum on my Converses right outside, which I couldn't entirely remove from my sneakers.

But my main goal was to get to play the chess hustlers in Washington Square Park. After dragging Joshua to the Chess Shop and making him wait for me while I carefully inspected chess sets I could never afford to purchase, I brought him down to the Park. The prospect of making the fantasy real was exciting and anxiety provoking. I threw myself into it with alacrity. I sat down at the first open table I saw. The first hustler I played against was an older man with a salt and pepper beard, a flannel shirt, and shapeless vest. He had a weathered ivy cap on. He made some sort of small talk, "I don't want to just take your money, girl. You play someone like me? You could lose a lot of money." and I said something along the lines of, "I'm a gamblin' man, son." I could see that this all set Joshua on edge, as the hustler didn't look particularly safe and there were obvious addicts about. But we set to work, each player with five minutes. I had my own clock running next to his, to keep things honest, and it ticked so loudly he complained. I stared at him through narrowed eyes and asked if he had had enough or if he wanted to keep playing. He stopped complaining, but I won with a minute thirty to spare. I won the next game, too, before moving on to another hustler, a shaggy-haired blond man with an unkempt beard who seemed to have fallen on hard times, wearing threadbare clothes in style three years earlier. I lost the first match against him and won the second. In total, I played five different hustlers that day, and I won eight out of ten matches. No one tried to cheat me, but I didn't run into any of the famous hustlers like Russian Paul, Poe, or Clayton. At one point Joshua grew bored and went off for bagels, his second time that afternoon, living up to his statement that he'd been eating them constantly since coming to New York trying to get enough carbs.

As we left, thirty dollars richer, I said, "Well, I can take that one off the bucket list."

"Oh?" he said.

"I've been dreaming of doing that," I said, "but I didn't actually imagine myself winning so often. I guess I thought that the hustlers were all like grandmasters or something. They're pretty good, but they're not masters or grandmasters. I would have won only one or two games against players with ratings that high." There was an anxiety growing in me then, separate from but intertwining with everything else I was feeling. I didn't know why I had wished to do this with him, or what I had hoped from it.

"I'll take your word for it," he said, smiling. "I don't really know anything about that!" Despite my words, the thrill of victory was deeply tainted with some brooding thought, a darkness I couldn't penetrate, that left me feeling I had failed. I felt more miserable than ever.

Afterwards, we, along with some others, went out to a house in Yonkers that belonged to a friend of Joshua's where there was a party that evening.

ↄ

There is a special thrill to a film where the final scene requires the viewer to view the whole thing all over again to properly grasp the significance of its events. It is even especially powerful if this is because of a final revelation that changes the perception not only of the viewer, but the protagonist also; for this appears less manipulative, and appeals to our sympathetic connection to the protagonist. It is hard to avoid making this seem like a trick because we find it hard to believe that the protagonist could have actually missed the most crucial fact in his or her life. Of course, the truth is that for this to happen, the protagonist must have been tricking herself or himself all along, and have dragged the viewer along with the trick; and that can so strain credulity as to seem false, even risible, a kind of duplicitous sorcery.

Of course, theater and filmmaking can themselves be likened to sorcery: a good performer "holds the audience in his spell."

Audiences, as a rule, do not like to be reminded of this. The simplest method is to utilize some on-screen sorcery; audiences love "The Sixth Sense" because the trick involves magic, and they know they were fooled, but it's a ghost story, so tricks are to be expected. Yet the trick in "The Sixth Sense" really has almost nothing to do with the magic; Dr. Malcolm Crowe lives in a world with spooky rules, but there is nothing spooky about the psychology: what leads Crowe to trick himself is the exact same factor that deceives people in ordinary life. Crowe is a proud man who failed in his most essential task and who now lives as a ghost among the living, eternally reliving the failure he can't accept or comprehend. What is this but a symbol of ordinary life, life exactly as it is, made sorcerous merely to throw a softening veil over the mirror so we can more easily accept what we see?

Now, filmmaking is more like prose than like poetry; poetry, like dance, idealizes human life and grasps life in its aspirational ultimates. By tracing the lineaments of ideality in each thing, the poet reconciles every lost and alienated existence, and that is his sort of sorcery. Prose, however, is drawn to realism. Where the magic makes a difference in "The Sixth Sense" is in the idea that Crowe *gets better.* How can he get better? To have failed in what one regards as essential is not resolved by having succeeded in a separate case. Hadn't Crowe helped countless children before Cole? Those successes didn't weigh sufficiently against the failure with Vincent; why should the new one do so? The magic helps us believe that the success will allow Crowe to find peace. Suspension of disbelief bleeds out from accepting a magical physics to accepting a magical psychology.

In a film like "Shutter Island," where the same essential idea is developed but there is no magic, psychological realism triumphs. Andrew Laeddis does not get better. "Is it worse to live as a monster or to die as a good man?" Only the poet knows the way between the horns of that dilemma.

⁕

I wrote all of that as a preface to saying that although audiences may find such tricks uncomfortable, they are profoundly true; a filmmaker, however, to get our attention, relies upon guns and explosions, murders and madmen and ghosts. A thousand people die a silent death, however, to one who dies a violent one.

Every line written below cost me blood. No hard thought will limit my advance.

It was a dark dawn, cloudy and overcast. It was raining lightly. I made myself a poncho and almost got sick as I pulled it over my head, feeling sudden revulsion. My head was spinning. But why was I so ill?

When we arrived in Yonkers, I was a mess of emotions. In my ordinary way I suppose I didn't let on to any of them. For some reason we had to travel in different cars and I wasn't with Joshua, which put me out of sorts. When I arrived, he was somehow already there, along with two other dancers, an actor, and a clerk at Macy's. (Some others would come by later.) I felt a redoubled sense of my being out of place, but there was really nothing to be upset about; so I put on my best face and tried to convince myself this face was myself. I was happy, carefree, silly, as I supposed they would expect me to be. Sybil and Marie were both absent, which made this easier—and yet, later on, also much harder. I think we played some games—Twister with dancers is a more strenuous competition than the norm—and some of them began drinking and smoking weed. I didn't, though I pretended to. I'm sure I seemed idiotic. Joshua put on a piece of music by a Polish composer—Arvo Pärt?—and said to everyone, "Now this, this inspires me!" He began to flow into the music, and I was transfixed. Then the others arrived, maybe eight of them, and interrupted him. I let myself fade into the background, confused, self-controlled, disquieted. At times I played at observing what I saw, but I remember nothing because my attention was so wholly focused inward on something I knew not what.

Inside, the storm of emotions was resolving into something else, though I couldn't have said what was preparing to be born. Night fell quickly, a crisp autumn night whose coolness was refreshing, whose lingering warmth made it hard to imagine winter. I went outside and let myself feel the air, smell the leaves, absorb everything the senses could bring me. The air was refreshing after the cloying warmth of the overfull house. (A feeling I continue to utterly hate to this day.) I could hear the sounds of the party behind me, and the contrast with the peace of the night. I could make out Venus and one or two stars; the moon was behind me, a pale gibbous. I wanted to leave my body and enter the world around me. I wanted to absorb its silent peace into myself. I could hear water, somewhere, but I was disoriented and could not place what I heard or where it lay in relation to me.

For a moment I grasped the scent of something wonderful and lost myself in it. I merely breathed, drawing the scent in, and willing myself to pass into its world to join it. However, I couldn't stay outside indefinitely. Even then I grasped the importance of strength and knew that one must be steel inside or lose one's chances in the tumult of time. So I returned. Inside, I found an acceptable chessboard, and after taking a seat in the corner at the dining room table I set up a problem from Judit Polgár that I had been working through when I left, one of her devious and delicious traps. This drew some curiosity, and when people understood what it was—a situation in which Black seemed to have the advantage, and the problem was to see how White could nonetheless pull out a devastating reversal—several people tried to supply possible solutions. These were as a rule either very poor moves or moves I had already considered and rejected, and in each case, I explained why the move wouldn't succeed. This earned me respectful curiosity.

"But what's the right move?" Joshua asked.

I often played the most crucial stretches of Polgár's games out for myself, move by move, before studying her actual solution to the problems posed by the situation, and I had not yet looked ahead to see what she had actually done here. However, it now came to me in a flash that the correct move was Bxd5 (which it turns out is the move she did make; how exact this memory is, whereas everything else about this night is wrapped in such murk and requires so much effort to excavate), and I showed this on the board. It was pointed out that Black easily captures the bishop that took its pawn, a *prima facie* poor trade, but I then demonstrated how superior White's new position was and how quickly it could force checkmate.

Most spectators' curiosity was exhausted before the explanation was complete, and soon I was again almost alone in my corner at the table. Joshua was greeting some new visitor to the house and an awkward young man came over to play with me. He was not completely hopeless. While we were still in the opening, Joshua came back over to me.

"That was great, Elizabeth," he said. "I mean the Park, too."

"I've been practicing," I said, "training, I guess, really."

"How fun!" he said, oddly. "Wouldn't it be really cool if you became a famous chess player like Polgár?"

I stared at him, searchingly looking into his eyes, those dark, inscrutable eyes for whose depths I yearned. "Yes," I said.

"That's great," he said, again. He laughed, turned away, and began remonstrating with crowd about their poor taste in music. "God, this is worthless! What are you thinking?"

"What's wrong with it?" someone said.

Everything, you fools! (My thought.)

"Everything," he said, and put on *Sound of Silver.* Once again he was flowing into the music, into it, into it, leaving me in the corner where I'd trapped myself with this awkward boy. I'm sure he took the fact that I was playing chess with him as a sign of potential interest. I couldn't concentrate on the game, but it didn't require my full concentration to eventually overcome his defenses and defeat him. Joshua told some girl how gracefully she danced, but it wasn't so; she was not going to amount to anything. I didn't begrudge him those words. He wasn't trying to flatter her, flirt with her, get into her pants—though I don't know if I would have begrudged him that, either, what was it to me if he did any of those things? Could she have taken what I wanted from him? Perhaps to answer that I should have had to know what I wanted, which I perhaps never knew and still don't know, but jealousy is a funny thing; I am sure someone can turn green-eyed and look sideways even at an armchair, for my jealousy has always been that absurd. It produces no tearful rages or blistering demands, but operates within the icy glacier of my lowermost heart, and what rages and hatreds I have known that never spoke a word! The dancing always dispelled these storms; when we danced, it was as if they had been annihilated in the past and had never existed at all. In this instance, however, what jealousy could there be? I knew he was simply being kind, ever so kind, to make her feel better about herself. So very, very kind, he was always so damned kind. Damn him, damn his laugh, damn his kindness. I forced checkmate and when the boy left, I remained seated for a minute, and then left the room. For so long did my steel last.

I went to the room where I was going to sleep and wrapped myself in a blanket. For a long time, I didn't do anything. Finally, I pulled out the *Swan Lake* LP, my most precious possession. I ran my hands over it lovingly. I had come with the intention of giving it to him, with the intention of freeing him—freeing him from my expectations, my clutchings, my curses, and I would free him the only way I knew how. I would give him the LP. I knew how he felt about the ballet, his superstitious fear of Odile. But, God, it was *Swan Lake*, blessed with Tchaikovsky's incomparable score, blessed with the loving embodiments of its music and motion by generation after generation of dancers. And I loved it. That was what mattered. I loved it, and I wanted him to have it. It had made me happy just to imagine being his greatest little fan, with him holding it and remembering me. Then I could free him, and it. I would be content knowing there was just a bit of me in his life.

I didn't know what to make of these thoughts. Finally, I turned out the light, and I went to sleep.

☙

I woke early that morning, before sunrise. The birds were singing and I had left my window open. I got up silently and, putting something on, went out on the porch. The crispness of the night before had become harsh and sharp. It was a dark, dusky dawn, overcast and pregnant with the chill of winter. I couldn't help remembering what had happened the day before yesterday.

After dance practice, we had made a stop at a bagel place before going up to Yonkers. "I can't believe how many bagels I eat these days," Joshua said. "There's so much dancing, though, and you've got to keep taking in the carbs to keep going." The people working at the bagel shop seemed familiar with him, and I guessed he must come here often. They offered speciality items, bagel sandwiches of various kinds, but he had a simple sesame bagel with cream cheese and I chose something similarly plain.

I wanted to say something to overcome the uncomfortable tension I felt in the air. The tension didn't exactly seem to be *between* us; it was something else, an unnamable absence or a spectral presence. He was joking about something, perhaps he sensed something amiss and was seeking to create levity; yet, this attempt at lightness was deeply disquieting to me. "Do you remember what you said that one time?" I asked.

"What do you mean?" he said.

"Beauty is the dance of two mites on the edge of infinity," I said, almost in a rush. The words were thick in my mouth and hard to bring out.

"Oh," he said. He was chewing his food. "When did I say that?"

"Summer two years ago," I said.

"Was that when I went out with you to the Outer Banks?" he said.

"Yes, we were out on that spit near Hatteras," I said. "You had the Wrangler, remember…"

"You know that place a lot better than I do," he said, laughing. "I actually sold the Wrangler. It wasn't much use in the city."

"Okay," I said, "but what did you mean when you said that, that beauty is the dance of two mites on the edge of infinitude?" I asked, giving him another chance to answer. *Please*, I was saying, and there was something half-alive inside me reaching out for its mother, brother, father, friend.

Now, this moment is crucial, but I don't know what to make of some of its features. I have considered it many times and, though I have understood it a certain way for many years, it now seems to me that I may have missed something in it, that all those years I misunderstood the significance of Joshua's look, the motion he made with his hand. More than anything else, my understanding of his meaning determined what I did when I left two days later, and if I misunderstood, I don't know what to think.

"Oh," he said. His hand was moving sort of nervously, in a way that was quite uncharacteristic of him, for whom movement was so purposeful. He didn't meet my eyes, and looked out the window at something. "I guess I really don't know."

Sometimes, the refusal to commit to saying something definite is as pregnant with meaning as any particular statement could be, or even more so, because of how it lets the meaning be born without an echo in the mind of the listener, like an echo without a source. What matters is the context, the passion refused or accepted, in making or refusing to make a statement. Refusing to commit to a clearly offered meaning, a meaning that invites personal commitment, means something very definite: a refusal of personal commitment. I have always understood him to have meant: *I know what you took that to mean, and I didn't mean that, but it would be cruel to say that—please understand.* Yet, was that what he meant when he looked out the window? Was that to spare my feelings? I saw some kind of pain flash by on his face. Was that pain his discomfort over sparing my feelings, or something else? He had often looked out the window in that way, even when he didn't know I was looking; and always, the hint of some private preoccupation or grief, suffering. Absorbed in my own pain, I drew all of these impressions around myself, and understood everything on that basis.

Today I wonder, and yet to wonder is to invite peril! The smallest doubt of this has already awakened feelings I can't perhaps control at all, and that threaten to drive me mad. What began with letting him out of the little shrine I kept him in in my mind may have led me to entertain thoughts I want too much to be true; and to think them now, of all times, when I hardly know whether I will live at all! But moreover how can I move from the thought of wishing to confess to him, which was already quite a daring thought, to the thought of wishing to be friends again? If he will even be willing to do so. It was I who left him, after all, on that day ... But that is assuming I am right to reopen these thoughts, for perhaps it was my younger self who was right in thinking that it was really he who left, and whose kindness kept me in a kind of sheltered orbit, never to again occupy the idyllic landscapes of his heart, his life. To wonder whether I was wrong is to wonder whether some seed of our relationship still endured that might yet be reborn and grow into something wonderful again. When I think this, I almost can't breathe for hope, as if a vast magnetism is drawing me inward on myself, and I don't know whether I can survive the thought that I, I who killed Sarah, could ever again have happiness in my life; and that is what it would mean to have Joshua again, in whatever way he would let me have him. In that thought, I crumple. What if he *didn't* mean "I know what you took that to mean, and I wish to spare you the pain of denying it"—what if, into that ambiguity, I had projected all my own anxieties and grief, and assumed he must be speaking in relation to it?

This is all a distraction. To wonder if I was wrong is not to wonder if I can hope again, but to wonder if I am guilty of yet another mistake, precursor to all the harm I did to Sarah. What I did spoke to him, as well, and may not have meant at all what I thought he'd take it to mean. But in that past moment, I stood on the porch, in the gray, dusky dawn. I again held the *Swan Lake* record in my hands, and again ran my hands over it lovingly. I could not free him as I had imagined, for to free him was to lay a claim to him, I saw that now; to do what I intended would mark him forever as *mine*. Giving him the record would give my jealousy the final say in our relationship (assuming, that is, that there was still a relationship). I sometimes had the thought of seeking out a boyfriend simply to make *him* jealous, which was also absurd, and in fact, I was always abysmally unsuccessful in dating; the image of Joshua always operated between me and any potential boyfriend, and by comparison, the boys I knew were all too awkward and dull. Sal, of course, had been an exception to that generalization; whereas the other boys had been like flickering lights next to Joshua's sun, Sal had been like a neutron star, whose infinite inward density set him apart, but I had another reason for not being interested in him, and in any case, he wasn't Joshua....

Well, this simpering has gone on long enough. What self-pitying introspection I have been wallowing in. High time to steel myself and drive in the nail.

I stood on the porch and watched that dusky dawn, the rain falling like flecks of deadening darkness, light as a feather but suffocating in their expanse. I didn't know what I felt, but there was a moment in which I grasped that I had no life with Joshua, that this had been a fantasy. I didn't think that it had been that common thing, a friendship of childhood that couldn't survive adulthood, for I was sure it had possessed something beyond that. What it had possessed, however, it retained no longer. The turmoil and confused agony relaxed, as I finally released whatever fingers were still grasping for him in my heart. The disgust I felt with myself eased into something else, something heavier that fell into the pool of my heart and sank to the bottom.

I went back inside and found Joshua where he was sleeping. My mind dreamed thoughts of him living a beautiful life and I prayed, one of the few times I have in my life, that he would live this beautiful life, even though it would be without me. I sat and watched him for some time, not counting the minutes but just contemplating his face, and finally, not wanting to lose my nerve, I quickly wrote a note for him in which I thanked him and said goodbye. I had told him I would leave this morning, but there was no reason I was leaving even before the sun rose except that I simply couldn't face the pain of spending more time with him and having it be like this. I felt I would break down if we continued. I could not live anchored in his harbor, never to come back to shore. I would have to find my own harbor and my own land. I bent over him, kissed him on the cheek, and gently placed the note within his hand. I walked out into the rain, started the car, and began the drive home.

ఌ

What had happened to the *Swan Lake* LP?

When I found the record in Sarah's apartment, I found the room spinning around me, unable to process what I was recovering within my mind. I didn't grasp how she could have had it in her possession, but it was not this thought that disturbed me most; rather, there was a nameless something that seemed most alarming, and which the simple presence of the record invoked. It drew spectral images of the past to my mind which didn't, however, resolve into anything firm or certain; it was like I had, while walking familiar grounds, found an invisible wall I had somehow never discovered before. One does not know what to be most disturbed by:

that such a wall exists; that one had missed it despite its presence in one's own most familiar haunts; or the anxiety regarding what, behind its secret barricades, one might find—all of these thoughts were upon me at once, and I leaned against the doorframe to catch myself, and fell like a deadweight into a nearby chair, sitting there for what seemed minutes unsure what was called for, or if there was even anything to think about; the more I rehearsed the facts, the less I felt I had to fear, for there seemed to be nothing especially odd in anything, except, of course, each time I returned my glance to her bed. The thought of her holding the record would set me dizzy all over again, and each time I knew I was in the presence of the wall. Not knowing what else to do, I made her bed, and then realized I ought to strip it instead, and did that.

When I left, I thought no more of it and had again forgotten all about the record until the second blow arrived. That was when Aunt Helena gave me the letter Sarah had sent her, which had again forced me to reconsider the record and how it could have found its way to her. This mystery, unlike the spectral disturbance I had experienced in Sarah's apartment, had a much more specific content. This specific content, however, belonged to what was behind that invisible wall, and its appearance opened a hole in that wall that began to allow other memories to newly appear, or to appear in a new light; and in the wake of Sarah's death and its grief, I drowned in confused misery, aware only that I had somehow done something very wrong, but unaware what it was.

I had not forgotten New York, but I had forgotten bringing the *Swan Lake* LP with me, forgotten holding it on that porch and stroking it with my hand; forgotten my intention to give it to Joshua; forgotten rescinding this intention; and in a final act of forgetting, had forgotten forgetting it in the car when I returned. For, as if having planned to forget, I had placed the LP in the back of the hatchback, but the rest of my luggage in the passenger seat. (It occurs to me now that I don't know what happened to the little knight I purchased at the Chess Shop; had it been in the back, too, or did it fall into some crevice?) When I went inside I naturally took only my luggage. Aunt Helena, of course, later came for Thanksgiving, and had borrowed the car until after Christmas, driving up and down the coast visiting her friends from Virginia to Florida. Within that time frame (prior to Thanksgiving even) I had discovered the Sacrum Arcanum, had fallen ill, had grown strong, had made my soul equal parts steel and crystal; and from that point until I entered Sarah's apartment, I never thought of the LP, or my intention to give it to Joshua, or what had happened to change my mind from doing so.

♍

I spoke with Simon about the friend, though not exactly as I have put these things above. There were long stretches when he said very little, although at points he asked very pointed questions. He seemed subtly preoccupied yet also attentive. When I had finished, he said, almost smiling, "Ah, yes—the friend." And I said, "If only the friend appeared in the that first moment, the instant you stood upon the dais, and you could support yourself with his hand—but here is the problem, and I am sure this is why Niakani gave up, it is that by the time the friend appears, you are already in the wrong, and he can't get down deep enough into you to pull out the anchor you sank in the wrong place.

"So you do not think that the friend, or the self-making passion, can redeem someone?"

"No," I said.

"But you do believe that it reveals the pattern for you, by which you could cinch up the self?"

"That's a funny way of putting it! Yes, in principle," I said.

"But not in reality," he said.

"No, not in reality, because the piercing of the heart is distorted, just as everything else is, by the false steps already taken. So what the friend reveals most clearly is not the pattern, but the false step. Yes, that I do believe. When the heart is pierced, and that perfect pattern goes down, down, into your heart, the blood that comes back up, the blood you will write your life in, that blood contains this dark, mangled thing, your false step, so that your whole life, you will never stop writing it down, dimly conscious of who you should have been, but most aware of this grotesquery in you that prevented you from realizing the principle of joy you had been given."

"I see," said Simon. "Perhaps that is indeed why Niakani had to stop writing."

"That is why I say it all hinges upon the possibility of a second infinitization, a reopening of possibilities for the self."

"I think Niakani believed in a second infinitization."

"Then why did he stop?" I said.

"Perhaps he discovered an insoluble problem in such a thing, of the kind I mentioned yesterday," said Simon. "Or perhaps he didn't fully grasp the essence of the problem."

"What do you mean?" I asked.

Simon was just quiet for a long time. I was trying to see through this maze of traps he was constructing on the board, to see what his goals were and how I could attack him, but I could not easily penetrate the depths of his interlaced defenses. I felt I was somehow being led astray precisely by my memory of the player he had been. This was interfering with seeing the board as it really was, and hindering me from adapting to the kind of player he was now. I played the cautious g3.

"You did not exactly explain the problem you mentioned in the beginning," said Simon, "the bit about being unable to avoid going wrong."

"That's the thing," I said. "I have the idea of the mirror and the ideal, and yet, it seems I cannot possibly grasp the pattern. The task of finitizing leaves me in perplexities I cannot escape; either I exclude the capacity for awe, and then everything proceeds easily, but the result is subhuman—ugly; or I include it, and then I become lost in perplexities I cannot solve regarding the inclusion of an indefinable element."[82]

"Well," said Simon, "perhaps the problem is different. Perhaps it is rather that melancholy itself is often inexplicable. One is held back from the ideal for reasons one cannot identify, and one becomes all the more melancholy for being unsure of the cause." He moved his knight to the center of the board, unaccountably exposed. This was when I noticed that he was playing much like Sal.

---

82 Ed.: There is something inexplicable in this explanation, which invokes ideas regarding the capacity for awe, and its relation to indefinability, not explained anywhere else in the notebook as if they were immediately familiar. Below is an attempt to understand what she means in this statement (perhaps drawn from final form of the Sacrum Arcanum):

Every individual begins as a bundle of properties—"finitude"—and has the task of bringing these into a condition of "unity, completeness, and harmony" through a process of self-conscious development she calls "finitizing." But literature is filled with attempts to depict "wholehearted" characters who are nonetheless mysterious in their inability to recognize or respond to anything transcendent (Diderot's Rameau's nephew, Dostoevsky's Svidrigailov or Smerdyakov, Cormac McCarthy's Chigurh). Perhaps, then, Elizabeth had an idea like the following: what such individuals lack is a proper human capacity for awe—the bowing down of the soul before something it recognizes as human-surpassing. But then she may have also been convinced that the "awe-inspiring" was somehow inherently indefinable, and this indefinability may have made it impossible to spell out this process of development ahead of time, or brought in an inescapable element of terror or an ineliminable possibility of error. This may have been the very way that "the friend" was supposed to help: to calm the terror and prevent the error. Then, perhaps Elizabeth felt that "the friend," rather than resolving the problems associated with the finitizing process, only increased the perplexities associated with it; for this very indefinability might seem to increase the probability that one will be unable to keep upon the same axis as the friend.

GOLDEN SLIVERS

Time present and time past
Are both perhaps present in time future,
And time future contained in time past.
If all time is eternally present
All time is unredeemable.
What might have been is an abstraction
Remaining a perpetual possibility
Only in a world of speculation.
What might have been and what has been
Point to one end, which is always present.
Footfalls echo in the memory
Down the passage which we did not take
Towards the door we never opened
Into the rose-garden.
              T. S. Eliot, Burnt Norton

I was staring at the board, and when I looked up, Simon's face seemed strange, as if his hair were glowing, or rather, turning almost white in the light. I shook my head, trying to clear it of memory. I ran my fingers through my hair and ended tying it behind my head in a makeshift bun. I moved my knight and placed it on e6, behind Simon's lines, supported on the diagonal by my bishop.

❦

I sat with Sal at the cafe, carefully observing his strategy. We always struggled to obtain a decisive advantage against each other, and in most of our games the victor won a narrow victory. I had won against Sal as much as I lost. I was playing White and, typical for myself at this age, had sacrificed material for a positional advantage I intended to use for a brilliant unexpected combination. I was sure I knew what he was up to but manifested an air of indifference.

"What do you think of all of these?" he said, waving his hand to indicate the people walking by outside the cafe.

"What do you mean?" I asked.

"What do you think about all the beach bums in this town?" he said.

"I don't think about them at all," I said.

"Exactly," said Sal. "And they don't think at all. *Res extensa sine re cogitante.*"[83]

"You're trying to trick me into giving away something. It won't work."

"No, no," he said, "I'm being serious, almost serious. Humor is the boundary line between the specious and genuine insight."

Sometimes, Sal took to these talkative moods and would verbally prance about, and one could hardly shut him up. It betrayed something anxious in his thought, though he never expressed the content of this anxiety. I said nothing, but continued to watch him, occasionally almost glancing at his rook, as if I were secretly nervous about his plans for it.

---

83 Ed.: "An extended thing without the thinking thing." Sal is making a riff on Descartes' distinction between material substances (*res extensa*: extended thing) and minds (*res cogitans*: thinking thing), which he regarded as immaterial.

He continued to stare out the window. "God, they are such insects," he said. "How else can you explain their behavior? Here we are, next to this magnificent thing, this *ocean*, something so powerful and inspiring it will put a genius about his task, and what do they do? They flit about like flies on a corpse, seeking whatever momentary sustenance they can find, resting in the dying warmth of their expiring lives. It's as if the greatness of it overwhelms them so much they are reduced to living as somnambulants." He spoke angrily, but his mouth betrayed a certain tension, and I saw pain in his eyes.

At this point, Sal paused, seeming to very much want me to respond, to acknowledge some secret in what he spoke. I said nothing.

"You're cagey," he said, "but I know you agree with me. Human beings can't live without the ideal, greatness, grandeur, whatever you want to call it ... what the Greeks called the *kalon*. The problem with the true criminal—I mean, with the career criminal, this petty being—is not that he's an immoralist but that he is subhuman in his lack of relation to the truly human things. I can tolerate and even approve a criminal who retains his relation to the ideal. I mean, isn't that why we admire great conquerors like Alexander or Napoleon, because they still have this hunger in them? That's what I liked about Ahab, you know, whaleman that he was, he still had it. Whereas that's not at all the case of more boring types, who are like these somnambulants, living without being alive. Everyone admires Milton's Satan, because he has greatness in him, but no one admires an imp like Smerdyakov ... one just steps on him, on his tail, kicks him aside. Or does one have one's own tail stepped on?" he concluded strangely, out of keeping with the initial discourse. His eyes refused to settle on anything in particular, as if he were looking for something he had lost, and then he moved his rook.

"I don't even want to argue with these people, if they happen to be clever, because what would it lead to? You can't argue with Smerdyakov, it's pointless, he's missing the necessary component..." said Sal, even now seeming to stare at something in the middle distance.

I moved my b2 pawn, and his mouth tightened. "Mate in five," I said, "or your queen in three."

෴

I began adjusting my play accordingly, as if it were Sal before me, and not Simon. I realized that, if he had been trying to understand Sal, he would have studied how he played and looked for the sensibility behind that suffocating maze of traps Sal liked to draw his opponents into. Only, the strategy was not quite Sal's, it was a kind of mixture of two styles in which Sal's was sometimes predominant.

Simon was silent for a time. Finally he made a little, unexpected move, and said, "Your argument raises an intriguing line of thought, but is missing its primary category."

"Oh?" I said. "What do you mean?"

"You speak of the irreversible misstep, but it is not clearly defined," he said. "Moreover, I think it mixes together two different thoughts about how we go wrong ... at least, this is where the metaphor of the tightrope walker pushes us, to a view in which the danger is that we will, somehow, not even knowing what we are doing, misstep, and ruin our life, along with that of anyone sufficiently entangled in it."

"Is that thought mistaken?" I said.

"It is missing a very important idea," said Simon. "Loss of self."

"I don't know what you mean," I said. My mind went back to that old discussion with Sal about keeping oneself, but the concept of loss I had used then didn't seem related to our present discussion. Besides, Simon wouldn't know of that idea. Or would he?

"The idea is not widely appreciated or understood," said Simon. "It occurs when the pain of developing the self becomes too overwhelming to be endured. To grasp it, we need to return to what you said about relational discordance—when the goal, as it is perceived by you and by the friend, breaks down. What makes this experience so difficult?"

"That you must lose the friend, lose the goal, in any case, lose the ideal," I said. "And, whatever you do, the self will disintegrate."

"Because these things turn the self against itself," he said. "Your commitment to them is unqualified, fundamental in your sense, they lie at the root of your concerns. So discordance among them produces the self-destructive dynamic described by your Niakani."

"You mean 'the crisis,'" I said.

"Niakani seems to suppose that what comes from the crisis will be a conscious choice of some kind," said Simon. "But, having further considered the matter, I think that is too limited a view. Niakani senses something of this in Kierkegaard, whose resignation knows too much to be the innocent resignation of Socrates or Dante, but doesn't consider what happens when the crisis lingers. For if the crisis lingers there is not this moment of pure 'infinitization,' as you would put it, when the self breaks open and the person faces this terrible opening of possibilities. No, that's a rare moment, indeed. What happens instead, if the crisis lingers, is that it becomes submerged and sinks into the person's mental background. The pain itself keeps it there, for to think the crisis is more painful than anything. To choose, in the manner described by Niakani, is a horror; too much hangs upon the choice, and the will, besides, has too little leverage over the outcome. To let it linger beneath the horizon at least allows life to be carried on in an ordinary fashion."

"I understand," I said.

"But even submerged, the crisis continues to operate with its disintegrative power, unwinding what the person has wound together," he said.

"What do you mean?"

"The crisis indicates that certain elements of the self cannot be harmonized with each other, but also cannot be eliminated. Correct?"

"Yes," I said.

"Can the crisis remain submerged if these elements come into contact?" he said.

"No, if the conflicting elements touch, it would be like an electric shock," I said.

"Then, to keep the crisis submerged would require isolating elements of the self—containing them, somehow," he said.

"And what would such containment look like?" I asked.

"First of all, since the submersion is more of a happening than an intention, a person would not immediately engage in such containment. So they would experience these shocks of sudden, sharp awareness several times, when the contradictory elements are brought into proximate juxtaposition. But from this series of shocks would come the key intention—a resolution to prevent the proximity from which the shock arises. This would be after allowing the crisis to become submerged, you understand; the intention therefore does not explicitly aim at resolving the crisis, only at escaping anguish. Nonetheless, the intention does imply, or rather, entail a kind of resolution to the crisis."

"What do you mean?" I said.

"*Willing* the containment of the offending parties means," he said, "also willing the continued submersion of the crisis; for the containment can persist only if it is kept below the surface and not consciously considered."

"I see," I said.

"The complication is that although the person's intention to contain is also an intention to submerge the crisis, the intention does not contain that description; if it did, we would face a different psychological configuration, as the person would be far more conscious of the submersion."

"I accept the distinction," I said. "How does *this* configuration develop?"

"The person wills submersion under the description of containment, but this requires the person not be conscious of submersion as their end. However, the crisis acts as an aversive motive—do you understand?" he said.

"You mean, the crisis provides a motive for action through aversive prods away from its object?" I said. "I suppose that is right, but since the crisis makes a prod in the opposite direction, as aversion, it functions very poorly."

"That is exactly why submersion answers the moment," said Simon. "When every direction is prod in another—then the only way to win, it might seem, would be avoid playing the game."

"Hmmm," I said.

"Let the crisis disappear for a while, for a day, a week, a month ... this may not be the explicit aim of the person, but what answers an aversive need need not be chosen under its own description. What is chosen is peace of mind," said Simon. "Only, the peace is an illusion."

"Yes," I said.

"Remember the terms of the crisis," said Simon. "The condition of the crisis is that someone has, first of all, found the pattern whereby the self could be sewn up and made whole, the melody in which every part is harmonized. The crisis postdates this discovery, and it involves a conflict within the self, in which it is the pattern itself that is embroiled in a struggle with one of the elements of the self. Yet, this element of the self cannot be cast aside, as it is the ground and conduit of the pattern. So you see, to leave this conflict submerged cannot result in peace."

"Because it means you've abandoned the pattern of the self," I said.

"That's right; and to have found the way you fit together, and to have left it behind, is to be in a state of disintegration, or, as Kierkegaard put it, impotent self-consumption," said Simon. "For as long as you wish the pattern submerged, you wish the self away; you wish for another self."[84]

---

84 Ed.: Søren Kierkegaard, *The Sickness unto Death*, trans. and ed. by Howard V. and Edna H. Hong (Princeton, NJ: Princeton University Press, 1980), p. 18.

"There is something that doesn't quite make sense about this," I said. "Seeking a new self is inconsistent with not knowing, not being conscious of, the submersion of the crisis and the old pattern."

"Is that what you think?" said Simon.

My head hurt. "I don't know."

❧

It occurs to me that this notebook is likely to be found without me. I wonder what will come of it? Will it be picked up by someone and hoarded, like the one that Sal kept? He often carried this notebook on his person, and he studied it carefully; I had a chance to look inside it once, and saw it was filled with spidery writing by someone or other, as well as copious notes in Sal's own hand—the first in black ink, universally, the second usually in blue and occasionally in red—marking and remarking what was already there. When asked where he had found it, he remarked: "Brooklyn, once." Then he smiled a kind of secret smile, the first time I saw his face genuinely lit with enjoyment, but there was something in the look that repulsed you, like the look of an unhealthy craving.

The notebook was just one of the things that stood out about Sal. He was three or four years older than the rest of us and, while he was certainly bright, there are many bright students, but he also had a distance I noticed at once, as if what he were thinking were never commensurate with what he said. He clearly kept back a secret of some kind, something essential to understanding him, and this secret both required and allowed him to be content with constant misunderstanding and disjointed connections with others. Some thought him aloof, arrogant, and far too full of himself. No doubt they were right, but those judgments all missed the fact of the secret.

The notebook was connected to the secret, somehow. He'd obtained it in some dusty bookstore in Brooklyn, where it had become mixed in with a number of other books—on psychology or criminology or related subjects. This was during his years out of school, for he had been kicked out of NYU over some kind of scandal, which his mother's money helped keep secret; it was then he made a determination to break off all ties of dependence on her, to make a life for himself. He made up his mind not to leave New York, though this meant he lived a very private, pennypinching life for three years. When he finally obtained enough independence to satisfy himself, he returned to North Carolina.

"What's in that notebook?" I asked him once, when we were playing against each other.

He stared at me for a long time, and finally said, "A true history of the human soul."

"That's why it's so valuable to you?"

"More valuable than anything," he said. "Only, I think it has a flaw."

"Which you'll expose?" I said.

"Which I will solve," he said. I wonder if he did.

❧

"The truth," said Simon, "is that the person feels the loss of the pattern as a void, a kind of hole through which the tidal forces of life enter and exit, disturbing him. He ought to have some integrated way of responding to events, life's pricks and pulls upon him, but, having submerged the pattern, he does not. These events may impact his various concerns in all kinds of ways, and the lack of a pattern will be felt. That void will therefore generate anxiety, a sense of nameless foreboding about the possibilities of the future, that must be filled with something."

"So the person does not, again, explicitly conceive of herself as seeking out some new pattern," I said.

"No," said Simon.

"Instead, she will see herself as merely settling an anxiety or uncertainty in herself," I said.

"Yes," said Simon. "For anxiety, unlike fear or desire, is not fixed upon a specific object as its answer; anxiety is attention to an indefinite multiplicity of possibilities in which the self has an uncertain future, and its answer is to resolve those possibilities into something fixed. So anxiety is associated with freedom; the more choices someone has, the more uncertainty over which choice to make, and the more these choices will impact that person, the greater the anxiety; and likewise, the more one's self is subject to the freedom of another, the more anxiety. So these disturbances, and the foreboding they create, need a something, but not a specific thing."

"But don't they need the pattern?" I said.

"Well, yes, that's so," he said. "But the pattern has been contained, so it can't to its integrative work. For if it could touch all parts of the person, which is required for it to do its work, then it could touch the subject which drove the crisis."

"I see," I said. "So the self begins unwinding, now; there is too much slack."

"The person needs a new pattern, then," said Simon, "something that emerges from the elements of the person, imposes order upon those elements, and projects the person into the future."

"It needs to be the pattern," I said, "but not be the pattern."

"This matter has been very little studied," said Simon. "So I must speculate here, unfortunately—with some body of material, but not enough perspective, I fear, to bring the material to a state of completion. The new pattern must have two qualities. It must integrate the elements of the person. And it must make the person forget the old pattern."

"But isn't the first going to be impossible?" I said.

"You mean, because only the pattern could do that?" said Simon.

"Because the first pattern has already been integrated into the person," I said.

"That is relevant," he said. "The new pattern will have to somehow integrate the old pattern into itself, as one more element among the others."

"But that's going to produce a contradictory state," I said. "A pattern is like a master factor in the self, with the right to

THE HURRICANE NOTEBOOK 313

condition everything else a person is and contains. You can't have two patterns."

"Can't you?" said Simon.

"I mean, you can't have two of them, and keep yourself whole."

"Now, that does seem right," said Simon. "No, you will not keep whole."

"So the new pattern is a time bomb," I said.

"So it seems," he said.

"But then what do you mean, the new pattern will take the old one as material?"

"Well, that is the hardest thing to think about," said Simon. He seemed to be intent, striving to remember something.

For a minute, we sat in silence, and we made some apparently meaningless moves on the board. But finally, I spoke. "I remember something Niakani said."

"Oh?" said Simon, looking up at me.

"He said something about the pattern, and the self-making passion, being like a gift ... an unexpected breaking through of grace," I said.

"Yes," said Simon.

"Then the new pattern will be different," I said. "It will emerge from oneself, so it will not be a gift," I said.

"No," he said. "It will emerge, you might say, from a darker place ... from some will for self."

"You might say, from that 'awful essence' of man," I said.

Simon started, and looked at me strangely. "Now, why do you say that?" he said.

"It's from *Moby-Dick*," I said. "When Ishmael has to describe the root of Ahab's madness. He describes how the conflict with the white whale, who ate Ahab's leg and nearly killed him, provided Ahab with a monomaniacal focus and self-organization— so that all he was became aimed at one goal, a confused goal in which physical and spiritual harm intermingled with one another to produce his single purpose of revenge. But, beneath all of

this—Ishmael says that there is some other element to his madness, the 'awful essence' we all share, the root of human grandeur
and human madness. In the Halls of Thermes, the natural water,
the natural infinitude, we contain in ourselves…"[85]

"Now that is something," he said. "I had forgotten… It would
have made a difference, too." His face appeared troubled.

"Perhaps I do understand. It's this awful essence that has us longing for grace," I said, "because those dark caverns of the self exist
only for safety and death. Whatever beauty arises from those parts,
arises to leave them and to stretch past them, toward heaven. Only,
no one can stretch out without setting her feet somewhere, and
even if a dancer can make you believe she flies and glides, she does
not; she too has her feet down in those catacombs. Thus, Niakani's
experience of grace is not our reaching up for heaven—it's heaven's
reaching down for us, an unrivaled miracle, just as Niakani said. But
that's what this new pattern has all wrong. It's the pattern we give
ourselves. Once we've sunk that other pattern down into the pools of
those catacombs, something eventually comes back up. It looks new
and fine to us, even if it has this mouldering air about it, for it meets
the need we have. The pattern, subject to my own will."

"A suggestive phrase," he said. "Yes, so there is a new pattern,
to help ease the anxiety, to cover over the gaps, and it includes the
old pattern in it, somehow, but subjected to the rule of self, and
this covered over, somehow … well, yes … specifically, you have a
problem because the true pattern involved openness to the world,
a promise of connection, and this would reduce that openness by
subjecting whatever it was that called you into being to your will,
or achieving your freedom from your connection to it, some kind
of independence for yourself. But, there's a more serious problem
than this. The new pattern acts as an integrating factor."

---

85   Ed.: The "Halls of Thermes" are the ruins of Roman baths beneath the Hôtel de
Cluny in Paris, now a museum. Melville, in *Moby-Dick,* uses the "halls of thermes" as a
symbol of humanity's buried, hidden essence.

"The first part is what I've come to understand," I said. "If the pattern is being written *into you* through your relationship with something else, someone else, then this will to self is a will to control what it is that is writing into you. But you can't have it both ways: direction of fit can be self-to-object, or object-to-self, but it can't be both.[86] The moment you bring in this new pattern you've made it self-to-object. You are writing your own pattern on the materials at hand. But why do you mention the fact that it is an integrating factor as a problem?"

"Because once the new pattern has been adopted, it conditions your thinking," he said. "It is a kind of madness. It requires a practical contradiction in your identity, and must erase the power of the old one while retaining its appearance. Prior to that moment, when you lose yourself, you can remember everything—afterwards, you cannot remember things, whatever it is you must not remember, or else become aware of the conflicts between the integrating patterns. In that way, your life appears seamless, as if your life were the single progression or development of a single set of goals, values, and aspirations, rather than the jagged discord of the pattern, the crisis, and the subsequent reintegration."

"Really?" I said. "That sounds pretty strange."

"It is strange."

"How do you know that is what happens?" I said.

"This new pattern, of course, has a constraining power—it has a force of its own, a force alienated from the person's own powers—and the person may experience that," said Simon. "He may feel heavily bound to something, he knows not what. This force is dependent, I am sure, on the force of that intention of containment—its ongoing life, as it were."

---

86 Ed.: This seems to be an extrapolation of a distinction operative in contemporary philosophy of mind, called "direction of fit," between mental states that are "mind-to-world" and those that are "world-to-mind." The main example of "mind-to-world" fit is belief. The main example of "world-to-mind" fit is desire. A belief is what it should be when it is "fitted to" the world; a desire is satisfied when the world has been "fitted to" it.

I laughed a little.

"But, it also affects how information is processed and stored—how it is categorized and dealt with, particularly in the instant after it leaves the conscious mind. It goes down to those catacombs below, where the grim will to self has its way," he said. "Nor is that all. It also affects, as you might expect, what someone will do—that is, new motives and intentions appear, and new goals. They represent that will to self, and are often disguised, tied up with other motive factors, so that, among other things, introspection becomes impossibly arduous. Motives are tied together in ways that make it always seem the case that a person seems, to himself, to act on one concern, when in fact, he enacts a different concern. Some intended actions may never be carried out; others are carried out very strangely; and always, the disruption of memory is ongoing, unraveling the person's ability to grasp what it is he is doing. Memory is a flighty mistress."

Simon was silent again, his eyes hazy and unclear. "Do you know what Sal's philosophy was?" he asked.

"Ahab happy," I said.

He smiled. "The first principle was truth in all things," said Simon. "But the corollaries he drew from it give you a sense of how he developed his idea. The corollaries were that truth in relation to one's own life is to be one, and that since we are all addicted to lying to ourselves, life is a *via crucis*, and becoming one is learning not to lie."

"We agreed on some things," I said.

"Well, well," said Simon. "So do many great adversaries. But what made his view distinct was what he counted as the necessary components of humanity that had to be fused into that 'one.'"

"He never fully explained this," I said. "How did this become relevant to you?"

"Well, do you think that self-knowledge makes for happiness?" he said. "Sal thought it made for despair; and the deeper the self-knowledge, the more complete the despair."

"That sounds true enough," I said.

"He thought this was due to the incompatibility of humanity's

components—in particular, the impossibility of coherently com-
bining our essential relationality, our sense of justice, and our 'awful
essence'—you see, that is why I started when you mentioned that,
because he used that phrase in his definitions. The awful essence
is our self-will, something he went to a lot of effort to pin down."

"His 'science' experiments," I said.

"Those were part of this, yes," said Simon. "He wanted to know
precisely what self-will was. He determined that it was Milton who
captured the idea most perfectly."

"Milton?" I said.

"In Satan's famous statement in *Paradise Lost*—'Evil, be thou
my good.' This captured the truth of it, according to Sal, because it
captures the most distinctive aspect of our will ... and this is what
comes up from the catacombs, so to speak," he said.

"What is that? Satanic pride?" I said.

"Perhaps so ... what he said, though, was that it captured our
need to assert ourselves and distinguish ourselves, to leave our mark
upon whatever would make a claim on us," said Simon. "Thus, our
attempts to know the truth, to form meaningful relationships, to
live in accordance with justice, all these attempts always encounter
a collision when they come up against this other element of the
person, the 'essence' of man. Hence, the despair of self-knowledge."

"Ahab was doomed by his own will," I said. "That part I understand. But why envision him as being *happy*?"

Simon went on. "Sal's special hobby, though, was what drew
our attention."

"What was that?" I asked. "Surely not something stupid like
murder or white collar crime."

"No," he said. "His hobby was bringing *others* to self-knowledge
and despair."

"I don't think that's a crime," I said.

"No," said Simon. "It's not."

"Then what?" I asked.

"Why must one envision Ahab as happy?" Simon asked, mostly

to himself. "If he goes to his doom knowingly, knowing his revenge upon the white whale is an impossible contest of his will in rebellion against the just claims of friendship or love or society, against God himself if need be—well, that strenuous course was what recommended itself to him. That meant, of course, living with a lot of betrayal, but I think the very frisson of going wrong appealed to him, which only appeared when one knowingly went wrong."

"That is a dark thought," I said.

"Yes," said Simon, simply. "But it was, on his view, nothing but a self-conscious grasp of the truth that governed us, whether we were conscious of it or not."

"Then what got him noticed?" I said. It was beginning to rain big, warm drops.

"You don't know?" said Simon.

I was silent a moment. "Sibley's suicide."

Simon sighed. "She wasn't the first."

For a time we were both silent. Finally, I spoke. "Simon. I have done something terrible."

"What have you done?" said Simon, more authentically concerned now than when we spoke only half seriously earlier.

"I can't remember."

"What have you forgotten?" he said.

"Something important," I said. The dimly lit dawn, as if dusk; the crawling clouds overhead. I stare out from the porch, sighing, and the sun doesn't rise. I want to crawl away. The street light turns off. The birds are singing.

"You found the principle in yourself, then," he said.

"The 'awful essence,' that grim, appalling apparition that rises from the dark caverns of the self?" I said.

"You have found it?" he said.

"Yes," I said. "Only, the thought is dim... I can't seem to make out its lines."

"It is the thought of rebellion," said Simon. "The thought of mastering your own fate." He stared at me, eyes penetrating, sharper than a razor. I wanted to be understood, and felt, finally, that someone could. "Do you remember what you said when I taught you to play chess?"

"What did I say?" I asked.

"You said: *I don't love the game. I just love the people.* It's why I never prepared you for tournaments."

"I said that?" Of course I did. We were sitting in a funny little café somewhere, I had ribbons in my hair (what for?!), there was a festive atmosphere, and I was laughing. He was serious, his face so severe.

"You did; and you said that you loved to *make the game with the other player*, and that was really too much," he said. "You wanted to make the other player win!"

"What?" I said. That didn't make any sense. That was not how I played. "Why do you say that?"

"You said it yourself!" he said.

"It must have been someone else," I said.

"But it was you," he said.

But that was what I had written of Joshua, just a few days ago. I was afraid of my own thoughts.

"What changed?" he said.

I was silent.

"You must excuse me for being so forward. My eyes have grown sharp for guilt."

I was playing him as if he were Sal, and suddenly made the move I had been holding in reserve for the moment he exposed his knight, a pawn move that threatened his knight but also revealed an attack by my queen on his h7 pawn. "Don't bother," I said. "In four moves I will be up a rook."

"'The plus of which,' as Lasker says, 'suffices to win the game.'[87] Very great cunning," Simon said, tipping over his King.

෴

87 Ed.: See Edward Lasker, *Manual of Chess* (New York: Dover Publications, 1947), p. 15.

The summer I was fourteen, Helena stayed with us for two months in the Outer Banks. She was a whirlwind of color and activity and Corona beer who never seemed to sleep. The sun was so overfull of happiness its rays shed its excess upon us. It was just our second summer surfing; she was far beyond us, like a goddess of the waves. We felt clumsy beside her grace. "Oh, the waves here are gentle little darlings," she said. "If you'd seen the way I was bailing in Hawaii last month, you'd tell a different story!" But we had not seen her in Hawaii, and to us, this seeming false humility made her more wonderful than ever.

Near the end of summer, a Wednesday when none of the adults were around, Sarah and I went out exploring and we took out kayaks and explored the little islands of the Outer Banks. We came up to one of these and scrambled through brambles and stiff grasses before reaching a tall tree that stood out upon the island, alone, towering over everything. We climbed it as high as we could go. Together

Joshua was sixteen that summer and came down to Hatteras in August, just when Helena was leaving for Jeffrey's Bay. It was also the first chance I had to show him the place that meant so much to me. He had his license now, and had a car, a 2001 Jeep Wrangler, and this was all so new it felt thrillingly wrong just to ride in it. It was our first opportunity to enjoy the freedom that comes from driving. We drove out to Hatteras, to one of the ORV beaches where you can take your four wheel drive. When we saw the wild horses, we jumped out of the car and ran out among them, laughing. They stared at us blankly, and we just laughed harder. We had lunch at some awful place that has been closed down now.

Sarah suddenly recited one of her poems:

A pirate, a wench, and a boatswain,
Pursued chests of gold at an auction,
But then, halfway there,
Fell into despair,
And realized they
could've just stole one

we managed to climb to such a height as we'd never reached before. The view over the ocean made me feel heady and alive but Sarah preferred to stare up into the branches of the tree. When she was staring out at the sea, she cut her finger somehow, and when she saw the thin line of blood on her hand, she got scared somehow and began panicking, breathing too quickly, and she couldn't seem to calm herself.

I helped her get down again, concerned for her but also disappointed I didn't get longer to stare out over the infinite ocean. We went back toward Hatteras and surfed there, showing off to each other everything we'd learned from Aunt Helena. When we walked back into town, we saw some boys near Ferry Bites, a little restaurant shack selling comfort food. It was the boys we'd run out on earlier that summer. We ran to hide behind the restaurant rather than confront them, giggling with our hands over our mouths and crouching down beside each other in the sand. She was wearing one of those

Limericks are inherently funny, so we laughed, but then we argued over which of us was which, while Sarah just smiled.

The Outer Banks spread out before us like possibility haunted by memory. We visited places old and new. It was strange to find out how much better I was at surfing than him. We tried to show Joshua how to surf, and despite how athletic and naturally graceful he was, we drove him into the ground. We explored caves and groves and islands, and walked miles along those sun-drenched shores.

I took him to the little cafés I knew and to funny and unusual spots worth spying out and seeing. And yes, we danced, we danced *Romeo and Juliet* in a park where a few individuals stopped to watch and smile, and Sarah smiled and smiled, still wearing her big sunhat, but there was a quietness and a stillness behind her face. One night we built a big bonfire and Joshua danced the part of Puck from *A Midsummer Night's Dream*. Puck of course does not dance any *pas de deux;* he always dances alone, for he

wide sun hats, we'd picked it up somewhere that day, and smiling as wide as a Cheshire cat.

We were sitting there looking at each other and wondering how long we would have to stay there when suddenly Sarah caught sight of something, and said "Oh!" She got up and ran out to someone standing near the line for the restaurant, a man with a mustache. "I'm sorry," she was saying. "I didn't know." The man nodded, but didn't say anything, seeming perplexed and unable to speak. It was the man who had been the assistant manager at Baskin-Robbins. Sarah walked back to me.

On the way home, the sun began to set before we got back. We set our towels out on the beach and stared out over the ocean. When it grew dark we lay down and watched the stars come out. One by one, they appeared, specks of light in an infinite darkness, communicating with each other across million year distances, speaking their beautiful parts even ages after their deaths. You whispered to me, "I get so scared

alone is self-sufficient in all the ballet, and this dance of Joshua's was the most marvelous and sublime performance I ever saw him perform, burning away in ephemeral greatness, caught in the uncertain light, the reflection of the sea, and gliding over the chance footing of the sand—everything combined to produce a strange effect, a hypnotism in which nature itself revolved around the dance to spellbind us all; in the final moment, because he could not be raised up above the stage (as Puck is supposed to, to conclude the ballet), Joshua instead cast himself in a great leap into the dark, yawning ocean, a leap that took our breath away.

He and I found a hill to go up near the shore where we could look down on the water. There was a little monument there, with four pillars and a roof, like a little shrine, and benches set to the side for visitors. From this hill, we could look down through the arching branches of some trees upon the water, and there we gazed out upon eternity. The stars twin-

sometimes, M. When we were up in that tree, and—the sea was so big, we were so high, and the tree ... It's too much. But when I'm surfing, God, M, when I'm riding one of those big waves, I feel like I can handle anything else life has for me. You know?"

You were looking in my eyes, hopefully, beseechingly. I smiled, and held your hand.

"It's like when you dance," you said. "It's the only time I feel beautiful."

I laughed. "Do you know why?" I said, instead of arguing with her.

"Why?"

I got up on my elbow and continued to hold her hand. "Beauty is a dance of finitude upon the edge of infinity, and the waves are so, so big. I love you. You are utterly beautiful."

She buried her face in my embrace and I held her. Up above, the stars shone down upon us, and when we looked back up, they seemed to smile at us with their infinite happiness.

kled upon the waves like dancers. "The dancers are all gone under the hill," I heard someone saying, and turned to find him, seeing only Joshua. His face was a little sunburnt.

"God, Joshua, it's too big, it's too wonderful." I was looking up into his sparkling eyes. "It's so beautiful."

"What is beauty?" he asked.

"It's all of this!" I said, spreading out my arms to indicate the world around us.

He laughed, and he held my hand, his other hand on my shoulder. "Beauty is the dance of two mites on the edge of infinity," he said. He was looking in my eyes, and I saw myself in his.

I wanted to seize him, kiss him, grasp him somehow, and this feeling confused me. I didn't want our relationship to be like that. I didn't know what to say, but I longed for his strength to support me, so I buried my face in his chest, and whispered to him, "This is the best moment. Don't ever forget."

✌

Sept. 8

> Go, go, go, said the bird: human kind
> Cannot bear very much reality.
> Time past and time future
> What might have been and what has been
> Point to one end, which is always present.
>   *T. S. Elliot,* Burnt Norton

I've reached the conclusion that, barring some miracle, I am going to die very soon. I am surprised, because I suddenly don't want to. Should I die, however, it greatly increases the chances that this notebook will be found without its proper interpreter. Well, I will do what I can to while away my time and see if I can finish it before that happens.

                    ☙

We began playing again. Simon played White. I played Black. "Can you really live the way that Sal recommends?" I said. "Embracing your own necessary incompleteness and incoherence with the highest expression of the ideal that you know? I don't know what he means by that, and I don't think that he knows, either."

Simon was quiet for a long time. "You know," he said, "the one thing I really know for sure was what I told you before." He was playing a very strange opening, something like the Flick-Knife Attack. I couldn't remember having studied it.

"Everyone is guilty?" I said.

"Yes," he said. "Do you know, I understand why you left, and didn't answer Pete's wager," he said.

"Oh?"

"Of course," he said. "That's the logical conclusion, if 'everyone is guilty' has a substantive meaning and a person is committed to not allowing the awful essence drawn up out of those catacombs of your heart from coming up and polluting the waters any longer. One must learn to live within oneself. It is precisely the friend and the beloved whom we most frequently betray. I used to allow myself the occasional dalliance with another human being, and in those moments, I would find a student, a friend, although a student was better, because it was easier to break things off. Well, you know what I mean," he said, referring to that time some years ago when he had taken on the task of teaching me chess, only to completely disappear 18 months later. "Friends, I've had just Rufus, but we're two neutron stars, all our fuel is in our guts, and we need nothing from anyone—so that's been easy. Love ... romantic love ... I always fall in love with the wrong person, so I never had any dalliances of that kind. Students were best; there's always room for a wall, but they allowed me to give myself the pleasure of being loving toward someone, in my fashion. I came to suspect this tendency, however, as love is not a dalliance; my practice was merely self-indulgence."

"But now you crave excitement?" I said. I hadn't seen him in such a confessional mood before, and wondered at it.

"This mode of life has left me feeling thin, stretched out, and empty of substance. That was the intriguing aspect of this case," said Simon. "It spoke to whatever was down there, Sal's philosophy did, for it is rare to find someone who knows the same truth you do and is engaged with it in all earnestness; and then to find the idea so strangely developed ... well, that was something."

"I don't think I could live with it," I said.

"Well, one must live with oneself," said Simon. "I wasn't sure I could do that any longer. There's another reason for that, which I'll get to. But if Sal is wrong, if the self is not the unfolding of your own necessity in time—contradictions and all—then we have to ask what he was wrong about. If the self is not just the unfolding of your own necessity, then there must be a point when you posited the self, when it could have been one way or another, and you chose to weave the self together the way you did. But, likewise, if there is such an act, it must be an utterly ordinary act, too, at least on the surface. Otherwise, how is it that it slips through the fingers of memory whenever it searches for the crucial moment of positing?[88] How else, unless it appears on the surface an utterly familiar act?"

"Well," I said, "that would make sense, I suppose."

"The Act, as I will call it, would have to be an act whose intention presupposes or entails a way of weaving the self together, whose performance does that weaving, and whose most lasting result is not whatever consequences fell outside the act, but the posited self," said Simon. "This Act would not be necessary but would be the agent's own contribution to his development. If this were so, then Sal's contention would be wrong: the self is not the unfolding of the person's own necessity in time, but a mixture of freedom and necessity. Is that entirely clear?"[89]

"No, it's not," I said. "I don't know what you mean by an act, or rather, an act's intention, presupposing a self."

"Since this is a hypothetical discourse, you'll have to forgive me for not having a detailed account to provide," said Simon. "Yet, I think it must be something like this: for an intention to presuppose a self, the intention must be of a specific type: it must intend the act under a description in which the act is specified as belonging to a certain type of self, and that 'self' be a possible configuration of the person as he presently is. Clearly, the person must also be in a state of flexibility, as you put it, for this to occur, and then the Act also implies the application of that idea to the person himself."

"I think you still need to make that more concrete," I said.

"Imagine a boy who suddenly finds the crucial things in his life at stake," said Simon. "He has grown up surrounded by gangs and

---

88   Ed.: Simon again uses the language of Kierkegaard's *The Concept of Anxiety.*
89   Ed.: It is worth noting that both Elizabeth's and Simon's conception of freedom is essentially a developmental condition concerning degrees of freedom, and not explicitly concerned with questions about the will's freedom from physical determination.

poverty and the pressing problems posed by such circumstances. Now a crucial moment arrives. Whereas before, he merely reacted to events and left big decisions to 'the adults,' he now sees that what happens really hinges upon his own decision. Perhaps he is offered a choice to help out in some minor way with a drug deal, let's say to act as a courier, and in return, his family will be better off. His father is absent, his mother is ill, he has several sisters. In a flash, he sees that it will all depend on what he does now. Well, what does he do? He must act. A child will act merely in response to the immediate situation and avoid positing a self, because what the child intends is something like 'get out of the fearful situation' or 'get the pleasant thing' or something like that. But now the boy you see is no longer going to be a child. Does he cooperate or not? Does he materially support his family or strike out into the unknown with a self whose only support is virtue?

"When he finally acts he must act under a certain description of himself, an idea of himself. Perhaps initially this idea is not articulate or even susceptible of verbal expression. It is, rather, a kind of image in his mind of a certain kind of person, the kind of person he takes himself to be or to be becoming, in these circumstances. It may take him a long time to be able to verbalize the self he has adopted. I assume that it took many years for Dmitry Karamazov to reach the pithiness of 'a scoundrel, but not a thief,' his summation of the self that was presupposed by his actions. His base desires he could not change, and he would pursue them, but he would pursue them honorably, and hence, he was 'not a thief.' Or so he supposed. The verbal description, you see, may hide as much as it reveals. What is fundamental is the organization of the person's concerns, a certain hierarchy of goods, a pattern of action and integration related to these.

"So, the boy acts. He cooperates. In that moment, his freedom appeared, and in that moment, it disappeared again, but all he did was agree to move the bag from one place to another, from one person to another person. In that little act, he decided the description of *himself* that would apply in the future. To say no would be to abandon his family, he thinks; and he is no traitor to his family. Perhaps this is even his verbal description for the type of person he has decided to understand himself as: 'not a traitor to my family.' But it is not the verbal description that is truly meaningful: it is the understanding of that implied in the act of cooperation. For what was entailed was a whole way of understanding not only his obligations to his family, but the proper way of relating these to others, to justice, to truth, to himself. It contained a way of responding to threats that was written deep into his soul so that when the circumstances reappear what was free appears as a repetition, and a repetition is not just a new instance of a past circumstance—for it is always easier to do something a second time—but a reappearance of a circumstance that this description of the kind of person he is, that was adopted in the Act, entails a clear answer for. Changing his mind later is therefore much harder than it would seem it should be because it would mean changing his mind about what kind of person he is after he had already let the Act define him in his own concerns and hierarchy of goods and pattern of relation to the world."

"I may wish to discuss this again later," I said, "because I don't know if I have an act like that in my life."

"That's my fault," said Simon. "I painted it too vividly, to bring the Act to light. I contradicted my own strictures that the Act would need to slip through the net of memory, whereas under circumstances like those the Act would be memorable. Most of the time, however, I think that the Act would be practically invisible; the key to finding it is grief that is awakened by going wrong combined with a deep awareness of what that Act posited, rather than an awareness of the concrete specificity of the Act. Most of the time, the concrete form of the Act will never be more than a hazy recollection, but what must become clear is the idea of oneself that it presupposes and entails."

"I suppose I'll accept that for now," I said. "I think I know what you mean."

"Good," said Simon. "The other thing is, if Sal is wrong, if the self is not the unfolding of the person's necessity in time, then there must also be a way of repenting this act and getting back behind it again, so as to redo the Act. There must be way of being so broken by one's incoherence that flexibility returns, so grieved that one is led to this silent act and able to grasp what it is that one must repent, and yet now so differently constituted, despite being the same person, that one can repeat the act of positing the self while correcting the error of that moment's first Act."

"Right," I said, "because if there is no flexibility, there can be no positing of a self; if no grief, no motive to change this act in particular; and if there is no way to avoid positing the same self, then Sal is right anyway, because you will freely posit the same self again and again, which has been my fear all along. For I don't see how to do it again without again becoming guilty again."

"Well, and so I thought, too, but it only produced more trouble … well … I will return to that later," said Simon.

"I don't understand something," I said. "I know you're sketching 'the Act' as a mere hypothetical, but are you meaning for there to be only one Act for each agent?"

"Oh," said Simon, looking somewhat relieved. "No, I don't think so, but perhaps it's a matter of degree. Perhaps each Act further defines us, but in the way that you suggested, in terms of an ever-diminishing range of interpretation as new concerns are added to the mix and the new whole, the original plus the new concern, and themselves mixed together."

"Is losing oneself an Act like that?"

"I don't think it is," said Simon. "It seems rather to be a pseudo-Act, an as-if positing of a new self that is, however, just an illusion drawn over the truth about the self you are. This illusion was the main reason Sal tried to study it and oppose it. He thought one must strive to fully and consciously embrace one's being, knowing everything. But if there is an Act, then the real danger of loss of self is its ability to mask the Act and make it impossible to get behind it again and repent it. For if the lie one tells covers itself up, then it will create a mist between the person you are and the person you were that you cannot bridge. For if you don't know what self you have posited, you will not be able to repent positing it wrongly and get back behind it again to correct the Act."

The rain was falling on us very hard now.

Simon began to say something, "And I'd wager—but oughtn't we to get out of this?" He was looking up at the weather. The horizon was very dark.

"Perhaps this was a mistake," I said

"Get inside," said Simon, putting his arm around me. By instinct, I stuffed the chess pieces into my purse, and we ran inside as the force of the storm increased.

Inside the house, the wind was battering the rain against the walls so loudly I felt, for the first time since Sarah had died, the spark of genuine terror. Simon immediately turned on the television and found the weather. There was a man jabbering, but I didn't hear what he said. What I saw was an enormous spiral of white turning up the coast past Florida, and now crashing into the southern coast of North Carolina. The man was now talking with another man about how two low pressure systems, one inland and the other at sea, that had created a funnel drawing the storm north.

Simon was strangely tight lipped. "Neither one of us watches enough television, apparently," he said, "or talks enough to other people about such things."

"There was no one on the beach this morning," I said.

"Naturally not," he said. "We need to get somewhere more secure." The howling of the wind and rain sounded sounded like a locomotive running over and around the house, and the wind somehow was moaning, or screaming, as if in agony itself. Every ten or twenty seconds, something struck against the house—a shutter, a door, something from the beach—I didn't know. Occasionally, there was a loud clanking strike, as if a chain were whipping in the wind.

So we went deeper into the house. There was a basement, which was clean, if rather bare, except for a corner that had been made into a wine cellar. Simon nodded, as if it confirmed some expectation he had held. The only furniture was a broken chair and a massive, marble table. In another corner was a cart with several large paintings, for which those hung above might be traded. In the opposite corner, a mat and some exercise equipment, including a large punching bag. The horrifying sounds of the storm were muffled above, whipping, whipping, whipping the house, and moaning constantly in hellish agony.

I tried to get some kind of update on the storm on my phone, but there was no service. Simon continued to look about. I asked him what for, and at first he didn't answer. When pressed, he said, "This house is old enough ... and I'm sure he favored it for that reason." The storm continued battering us above, battering and howling as if yearning to get inside and furious at our barring it.

"Are you looking for the smuggler's tunnel?"

"Yes," he said, "did he tell you about that?"

"He said that the house had one, and that he used it sometimes. But I didn't see it when I was here," I said.

"Well, that's confirmation that it's here anyway," said Simon. We then searched together for the hidden entrance we guessed would be there. I don't think I'll ever forget those moaning howls and screams the storm lay on us; and it went on for hours. But we found the false wall that led into a smuggler's tunnel relatively quickly. As Sal had said, it was dark and not particularly safe looking. However, the area immediately within the tunnel, just past the hidden door, contained a large painting and a box of rare pipes. Simon went down the tunnel a ways, then walked back. Back inside, he pulled out the pipes, found the tobacco, and lit it, smoking while I set up the chess pieces in the dust. We played off and on, but external circumstances interfered with our concentration. Occasionally, we broke off from it. I wrote in my notebook while Simon tried to nap. When that didn't work, he took down the training bag, lay it on its side, and lounged against it smoking the pipe. The game dragged on, developing into a cagey, defensively-minded game of feints and strongly prickly structures. We spoke, but the conversation would be hard to convey, for it was broken and confusing, and there were long gaps. Yet our talk also became extremely intimate, as if we were lifelong friends who had proven ourselves to each other in many bearings of the soul, and were not merely seeing each other for the second time in many years.

"You asked if I was one of those philosophy majors who becomes a lawyer," said Simon.

"Yes," I said. That seemed an age ago.

"The answer is no," said Simon. "I actually set out to become a priest."

"A priest!" I was surprised, though in hindsight, this made perfect sense.

"Yes, I intended to become a priest, and I very nearly took vows, but at the last minute, I went to law school instead," said Simon.

"Why was that?" I asked.

"It would be hard to explain," said Simon. "Well, that's not true. I suppose you already understand. Father McBrien, you see, was always saying that what someone needed was a new king in his heart, and I didn't see how I could ... well ... I may not have fully understood what he meant at the time. The king, you see, is like the awful essence we discussed earlier."

"You've lost me," I said.

"I did foul that up," said Simon. "Father McBrien—he was my spiritual director in those days—had this metaphor he liked to use for the human soul. He said that in every soul there is a prophet, a priest, and a king; but the king must die and a new king take the throne or else the prophet and the priest would both be strangled."

"And the old king is that awful essence that Melville wrote of?" I said.

"That's right," said Simon. "The prophet is what speaks the ideal into your life and confronts you with transcendent authority. The priest is what draws you out of yourself into the world to serve others, in submission to this ideal that has been stamped on your soul. Well, I always thought I grasped those well enough in my own life, but it was the king who threw everything off, and what I found was that the king in my soul couldn't help but strangle the prophet and priest."

"I understand the prophet and priest," I said, "but what is the king?"

"That was what I never did understand," said Simon, "and Fr. McBrien could never explain it to me. That wasn't his gift, you see. He was a lovely man, a loving man, and he loved children, he knew how to speak to them. He knew how to make theology vivid and explosive. But when I pressed him to make it clear to me, to make it philosophical, I couldn't get anywhere. 'Let the old king die!' he would say, 'Then the new king can reign.'"

"What 'new king'?" I asked.

"He meant Christ, of course, true prophet, true priest, and true king," said Simon. "Still, I didn't see what that meant, and what I did grasp, I couldn't accomplish. You see, I had the idea that the king must be what you loved most in life."

"That makes sense," I said.

"So submitting to a new king must be to stop loving what you love, and loving something new, namely, God in Christ," said Simon.

"That follows," I said.

"If I had been a slave to alcohol or sex or anything of that sort, then I would not have hesitated to follow that advice," said Simon.

"Not that there is anything *easy* about giving up such things. That's obvious enough. It would have been straightforward, however: give up the self-destructive, other-destructive sin and embrace the healing new love!"

"Yes," I said. My icy soul, which despised such things, knew exactly what he meant.

"Yet, and I know this will seem paradoxical maybe, or strike you as strange, but to me, it's been love for others that predominated," said Simon. "The love I had … I could imagine giving up, but only in the most choked way, and you see, it was this love for certain others that I could never sacrifice, and which, in fact, was tangled up with the both the priest and the prophet in a thousand ways. The main thing, though, was that sacrificing it was unthinkable, and I couldn't see how I could do it, or how it would be right to do it." I thought immediately of Joshua, the glory of the light shining around him as he danced, and all the searing adoration of my heart fixed upon him. But what could I give to someone to whom I had nothing to give? His life and mine had parted irreparably years ago. And then I thought of Sarah, standing there wearing one boot and one sock, and I felt keening sorrow. To her also I could no longer give anything. Simon went on, saying "I would read about Augustine and his friend, whom he said he loved too much, and how he said that love could be subordinated to a great, overpowering, infinite love for God, and I didn't understand how he could say such things.[90] I knew it was a flaw of some kind in myself, but I thought it each time I read that passage in the *Confessions*, no matter how many times I read it."

"Perhaps I understand," I said.

Simon watched me with his slitted eyes, the smoke from his pipe hovering between us. The smell was pleasant. "Yes, perhaps you do," said Simon. "Maybe I was wrong, though, and McBrien was right."

---

90   Ed.: See Augustine's *Confessions*, IV.4.7-IV.7.12.

"How so?" I said.

"Well ... Christ's command was to love God with all your might, all your heart, and to love your neighbor as yourself. Love for self, however, is ambiguous, which makes the command ambiguous, too," said Simon.

About this time, the banshee-like intensity of the wind decreased to mere howls, then quieted to moans and whispers. We went back upstairs. Remarkably, the television was still on, saying something, but the area was strewn with shards of glass, broken pieces of wood, and debris from the beach. A large umbrella had, likely after piercing the windows, been flung into the kitchen and scattered whatever had been left out on the counters. The humidity felt like an assault. The rain was still pouring, falling at 45 degrees, as much horizontally as vertically, and occasionally there was a kind of whipping whooshing sound, and the wind and rain would suddenly shift direction. Pieces of paper and other light debris were flitting about in the air, those that settled upon the ground replaced by new ones picked up by the wind elsewhere. They swirled about us, pregnant with uncertain signification.

Out the shattered windows lay devastation. Not only had the waters risen, their choppy waves pummeling the shore, but the long pathway up to the house, which rose up a bluff, was crumbling in several places beneath the storm's fury. Long shafts of earth had fallen away into the sea, blasted by its winds and rain, barring our way back to town. The spark of terror I had felt earlier grew into something else, something worrying and active, a dark, constrained anxiousness. I occasionally heard the sound of rocks and earth breaking loose from the bluff and falling into the waters below.

Simon stared out at the landscape, calm as if he surveyed such every day, a black pillar surrounded by swirling light and darkness. Looking at my pink Converse, he said, "Your canvas shoes are no good," he said. "Wait here for me. Check for bottled water or anything else we can use." He wrapped himself in a coat he found in one of the closets and went out. When he returned, I had found a case of bottled water, nearly unused, a first-aid kit, a large flashlight, a smaller flashlight, a blanket from the couch, and some large unused trash bags that could function as ponchos in a pinch. The wind was a moan again, and as much rain seemed to come into the house, flying sideways, as not.

"It's just the eye of the storm," he said. "Quickly—back into the basement." The rain was falling harder, and the wind had picked up. The smell of roses suddenly became sharp.

We went down, closed the door, and again descended into the basement as the storm winds struck the house, shrieking about us.

"How bad is it?" I said.

"It's much worse than it seems," he said. "The whole house may slide into the sea."

That tiny tendril of terror thrilled again. "What?"

"We should go down the tunnel," said Simon. "Perhaps, that way—" and we began exploring further down the tunnel with the flashlights. There was a sound of dripping water every now and then. The tunnel walls were of something like brick, rough and unfinished, but in places there seemed to be inserts of slate. These had been decorated with reliefs and inscriptions, which had, however, been worn away, and now had such vague and partial appearances as to suggest anything at all, depending upon how the light shone upon them. One looked to me to be the face of a man, though Simon took it for a large barrel; beneath it were written letters that couldn't be made out but might have read "...sicut alienum..." Another seemed to show a lion, but Simon thought it a grinning mask; beneath it were letters that might have read "...orum infinitus es..." These alternated with large iron rings that protruded from the wall and that may have been for the purpose of holding torches, or, I suppose, prisoners. The arches, meanwhile, were all of slate, and though there were minute signs of detail work here and there, they seemed to have been constructed with strength rather than fineness in mind, though strange, horn-like protuberances of rusted away iron emerged from every third keystone. The air was oppressive; even with the storm assaulting the world outside I didn't feel wholly certain we weren't headed toward a worse fate.

"You know, something happened a year ago … fifteen months ago, really, something that shook me," he said.

"What happened?" I said.

"I was visiting your father," he said. "I don't have time to explain why—it was the Ratzschel case—anyway, when I was there, I over-heard Sarah talking with your mother. She was saying how much she missed seeing you dance and all your imaginary adventures in the Outer Banks. I walked into the room at this moment, and your mother was saying the kinds of things people say when they are trying to sound sympathetic but they do not actually take some-one's concern seriously; and when Sarah persisted in describing her unhappiness, your mother concluded by saying 'Oh, people always have to leave things behind when they grow up.' Well, Sar-ah stopped talking, that's for sure, and I'm sure no one saw what was on her face—but I did. There was an inwardness in her expres-sion that I knew too well, when someone has tried to express a pain that cannot be communicated, and brings the pain back within oneself. Well, I didn't do anything, and didn't say anything, though I might have. I've spent my life punishing the guilty, coming along after the fatal deed is done, but I haven't ever saved anyone; I was never any good at it, because once I grasped for someone, I could never let them go again. So I said nothing, and went away."

The wind was howling like a banshee. I had no reply.

"I didn't become a priest because I knew I couldn't serve anyone, love anyone, faithfully; I meant, I knew how to devote myself to some-one, but not how to do it without ruining things somehow, because I always seemed to love too much. But I couldn't give up loving others and love only God, which is what I took McBrien and Augustine and everyone else to be recommending. So I walled myself off in 'everyone is guilty' and kept to myself, thinking this would at least keep me from becoming guiltier ... I knew I couldn't fulfill the call I was given, but I could at least pursue the guilty and bring them to truth."

"But when you saw what happened, you saw it didn't protect you," I said.

Simon sighed. "You must understand that it wasn't just you who failed Sarah. I, too, share that blame."

"But how could you have known, from that little incident—" I said.

"You see ... well, it's all too absurd," he muttered. "Anyway, I did understand, and it was then, I had the dream ... it would terrify me and almost debilitate me, this dream. I knew it meant I should act, which is to say, not act. Well, forget that. Anyway, I waited much too long. Too long. You see, I thought I knew the best course, and that was to keep away from her, avoid becoming guilty again. But instead, following that philosophy of guilt only became a new source of guilt. I see now I have never escaped the call, for here I am."

I didn't know what to say. We continued down the ancient tunnel, which had recently been cleaned and reinforced at certain points, but the strange, uncertain faces—or whatever semblances were on the reliefs—began to seem to me more and more like horrors. There were tears of compassion and grief in my eyes.

"Now, the thing is, what I wanted to say above, earlier, is that self-love is ambiguous," said Simon. "This is essential, forget the storm, you need to grasp this. 'As you love yourself' can indicate the reality, vividness, and presence of your own concerns to you—your sensitivity to them, your appreciation for them—but love for self can also have another side. Someone can love another person and even in this love love only himself. Force this person to need him. Read his purpose in this other person's life and determine to control the other person and the terms of this devotion."

"You're talking about the awful essence again," I said.

"Right, of course," said Simon. "So you see how the ambiguity of self-love leads to ambiguity in all other loves. Even love for God, no matter how big it is, no matter how monomaniacal, can be totally mastered and under the sway of such a principle of self-love, by referring everything back to itself, to make God into its own mission, its own project, its own system of power. So the same thing follows from the other side, you see? The ambiguity."

"I suppose so," I said.

"Then you'll understand about the King better than I could," said Simon. "The king in the soul is the master factor that unifies everything, a kind of ruling and subordinating principle. With the right king, submission to the principle which would purify, not replace, the prophet and priest. A new way of loving what you love."

"You're moving through all of this much too quickly," I said. "What do you mean, it would purify, not replace them?" We passed by what might have been an ox-cart, or a great sailing ship, or perhaps a monkey on a couch; beneath it read what might have been "...ebus et tribus..."

Simon slowed down. "In your way of talking, you see, the friend awakens the priest in you, or as Niakani said, the self-making passion is an act of grace.[91] It comes from beyond you, it isn't of you, but brings you to life; and the ideal, you know, as you put it, contains a transcendent, authoritative word, which you must apply to yourself. So let's suppose that both your highest ideal and your most decisive loves for others, in a sense, arise from beyond you. That is, what is *in you* was the capacity to become related to something outside of you, whereas the ideal and the friend stand outside of you. The question is the master conditioning factor in your heart."

---

91 See p. 100, this volume.

"You're still going too fast," I said.

"I don't think we can move slower," said Simon. "But … well. Here. A self is an intentional stance of some kind toward the factors making up one's own person; it's a way of understanding them and relating them to one another."

"I do understand that," I said.

"So some factors of the self may have the right to condition or limit other factors. In particular, one factor may be a master conditioning factor, a concern that has the right to condition all other factors."

"Ah," I said. "And that's the king?"

"Right," said Simon. "The king is not the biggest, it's the most authoritative. So it need not be a dominant end: it need not condition all other factors in the sense of reducing them to means to a single end. This is perhaps what always confused me in Augustine. Perhaps Augustine was himself confused, but I always took him to mean that we had to drop every other love and love just God; and then love others 'in God' in a way I couldn't comprehend.[92] Now, though, I think McBrien might have been pointing at something else. If the self is like a recipe, the master conditioning factor is the will toward the recipe, a will that either shows the other factors how to get along or locks the person into endless contradiction, and the embrace and release of the self to God could itself be such a will."

"But what do you mean by a 'will' toward a recipe, toward a self?" I said.

Simon was lost in thought a moment, seemingly unsure what to say. There was concentration, but also immense pain, upon his face. Finally, he said, "You're a dancer, you would understand what I mean when I say it's accepting the idea of the self in the mood of dancing."

"Actually," I said, "I don't know what you mean."

---

92 Ed.: See Augustine, *De Doctrina Christiana*, I.22, 27.

"I'm sorry, I'm only grasping this now," he said. "I am not yet articulate in it. Where does a dancer find her idea of herself?"

"In the music and in the choreography," I said. "She accepts those into herself and freely reflects them in herself in the act of the dancing."

"And I suppose even if the dancing was improvisational, a dancer would still find her 'idea' of herself in the music, not simply in herself?" he asked.

"Yes," I said, "although perhaps also in herself."

"Including the passions she was supposed to embody and enact in her dancing?"

"Especially those," I said. "They are in the music, and she then finds them also in herself."

"Yet it's not the passions that reign, it's the dancing master," said Simon.

We had now reached the bottom of the tunnel. Before us rose up a large archway weathered to the point of almost seeming a natural construction; over the generations the water had made the hand of man invisible. Doors had been installed recently, leading outside to the wharfs, as well as a kind of side compartment on our right, a closet four or five feet high and a bit over three feet wide. Above the door to the side-room read the easily legible inscription:

VERITAS SUPRA OMNES
Tristia fortitudo est [93]

The outer doors were hanging loose, having been blown open by the storm outside. The wall opposite the side room, on our left, contained a dozen of the iron rings we had seen occasionally on the trip downward. Water and loose debris was halfway up to our knees.

---

93   Ed.: Sal, perhaps inspired by the broken inscriptions on the wall, apparently gave into a taste for the dramatic. The inscription reads: "Truth over everything. Sorrow is strength."

The wet walls showed the flooding had recently been much higher, and had receded to this level only due to the passing of the eye of the storm over the house. The wharf outside was badly damaged, but it seemed that it may at one point have been sufficient for several boats. There was only an upturned dinghy outside now, its white hull with a blue stripe running around its sides bobbing in the water.

The closet was secured by a combination lock, which Simon opened on the third try.

"I always scoffed at television shows where profilers could guess passwords," I said.

"Oh?" he said, smiling slightly. "The Lord turns evil to good."

Inside, the closet was about three feet deep. There was a little bookcase along with some books and a few documents, but far less than the room had the capacity to hold. There were also a few odds and ends. Simon flipped through the documents, scanning their contents. They were quite dry. He pulled out the book shelf and threw it up the tunnel. There were also some loose pieces of paper written upon by hand. I glanced at one, that read:

1. Truth above all things
    1.1. Truth in relation to one's own life is: to be one
    1.2. We all lie to ourselves; to be one is to stop lying

2. To be one means: *oneness of purpose*
    2.1. Singleness of purpose requires self-mastery
    2.2. Self-mastery is to hold *everything one is* in one's hand, ready to deploy it at once in pursuit of a single futurity or pattern of being, *one's purpose*

3. *What a person is:*
    3.1. What is *highest* in man: "grandeur," *greatness*, magnitude, power, and also, *virtue*, that is, goodness, nobility, beauty

3.2. Our essential context, relationships, immediate entanglements
3.3. The body, our immediate power over our environment, our susceptibility to the power of other beings
3.4. The mind, our openness to what is—to oneself
3.5. What is *deepest* in man: our "awful essence," chiefly *ego, will to distinguish oneself from all else that is and leave a mark upon it*

This section was X-ed out with a blunt pencil stroke, with the appended note: *Mistake here. REVISE.* Then, in blue pen: "Can attunement include both *loosening* and *tightening* of the frets?"

4. Self-mastery means that one must be master of one's immediate entanglements, or else lose oneself
    4.1. Therefore one's purpose in these entanglements must be made to contain both one's grandeur and the "awful essence" of man
    4.2.1. Two failures. Ahab and Nietzsche.

5. Keep oneself: do not forget

Another pencil scrawl: *Elizabeth Hyperion—!*

5.1. Grief is strength

"This seems to have been where Sal kept the journals he studied," he said. "You had better get in. There's room for only one person, and I guess you're probably nimble enough."

"You can't sacrifice yourself for me!" I said.

Simon was throwing the blanket and other supplies into the closet and kept only the pipes, a poncho, and a bottle of water. "I don't think we have much time before the tunnel floods again," said Simon, "but I doubt that more than one of us can safely remain in the compartment. I don't know if I will survive this, but you must. I didn't save Sarah. You may blame yourself, and that's … but perhaps, though, after all this time, I'll save someone." He laughed.

"Why are you laughing?" I asked.

"I laugh at Christ's sense of humor," he said. "I tried to abandon the priesthood, but the great choreographer hasn't let me go so easily. Well, maybe all are called to be priests in some fashion, to make our sacrifices and complete 'what is lacking in the sufferings of Christ.'" He waded out onto the submerged wharf and, with an effort, flipped the boat over. Its mast had been broken, sails were nowhere in evidence, and the little motor was probably flooded, but there were also a set of oars fastened within that remained intact. "And, you see, I've always wanted to go out in a boat in the middle of a storm. Now my dream will be fulfilled."

"That's mad," I said, shaking my head.

He stood a moment, then shrugged, and lit the pipe in his mouth.

"Well, I see I won't get to finish my discourse," he said. "I hope you can figure it all out better than I have. Follow your grief to the center of your being, and release your grip."

We stood for a moment and understood one another. "Take your place among the dancers, Simon," I said. "Fly."

He smiled and placed his hand on me. "Remember," he said, "may you find the peace I never did." And he closed the door.

That was the last time I saw Simon.

BROOKLYN, ONCE[94]

The rain fell in peals while he worked inside silently, efficiently, writing in the small circle illuminated by the desk lamp. His dark, oiled hair shone in the light. He quickly finished the letter and sealed it in the envelope before going out, dropping it in the nearest mailbox and taking the subway to the Boy's Club on 59th street. When he arrived, the rain stopped falling, and he went inside with a smile on his face, greeting each of the boys and young men one by one, laughing or frowning or giving a punch on the shoulder as appropriate. He was distracted but pretended it was a normal day. He was coming here for the last time, probably. A few hours later he cleared out his locker and put the contents in a black duffel before heading back to the subway, this time taking it to Carroll Gardens.

When he arrived at the almost century-old library, he found Fr. McBrien sitting beside one of the fireplaces, as was his custom,

---

94 Ed.: This short piece, written in a neat, spidery cursive script was found inserted in between the pages of Elizabeth's notebook. It is unclear where it came from—from Sal's closet or from Simon's briefcase—but its placement in the middle of her own account seems purposeful. I have therefore included it here in the published work.

reading a newspaper. He knew he would be here because of his affection for the painting above the fireplace, a large reproduction, 6' x 8' like the original, of Rembrandt's *The Return of the Prodigal Son.*

"Father," he said, simply.

"Simon," the other said, in a weak voice, but with a smile.

"I have decided," said Simon.

"And?" asked Fr. McBrien.

"NYU," said Simon.

"Ah," said the other. "Not the Passionists, then?"

"No," said Simon. There was a moment of silence. "I was thinking about what Scorsese said."

"The director?"

"I read about an interview with him," said Simon, "where he mentioned that he almost joined the priesthood. The writer kept making it out that if Scorsese hadn't been a director, he would have been a priest."

"I've heard that," said Fr. McBrien.

"There's something rotten in that," said Simon.

"Oh?" said the other.

"Well, either he had a calling for the priesthood, or he didn't," said Simon. "If he did discern it, then becoming a director was a sin, it was rebellion and despair."

"That's so," said Fr. McBrien.

"Or he didn't have a calling for it, in which case, he shouldn't put forward this idea that if he hadn't chosen to become a director, he would have become a priest. But putting yourself forward when not called is another kind of sin and rebellion. Or it's all lies and nonsense, just the marketing of another desperate man grasping for self-importance." He spoke angrily, voice rising higher than seemly in the setting of the library.

"That's so, too," said Fr. McBrien. He coughed a bit before going on. "But I think you're being too hard on poor Martin."

"What do you mean?" asked Simon more quietly.

There were sounds of books being stacked and set, and every now and then the sound of newspaper being shuffled, folded, opened and closed. He noticed that Fr. McBrien had closed his newspaper.

"Fr. Principe, you know, he told me all that before," said Fr. McBrien. "In his own words, of course ... but the words make the difference. Francis said that when Marty went to seminary, he learned that you can't become a priest just because you want to, that you need to have a real calling for it."

"I see," said Simon. "Then perhaps it was the writer who muddled it up."

"No doubt," said Fr. McBrien. He seemed quite weak, to the point that Simon became concerned that the old priest might be even closer to death than he had thought. In the silence he could hear not only the sound of papers and books, but the faint cries of children playing outside.

"Are you happy cooped up here?" Simon finally said.

"Oh, happy enough," said Fr. McBrien. "I have memory, which for an old man is a lot, I have many things I can recollect, even some pleasant memories, and of course, I can read. If it weren't summer, though, I might be tempted to despair. The children's voices make me happy. They give me hope."

What is silent, on the other hand, is present by its absence, thought Simon. A strange thought, however true, and in this connection he recalled Kierkegaard's "The most painful state of being is remembering the future, particularly the one you'll never have."[95] A dark feeling made him wish he could throw himself down, to sleep and sleep, and to somehow—

---

95 Ed.: Although this sounds like something that would be said by his pseudonym "A," in fact Kierkegaard is not recorded as having said this.

"What about you, Simon?" Fr. McBrien finally said. "Have you been called?"

"What is a priest, Father?" he said.

"A man who stands between man and God," said Fr. McBrien.

"Who represents God to men, and men to God, is that right?" said Simon.

"Yes," said Fr. McBrien.

"I once heard someone say that the main thing for a priest was to stand with the poor," said Simon, "and I agreed with that. To be God to them by letting them know God had not forgotten them. That is a powerful and meaningful task, a fitting task God would give to priests. 'Blessed are the poor.' 'Caring for the widows and orphans in their affliction.' But..."

Fr. McBrien watched Simon with eyes soft with compassion. "I know," he said, simply.

"Now, I see that can't be all … the priesthood should be concerned with peacemaking, and that means striving against evil," said Simon.

"Of course," said Fr. McBrien. "That is implied in the call to the poor, that the priest stands not only with the poor, but for the justice that makes, that makes—" Here, a coughing fit.

"Yes," said Simon. "Surely that's right, but … the fight is with evil, not just with bad men, but evil itself, 'for we wrestle not against flesh and blood.'"

"Yes," said Fr. McBrien. He seemed as if perhaps he would have wished to say more, if he could catch his breath.

Simon went on. "How can I fight it, Father, when it's inside of me?"

A pained expression crossed Fr. McBrien's face. He coughed again, and finally said, "Simon, what is grace?"

"An unexpected light, an undeserved blessing," said Simon.

"In all cases but one, a sinner being used to save sinners," said Fr. McBrien. "There was just the one case where it was different, and Christ died for us, *iustus pro iniustis*. The priest is a link in the chain of grace, a sinner being used to save sinners."

"You don't understand, Father. You're a holy man. I'm—"

Fr. McBrien was laughing, a silent laugh, that gave way to coughing. "No, Simon..."

"But can a sinner save sinners?" said Simon. "Can he do anything but make things worse? Bruce—"

"That was bad, but we're not talking about Bruce," said Fr. McBrien. "This is about you, Simon. Hard cases make bad rules."

There was another long silence. Somewhere, the sound of a large book being slammed shut.

"What if it isn't the exception?" said Simon. This was the moment he dreaded. "What if it isn't possible to be a priest and a sinner together?"

"Luis was a hard case," said Fr. McBrien.

Simon felt his skin burning. He felt numb with too much feeling to answer.

"A priest is a man who stands between men and God, it's true ... one who brings the people's troubles to God and serves them on God's behalf," said Fr. McBrien. "Yet there is also in every a soul a kind of priest, a love that will draw it into service and which will seek to intercede for others. A prophet, too, yes, that speaks the natural law to the person and afflicts him like Jeremiah or Amos when he falls short of that ideal God planted in his heart."

"Yes, and now the prophet denounces the priest for his effrontery and folly," said Simon. "He unleashes 'Thus saith the Lord' as often as Elijah against Ahab, but the priest is no good and that was his sin. He should have left this business to others." He could never divide his self-will from what he was doing. It was too much, invisibly united with everything he touched. And then, to see it unravel ... everything turn to nothing, not just once, but...

"Simon..." said Fr. McBrien.

"I used up all my strength the first time, getting him out of the Ñetas," said Simon. "I was as bold as St. John with the bandits when he went after Marcus.[96] But later, when his family was suffering ... I saw what was in his mind, and I didn't have any strength left to do it all again." Yet, *had* he seen it, or had his own anxiety placed it there? Everything became so ambiguous the second time. Self-will was always there, always twisting in among everything, endlessly repositing the past into the present, the future. When he felt the wall again, the saccharine coolness, that was too much proof that Luis was hiding something. Only, was the wall the cause of his suspicions, or the result of them? Once it was there he had become even more suspicious, and then, whom was Luis to turn to? ... And then ... The second time exposed the point of weakness in himself, the one he thought he had crucified the first time, that point of weakness was never healed. Fool he was for thinking it could be erased. That single, indefinable point of weakness, that faints in the struggle with evil, writhes away from every resolution.

"The loneliness is not good for you," said Fr. McBrien.

"I've always longed for a friend who fully understood me," said Simon. "That would be, as Kafka said, like having God visibly present with you. Then it would be easy to do anything. And I thought, you know..."

"Simon," said Fr. McBrien, "did not Christ say, 'Take up your cross *daily*'? Another person is always a mystery. 'Misery is the

---

96   Ed.: Clement of Alexandria tells a story about the Apostle John, according to which John entrusted an orphan named Marcus to the care of a church elder before he left Smyrna. When he returned, Marcus had become a captain of bandits. Distraught, John stormed the bandit's stronghold and demanded to see their captain. Expecting another victim, the bandits did so, but John's appearance and entreaties shocked Marcus so much that he fled. John chased after him, crying out, "My son, why do you flee from me, your father, old and unarmed? Pity me, my son! Fear not, you still have hope of life, I will pray for Christ's forgiveness. If needs be, I will take your death, as the Lord died for us. For you, my son, I will surrender my life! Stop now and believe, Christ has sent me to you today!" Humbled and shamed, Marcus fell to his knees and repented. See section XLII of "Who is the Rich Man that Shall be Saved?"

state of every soul overcome by friendship with mortal things and lacerated when they are lost.'[97] One must love all human things with awareness of the human condition, and love God more. Otherwise, such love can only produce grief, anger, and horror. All of life is a *via dolorosa* and accomplishment of God's will lies in the hands of God. Take up your pains, your weakness, take them up like a cross, and hold them up, cry out to God that you are releasing them to him, you have no power to accomplish his will, but will walk toward Golgotha still."

"Father, that all sounds good, but ... what I find is I am no rock, nothing can be built on me," said Simon. Fr. McBrien's advice tasted like ashes in his mouth. "When I look backward over my path, I see guilt in everything, and I can't give up anything."

"You are very close, Simon," said Fr. McBrien. He lay his hand on the younger man, gently. "I am dying—"

"Father—"

"No, I am dying, and yet, I feel healthier inside than you seem to be," said Fr. McBrien.

"I'm sure that's right," said Simon.

"The way of grace is always open, Simon. You must only open yourself to it ... become the father, and become the son." He was gesturing toward the painting that watched over them, the reproduction of Rembrandt's *The Return of the Prodigal Son*. It displayed the warmth and vivid colors common to the painter's works, along with his uncanny grasp of shadow and light. The father and the returning younger son dominate the left side of the painting. The father embraces the son who kneels before him to humbly receive his embrace, accepting the grace he holds for him. The father's gentle hands seem to radiate light, illuminating his face and the back of the son. The son's feet are barely covered.

---

97   Ed.: See Augustine, *Confessions*, IV.6.11.

One sandal has fallen off and the other is breaking apart. The father's red cloak, like a bird's wings, seem to offer protection. Four other figures appear: on the right half of the painting there are two figures, and the light that seems to radiate from the father falls on these two figures' faces and hands: one, the elder son, dressed as a Pharisee, whose face is troubled and whose hands are tightly clutched together; and a publican who observes the scene as if seeing something for the first time, his mouth slightly opened, his hand clutching his clothing as if to hide himself in. Behind the father are two other figures, dimly seen: one curious woman and another too busy, apparently, to pay attention to the momentous event of the younger son's return. The contrast of the warm light of the embrace with the darkness elsewhere throughout the painting makes the embrace the center of the painting and the responses of the onlookers the primary, and perhaps only, other matter for the observer's consideration.

Simon felt new pain. "I wished to be the father. To welcome Luis back. That was..." He closed his eyes. "But I don't see myself anywhere in the painting. I'm not the returning prodigal, not the stern elder brother, not the curious publican, not the daydreaming bystander, or the too busy one ... not the father."

"You are very close, Simon," said Fr. McBrien.

"I feel more distant from God than ever," said Simon.

"It cuts you deep," said Fr. McBrien. "Topple that king in your soul, and let the new King reign."

"I've prayed and prayed," said Simon. "Nothing gets better." The love, and so the grief, was too much a part of his soul. He couldn't replace it with something else. No matter how big a new love is, one can't cast out what has become a permanent part of the soul.

"Wherever the human soul turns, other than to God, is fixed in sorrow, no matter how worthy the love is," said Fr. McBrien. "Everything mortal dies, but under the true King, even what is dead can be raised back to life. Turn, in the grief of your heart, and let go. Let Christ reign in your soul and release every grief to him. The prophet in your soul may excoriate the priest, but it's the king who must be toppled."

"Who is that king, Father?" said Simon.

"Yourself," said Fr. McBrien. "Let the love of God take that place and Christ will reign in your soul instead."

Simon wanted this to be true, but didn't know how to make it true. The guilt and the love were so close as to almost be one and the same, and the love had been infinite. There was therefore no way to leave it behind for anything else. He felt that his love for God had grown cold, somehow, strangely dim, but he couldn't make himself want the monkish existence that had once appealed to him. He loved the people he loved too much. Could he cast all of that out to love God alone, now?

"The embrace of the Father and the Son is the essence of every-thing, Simon, it's the essence of the Godhead and the essence of the Christian life. It's true love. He's cut you open—"

"With what cuts!" Simon interjected violently. After a moment, he went on more quietly, "But after all, it was I who have done the cutting … and what I have found…"

"What have you found, Simon?"

Simon had too many thoughts to answer easily. Finally, he said, "I am sure it was my suspicions that drove him to feel he had no safe place with me, and yet, I knew what temptations he faced, with his family's poverty, his mother's poor health, and those friends … Paco was already halfway in, and I'm convinced that the girl, Marisol, she was much more than halfway in with all the wrong people, and she certainly knew what she was doing. Oh, what am I doing, rehearsing my suspicions again? Besides, I know I myself winked at it all too much." It was false that man's heart contained no good things. It contains true things, friendship, admiration of noble deeds, even worship. But there a creeping, strangling vine, a desperate self-will or self-hatred that would, if it could, find home in the cracks and openings of all these things, which was ambiguously involved in everything and eventually cracking them all to pieces.

"You know that the heart cannot be healed until it's torn open, and the place of royalty given to the embrace, self replaced by the new and growing force of a new King," said Fr. McBrien. "That is what Rembrandt knew. When the man gives up grasping to instead be held, then he is free."

The two men were silent a long time again, to the sounds of the children outside, and the rustling inside.

"He calls us not just to embrace the father, as the prodigal does, but to be the father ourselves," said Simon. "And I have tried to be that father, to offer the uncalculating embrace that receives the sinner back without any consideration of the possible pain that it opens oneself to. Yet, considering that vulnerability only magnifies the despair I feel. What strength it takes to love sinners! Knowing oneself a sinner too!" Fr. McBrien was right to say that another person was a mystery, and he thought of something Heidegger had said of mystery—that it "shows itself and at the same time withdraws."[98] Another person is an eternal mystery, and that is why no one can charge in without suffering, for the charge always ends at the base of another ravine; and that is where the ambush lies. The other, oneself, both are always already guilty.

Fr. McBrien didn't say anything, and for a time both were silent.

Finally, Simon said, "To place myself there ... in that holy circle ... would mean seeing myself as something other than guilty. But I am guilty all the way down."

"Is that all you are, now?" said Fr. McBrien. "Even now, Luis would not think so."

---

98 Ed.: Martin Heidegger, *Discourse on Thinking*, trans. by John Anderson and E. Hans Freund (New York: Harper Torch Books, 1966), p. 35.

"It's not all, but—but it's the core of who I am. The second time confirmed it—the repetition of guilt in everything, farcically guilty in everything. I couldn't—the anxiety I had over him—God, the Ñetas—"

He was stopped short by Fr. McBrien hand on his face. He might have been trying to trace a cross on his face, but his hand was too weak. His fingers felt cold. "Simon..." Simon grew still for a moment. "I won't tell you your grief is wrong. Sadly, it's right. It's all you've been and done. But Christ is calling you to the embrace, and that grief will guide you there."

"I cannot be a priest, Father," said Simon.

"But are you called?" said McBrien.

"The embrace you describe is too terrifying for me," said Simon.

"What terrifies you, then?"

"The thought of ... I really don't know. But I can't do it again."

"Do what?"

"Lose again," said Simon.

"Lose one you love?" asked McBrien.

"And someone can't be a priest without love."

"You can't be a *man* without love," said McBrien. "You can't be human."

"Nonetheless," said Simon. "There is a way..." He knew he was speaking strangely.

"Why can't you?" said McBrien.

"I feel I am ... an impossibility. And the impossibility of it all is the pain." He knew that expressed the idea too weakly, but he lacked the words. He was oppressed at the thought of the future he would "never have."

"Calling is a suffering, Simon," said McBrien. "An enjoyment, but also a suffering."

Simon said nothing.

"A hole torn through the heart's walls separating you from those you are called to serve. If it's there, you can't deny it," said

McBrien. "He's calling you to stand there for them, to be God before them, and to stand for them before God. You can take all that suffering and take it into that embrace, be before God for them, and be joined by his embrace in turn. Let Christ be the King and the great love of your heart, and you can do it still. Or you can say No to the embrace ... and, refusing to perish with those you love, begin the long road to perishing yourself."

"The only thing I am good at is finding out guilt, Father," said Simon. "That's the only thing I understand."

"Do you, then?" said McBrien.

"Everyone's guilty," said Simon. "In law I can at least remain devoted to that. I won't wrong anyone."

"That won't end the suffering," said McBrien.

"At least it won't happen again," said Simon.

"It will happen every day," said McBrien.

"I won't do it again," said Simon.

"And what did you do?"

"My suspicions—"

"Luis also had his choice in the matter, Simon, and he chose what he did. You didn't choose that for him."

"But would he have, without me?" asked Simon, painfully. "That's the question I can't stop asking. What use is a priest who makes others worse?"

"Oh, Simon. As deep as your despair is, just so deep will your love be, your unimaginable pain will become an everlasting pool of love beyond understanding."

"As deep as my love is, so deep will my guilt be, Father. Infinitely deep," said Simon.

"Then you need only come," said McBrien. "You see the world with wounded love, wounded by your own sin. You have sinned before heaven and before men, and you feel the pain of it in all your depths. You know the old Simon must go. He cannot last any longer. Accept the new King, accept the embrace, and let it be your new essence, let it creep in through the cracks that guilt and pain have torn through your soul. Say in your soul: 'This is who I am: the son,' and let the embrace become your principle of living; what you have received, offer, it will confirm it in your soul, and you'll be born again, a priest and co-worker with God forever."

There was silence between them for a long time.

"I can't," said Simon, finally. He would never be able to escape, resign, or replace the concern that so defined him. If he joined the Franciscans he would do so, could do so, only to serve the troubled youth that stand on a razor blade between hope and despair, but the echo of his failures would resound in every act of service. Repetition is hell.

"Then you'll go to NYU?" asked McBrien.

"And those I love will all be better for it," said Simon.

He got up and bent over, holding the old priest gently around the shoulders and kissed his cheek. The latter sighed, but returned the awkward embrace, and there was something in his eye that suggested he had not given up yet. "I appreciate all you've done, but forget about me, Father," said Simon. "That will be for the best."

"*Pax Christi tecum*, my son," said McBrien.

Simon went out and didn't look back. The rain was falling violently outside again when he came out of the subway by his apartment. Looking out upon it once he was safely inside, the rain filled him with loathing. The Upper Bay was full of dark, churning, polluted waters, and he wondered what flood it would take to wash them clean again.

The Rose-Garden

La mer, la mer, toujours recommencée
Paul Valéry[99]

---

99   Ed.: A difficult verse to translate; perhaps "The sea, the sea, ever renewing" ("The Graveyard by the Sea," in *Charmes; ou poèmes* (Paris: Éditions de la Nouvelle Revue Française, 1922), p. 38).

Sept 9

When Sarah was ten, she had a friend named Lucy Strange. She was eleven and had moved to Greenville only the year before, and would move away only a year or two later. Lucy was obsessed with the idea that the assistant manager at the Baskin-Robbins was hiding something in one of the freezers in the back. What she supposed this to be was never clear to me. At one point she thought it was a body, but at other times, she seemed to think it might be money from a bank heist, or even an alien. The one thing she was sure of was that there had been a crime and he was hiding the evidence in the freezer in the corner of the backroom. Sarah finally became completely wrapped up in this suspicion too, to the point that they began to make plans for how they would expose the crime and defeat the assistant manager's nefarious plans—whatever they were. They drew up maps and planned out how they would get in, how they would distract the employees long enough to allow them to get into the backroom, and what they would do once they made it back there.

The assistant manager, a man with dark blond hair and a short mustache, had this strange habit of licking his lips while making a kind of circular motion with his jaw, always to the right, and what made this especially disconcerting was that he commonly combined this with shifting his gaze to the left at the very same moment. I have always attributed this fantasy of Lucy's to this nervous habit of the assistant manager, as I can't otherwise explain what made her become suspicious of him.

This grew to such a head that they actually implemented their impossible plan. While Lucy distracted the employees with a bag full of marbles and plums that she dropped onto the floor, as if by accident, and upon which she dropped her ice cream cone (again as if by accident) while stooping to pick them up, wailing in an impossibly high pitched voice, Sarah sneaked into the back and opened the freezer that they believed concealed the assistant manager's crime. Lucy's wailing concealed the scratching as Sarah moved a crate toward the freezer so she could reach the upper shelf—then, suddenly, a great *thwump* as something heavy and frozen fell upon the floor, and while the employees were busy trying to help Lucy, Sarah came running out from the back. Her face was white and she grabbed Lucy and me and was screaming for us to run. "Just run! Run!" she said.

It turned out that the freezer had contained the assistant manager's dead cat, which had died two weeks earlier. The assistant manager didn't know what to do with it and didn't have the heart to cremate or bury the beast, so he had done the only other thing he could see—he had frozen it. Sarah hardly spoke for a week, Lucy moved away again at the end of the summer, and I never mentioned it to her. It would have been funny, but it couldn't be, and it passed into the stillness of her life.

MACRINA

From within the watertight closet, I could hear the storm rage outside, but the sounds were dim, distorted, and confused. At a certain point they became muffled and everything was almost peaceful, haunted by strange noises that arose and passed away into nothing out in some other world outside the safe. I wrapped myself in the blanket. I knew that the waters had flooded up the tunnel and that I was now sealed inside the closet as effectively as possible.

Time passed in unknown intervals. Outside, the storm howled, and I wondered if I would know if the house had been dragged down the cliff or not. I wondered whether Simon had escaped, if he was still alive. It's hard to describe those hours in the closet. They were the worst hours of my life, but so featureless and indistinguishable that no speech could adequately convey what they were. The dread grew every moment, exponentially so when from time to time I felt the ground shifting and wondered if everything would come crashing down upon me while I could do nothing to escape.

Finally, there was a kind of silence. It endured for so long I wondered whether I would even know if the storm had ended.

What would I hear when the storm ended? How would I know if the water had receded? How long would it take for the water to sink back down again? The door could not be opened until the storm surge had receded at least that far. Was it raining even now, piling up further inches of water above me? I was sure this thinking was confused yet I was also becoming so claustrophobic in the safe—I could not stand upright, as it was only four and a half feet tall—that I ardently wished to open that door and swim for it, just to get out of the dark, cramped space. Equally alarming, I discovered that there was water inside the supposedly watertight closet. I tried to find the source using the flashlight, but could not determine whether it was coming from the ceiling or from around the door. So gradual was its growth that I almost gave up caring about the problem; even after hours of growing it was only a dampness on the floor, yet if the hurricane had cracked the rock wall, it could crack further still, and perhaps everything would come apart or come crashing down upon me.

Moreover, my mind was swirling with the possibilities unveiled by the last discussion with Simon, as I tried to reconstruct a true history of the past four years, and continually saw the events of my own life, which had seemed so clear-cut, in one new light and then in another. My mind felt like a spinning kaleidoscope in which nothing would come properly into focus. Much of what I wished to understand I have recorded above, as it now seems to me; I stand by those records, to the extent I can, yet I feel even so that I have left the most essential part out. For there were other thoughts and feelings I felt I could not communicate or write out, not yet, and not in such a form, if form there be for such thoughts. The searing memory of that morning in New York, so long suppressed, was now continually, painfully present.

Time passed. Eventually, I became sure that the flood waters were receding and I would be able to open the door soon. The closet was some five or six feet above normal sea level and the water had only to drop that far, or nearly that far. When I considered it carefully, I knew that even when it had fallen far enough for me to open the door, I would still have to swim. I had the wherewithal to collect a few things I wished to bring with me—the notebook, two bottles of water, a flashlight, and a couple of other items—and to place these together in one of the plastic bags, reinforced by a second bag I wrapped the whole in. I tied these together with a piece of cord that I tied close to my back. I believed I understood how to tie a slip-knot, but I was unsure whether I actually managed it. If I had succeeded then I could release the package if it seemed to hamper me.

Finally, concentrating my mind and body upon the task, I ventured to open the door. There was momentary resistance before water immediately began to come in over my feet and came into the closet. The iron rings confronted me along the opposite wall; several were darkly dripping, while two or three were still submerged beneath the waters, for the water was still two inches above the base of the closet's door and the tunnel descended steeply at this point. In the narrow light of the flashlight I could barely make out a few inches of clearance beneath the archway's keystone. I would need to dive if I wished to make it out, then, and then—what currents would I be caught up by once I exited the tunnel and found myself in the free and wild ocean, driven by what winds trailed behind the great storm that had only barely passed? For some time I contemplated the water before me, and the longer I did so, the more terrifying it seemed to me; and yet what safety was there in remaining as I was? Sometimes I daydreamed of the waters descending, rescuers finding me, even Simon himself doing so; but there was something of weakness in these thoughts. Other times, I considered that the house above was likely destroyed, and the upper parts of the tunnel, too. It was not clear that the tunnel was stable any longer, or that it would be safer to remain than to dive, and to swim, and to seek the chance for life outside. The water itself seemed to be trying to communicate something, but what that might be, of course, never came into focus; when illuminated by the flashlight, its reflections and tremors showed me everything above the waters in the tunnel in distorted clarity, the iron rings that remained above its surface now appearing to double in number, gleaming with what seemed a wicked purpose. The more I held the flashlight out, the more I wavered, as I attempted to inspect my environment and became increasingly aware that I could not very well bring the flashlight with me, and that the environment that revealed itself to my inspections was utterly unlike the environment I would experience in actual diving. Still, it was hard to put the light away, for it always seemed that I might notice some crucial fact I had hitherto missed, and the utter darkness of going lampless was, frankly, terrifying.

"Remember," I heard Simon's voice again. "Remember." So I made up my mind, concentrating myself entirely upon the wish to fulfill the chance that had been given to me, regardless of the folly of casting myself into the waters. My fate was out of my hands, but I would cast myself in and swim with whatever movements I could make. I turned the flashlight off and tossed it back into the closet. There was utter darkness now, and I hesitated. I hoped the second the flashlight in the bag would make it. I hoped that I would make it. There was only darkness. I dove.

The first movement was easy; I threw myself into it, and dove beneath the surface. I had swum all my life and was an excellent swimmer. That, however, had always been under ideal circumstances. I had never swum in a hurricane before, and the necessity of diving beneath the surface in order to escape the tunnel meant that for a few short but critical moments I would be completely unable to see where I was going or what I was entering into. Those same moments, however, called for utter concentration of purpose as I absolutely had to escape the tunnel and the choked area of the wharfs where I could easily strike my head or become trapped beneath the dock.

Once I was beneath the waters, it became a desperate struggle;

the currents that warred against me were more powerful than any I had ever faced or tested my body against. It became clear that my strength would not be enough, but I had to swim nonetheless and make the movements, or I would be thrown against the walls and drowned. I therefore swam, and when I caught a current, I followed it as far as I could, hardly grasping my own spatial location any longer, but striving and being carried not knowing which was master or whither I was being taken. I thought I had made it outside of the tunnel but could not rightly tell, in the utter darkness and disorientation.

Suddenly, I was caught in something else, a current beyond my strength, and then hurtled outward. I needed to breathe but I dared not open my mouth or inhale. I was spun about at least twice in the current and I struggled to somehow regain control of the path I was taking, but realized in some way that I had better prepare myself for the critical moment when I could finally get my head above water—for surely I was beyond the wharfs now!—and that my concentration should be set upon this moment rather than trying to struggle against a force I could never control. Waiting for this moment, I was suddenly jolted and struck something forcefully. Pain exploded in my side—it felt like I had been struck by something like a branch right below my ribs—but I felt something solid, and I spent my last strength trying to grip and pull myself toward this, whatever it was, and then, all of a sudden, my hand felt grass and my head was above the water again. There was water and air in my mouth and I put my other hand out, gripping only dirt, but kept reaching until I found another handful grass. I pulled myself with all the strength I had left up onto whatever it was I had found.

Lying facedown on this patch of ground and breathing heavily, I smelt the sweet air of a North Carolina night on the coast. My arms and legs burned and my right side was an agony. When I finally felt able again to move I pulled myself entirely up out of the water and rolled onto my back on the land. A large fallen tree branch lay alongside me on the shore. I looked up and it was dark, though I thought I saw the branches of trees and ravaged dunes. The stars shone above me. They were bright, clean, innocent, silent. I was alone.

As I stared upon them, I wept. Each seemed to pierce me with its light, and the memory of Sarah, the thought that she herself had drowned in these waters I had just emerged from, overwhelmed me, and in every memory I could not erase the intimations of future happiness that never came to be. But, oh, Sarah. I will not forget.

⌀

Lying there beneath the stars, in agony from the storm's assault on my body, I had a fitful but dream-filled sleep. Many of the dreams are elusive and seem to disintegrate merely at the attempt to remember, slipping through my fingers, but one is vividly emblazoned on my mind. I will recount it here.

I was walking into a coffee shop and I saw Simon there, and a man I knew, though I had never met him, to be Fr. McBrien. He was smiling.

"Teacher!" I said, in surprised joy.

Simon smiled at me gently as I embraced him. We were walking out of the coffee shop, and outside he said, "Don't hold on to me," he said. "But go, and find the others."

"The others?" I said. And Simon was gone.

Along the shore I saw enormously many others, men and women, and all of them said that they could not answer my questions, and that I must keep going. Always they went hand in hand, each in a great chain holding the hand of others. Tall, willowy women, enormous, thick-bearded men, small, round women, olive-skinned men with shaved heads and garlands around their necks, I went along and along, and I found no one I could remain with or call my own. "Are you the one I am looking for?" I began asking, again and again, and always the answer was, "No, I am not the one. You cannot hold me. But go on, go on, go on, and you will find them." Then, in their happiness, they would return their gaze to the sea and the sun, and many of them were singing with each other, and though they did not all sing the same song, or even sing in one language, it was somehow altogether just one song that all sung. Endlessly I seemed to follow this chain along the shore until finally, as the sun was setting, I found a woman with a complexion like coffee with cream sitting alone on a mat. There was a brazier with an open fire between us over which she was roasting green coffee beans in a pan.

"Please join me," she said, and I sat down opposite her. I didn't know what was expected of me, so I folded my hands in my lap and stared down into the brazier. The flame was gentle, warm, and red, and burned among dark embers; but deep inside it seemed to have a spark of white fire. There was incense burning somewhere. I could not quite recognize the scent.

"Why have you come here?" she asked.

"I am supposed to look for the others," I said.

"Ah," she answered. She said no more, but was looking down at the beans in silence.

"No, actually ... I think I am supposed to find them, and tell them something," I said.

"Oh?" she said. "And what are you to tell them?"

I didn't know what to say. Shouf-shouf-shouf went the coffee beans roasting in the pan. I felt the warmth from the fire.

"Who are the others?" she said. She smiled.

"I don't know," I said.

"Then how will you find them?" I didn't answer. She was stirring and shaking the beans, which were growing dark.

"Will they find you?" she asked.

"No, I mean ... I don't think so," I said. The aroma of the beans was growing very powerful. For a long time we sat and neither of us said anything. She began to crush the beans with a pestle and a long-handled mortar. This went on for a long time, and I began to feel very sad. Finally, I looked up, and I saw that the sun had fallen beneath the horizon. There was only a glowing line of fire along the infinitely extending waters, and the crashing of the waves grew gradually more emphatic.

"Take this, my daughter," she said. I looked back at her. In her dark but luminous face I felt an enormous kindness and I took the cup of coffee from her. Somehow while I had been looking over the ocean she had already put the grounds in the jebena and made the coffee.

"Thank you," I said.

"I am afraid I have no popcorn," she said.

I must have appeared confused, for she looked amused.

Looking off a little toward something out of sight, she said, "Because it is a dream."

"Oh," I said. And I sipped the coffee, which was warm but not too hot. Very quickly I began to feel life awakening in me again.

"Why did you come to me?" she asked.

"Because I have no one," I said.

"Ah," she said.

"I did have someone, but I … I let her go," I said. "I let her fall into the ocean and be carried away."

Then I wept, but the woman's luminous, dark face kept holding me in her kind eyes. I stared into her eyes until finally my eyes were clear again, and it was as if I would fall into hers.

There was a hand upon my shoulder. I could not see him, but I knew it was Simon.

"You must go now," she said. I looked down, and saw that I had drank all the coffee. "Return to the river." I never saw him, but Simon walked with me as we went upward and inland, and the journey was many miles, but it seemed to take only a minute. He was behind me the whole distance and his hand was on my shoulder. We were well into the hill country and there was a great river surrounded by towering trees. Everything around the great river was bounding with life, and the great river led down to the sea.

"Wake up," I heard Simon saying. "You must wake up."

And I was pulled into the river.

༄

The grey, dismal dawn came, and went, and the day came, and went, gray, rainy, and choppy. When I woke I was sore and in pain everywhere. I was on an island in Cape Fear Basin. There were trees towering above me and all along the shore, many of them damaged, but most still standing even after the storm. I walked about the island, for it was not large, perhaps a hundred sixty yards in circumference, and found among some of the foliage a wooden carving of a head, looking as if it had been broken off from a ship's prow, and left here some ages ago. The island was only a few feet above sea level and had clearly been flooded during the hurricane.

I found that the packet I had tied to my back had made it intact. My notebooks and everything else were dry. I pulled a poncho on. It was warm, but the rain continued to drizzle. Near the center of the island, someone had once built something—perhaps a tower to watch from, or some kind of hut in which to hide from eyes on land—but the structure of wooden logs was now decaying and crumbling apart. It still provided a degree of shelter in one corner, and I used it to provide protection from the rains that came in from the southeast.

I didn't see anyone nearby, and certainly not Simon—not his little boat nor any other boat, anywhere. The devastation wrought by the lately foreseen hurricane must have been widespread. None of the ordinary ship traffic was in evidence. I did see what looked like a Coast Guard vessel in the distance; they didn't see me, and I tried hailing them with the smaller flashlight I had stowed in the bag, but I didn't get their attention and gave up, saving the battery for later.

Hoping for some kind of rescuers, I've instead spent my time writing. I've done nothing but write now for two days, drinking water from the river when the tide is going out and the freshwater was going out. There is nothing to eat. I crave omelets.

The humidity is almost making my hair stand on end. I'm sure that there's another storm coming. Perhaps it's a second hurricane; whatever it is, I don't expect to survive it. I'm sure it's my imagination, but I still catch the whiff of roses. Imaginary or not, I'm glad for their fragrant presence.

Simon told me to remember. But if I'm dead, how can I remember? So I have written it all down, whatever I can. When I'm done, I'll wrap the whole thing in the other bag I have here, the one I meant for a second poncho, and tie it together with a piece of cord that I grabbed from the house without thinking. Well, Simon, I'll save it, if I can, and if someone finds it, they'll at least know you saved someone. It was only for a little while, but isn't that all anyone can do?

Still, I don't wish to die. I think I need to swim outward, toward the ocean. The current is pouring out from the basin right now so forcefully no other course of action seems safe. That is madness unless I can catch a boat or ship out there. I don't see any other way, however, and in the absence of alternatives, perhaps even madness becomes sane. One way or another—when the storm comes, I will be swimming. I would rather do the diving myself.

☙

When the pattern goes down, it comes back up dark, bloody, twisted, and we write our life in that blood.

Mom and Dad. I'm so sorry. I didn't mean for you to lose both daughters. That's another crime for which I'm not big enough.

Joshua, if you ever read this, I forgive you for not knowing how to answer my questions. Please have a wonderful life. What could you have ever said? I don't know what I wanted or what I want now. I'm sorry I couldn't have been better. Play something sad. You'll know what. Just this once, though: Don't laugh.

Oh, Sarah. The storm is coming. I want to live.

ACKNOWLEDGEMENTS

In bringing *The Hurricane Notebook* to publication, I was aided by not many but still by several significant individuals.

This book was made possible in part by support from the Institute for Scholarship in the Liberal Arts, College of Arts and Letters, University of Notre Dame. The Institute provided support for the book on several occasions.

The support of my family was essential. My maternal grandparents, Maudeen and Alan Knights—whom I knew only as "Mum" and "Babar," and whose official names still seem false to me—passed before Elizabeth ever put pen to paper, but were crucial for teaching me the value of everything written down and the perilous glory of art, literature, and theater. I thank my mother, Julia Jech, who corrected typos in the typed manuscript—typos that sometimes seemed to reproduce so quickly as to be ineradicable—and my father, Jon Jech, for the taste for what is rare, unusual, and finely done, and the ability to distinguish between that and what is simply nonsense.

I also must thank my wife, Koelle, a thousand times, for her love and patience while I worked on a very unusual, and at times quite uncertain, project, through many strange turns, even as the publication date retreated ever further into the distance. Her support provided both moral and material support.

I owe special thanks to Megan Fritts, whose irreplaceable editing work the Institute funded, and whose help and enthusiasm for *The Hurricane Notebook* went far beyond what could have been required of anyone. Her understanding of Elizabeth's mind and ideas, and of Elizabeth's relationships with Joshua and Sarah, often exceeded my own. This intellectual sympathy no doubt was the reason for her ability to decipher what Elizabeth had hidden. Without her ongoing support and insight everything surely would have come off in a much shoddier and inferior manner.

I thank Andrew Helms for his unexpected and gratuitous support at an important moment, and for his help in making me notice Elizabeth's essential likeness to, and difference from, Socrates. The latter always doubted claims of knowledge (beginning with his own), whereas Elizabeth doubts claims of innocence (starting with her own). Indeed, it was this aspect of her thinking, perhaps more than any other, that provided the most shocks and surprises to me, as it is what seems to enable Elizabeth—to a degree surpassing my own capacity—to "think the hard thought."

I have to thank Philip Mendola for his comments made what seems a lifetime ago, at the very beginning of the project. His helpful and encouraging words, along with his open honesty, were irreplaceable and more instrumental than he probably knew in bringing the notebook to the light of day.

I must also thank Tom Morris, formerly of Notre Dame, currently of Wilmington, who believed the notebook should be published as much as I did, and who did so much to get the final product off the ground; Sara Morris and Abigail Chiaramonte, whose work helped perfect the final product; Claire Wolford, whose proof-reading of the book proof was so insightful; and if one can thank a place, I must thank Wilmington itself, for Elizabeth's story is surely a Wilmington tale, as much as the legends of Blackbeard, the actor turned theatrical pirate (who feigned to set his hair on fire to intimidate), the life of Abraham Galloway, escaped slave turned Civil War hero and statesman, and dozens of other inspiring, horrifying, and whimsical historical and legendary tales.Perhaps Elizabeth M. did not live as large a life as many of those who figure in such stories, but not many do, and in her notebook she shows as much as they the unexpected way in which all are interconnected with each other and with the places in which we grow into ourselves, and the depth of the human soul, which—like the tunnels beneath Wilmington—hides so many secrets, and even secrets behind those as well, above all the secrets of sin and repentance.

Finally, the greatest thanks go to Divine Providence, through which the notebook so unexpectedly came into my hands.

THE BOOKS OF WISDOM/WORKS

Wisdom/Works is a new cooperative, cutting edge imprint and resource for publishing books by practical philosophers and innovative thinkers who can have a positive cultural impact in our time. We turn the procedures of traditional publishing upside down and put more power, a vastly higher speed of delivery, and greater rewards into the hands of our authors.

The imprint was launched with the Morris Institute for Human Values, founded by Tom Morris (Ph.D. Yale), a former professor of philosophy at Notre Dame and a public philosopher who has given over a thousand talks on the wisdom of the ages. Wisdom/Works was established to serve both his audiences and the broader culture. From the imprint's first projects, it began to attract the attention of other like-minded authors.

Wisdom/Works occupies a distinctive territory outside most traditional publishing domains. Its main concern is high quality expedited production and release, with affordability for buyers. We seek to serve a broad audience of intelligent readers with the best of ancient and modern wisdom. Subjects will touch on such issues as success, ethics, happiness, meaning, work, and how best to live a good life.

As an imprint, we have created a process for working with a few high quality projects a year compatible with our position in the market, and making available to our authors a well-guided and streamlined process for launching their books into the world. For more information, email Tom Morris, Editor-in-Chief, through his reliable address of: TomVMorris@aol.com. You can also learn more at the editor's website, www.TomVMorris.com.